KACHKA

KACHKA

A RETURN TO RUSSIAN COOKING

BONNIE FRUMKIN MORALES

WITH DEENA PRICHEP

PHOTOGRAPHY BY LEELA CYD

FLATIRON
BOOKS
NEW YORK

www.flatironbooks.com

Book design by Karen Koch
Photography by Leela Cyd
Illustrations by Roman Muradov
Endpapers © National Geographic Maps/National Geographic Creative

The Library of Congress Cataloging-in-Publication Data is available upon request.

ISBN 978-1-250-08760-7 (paper over board)
ISBN 978-1-250-08920-5 (ebook)

Our books may be purchased in bulk for promotional, educational, or business use.
Please contact your local bookseller or the Macmillan Corporate and Premium Sales Department at
1-800-221-7945, extension 5442, or by email at MacmillanSpecialMarkets@macmillan.com.

First Edition: November 2017

10 9 8 7 6 5 4 3 2 1

In memory of my babushka Rakhil Moiseevna Frumkina.
Though we never met, your courage, tenacity, and wit move me every single day.

CONTENTS

содержание

✦ ✦ ✦

KACHKA

INTRODUCTION

WHAT IS RUSSIAN FOOD, ANYWAYS?

When most people think of Russian food, they go blank. They think of borsch—if they think of anything at all. But the real picture of Russian food?

Before its collapse, the Soviet Union covered a full sixth of the earth's land mass with growing seasons ranging from pomegranates to permafrost. The resulting canon includes carefully composed bites full of briny-sharp pickles and smoked Baltic fish; the saffron-and-cilantro-scented Silk Road legacy of the easternmost republics; French-inflected holdovers from czarist palates; and fragrant wild berries and heady forest mushrooms preserved from too-brief summers. It's far more than cabbage and beets—although if you know what you're doing, you can also create beautiful dishes with these salt-of-the-earth ingredients. And no matter what the region, it's not just hearty warm-you-in-winter dishes, but also garden-based summer feasts, and *zakuski*—the bright and varied little mezze-like bites that enliven any celebration, and come with their own ritualized etiquette of hosting and toasting. And it's this food—and feeling—we bring to Kachka's table.

YOU'RE OPENING WHAT KIND OF RESTAURANT?!?

This lavishly set table—the one I grew up around as a child of Soviet immigrants—is barely known in the New World. My husband and I learned this over and over again when, in 2013, we set out to open Kachka in Portland, Oregon. When you open a restaurant, you meet a lot of faces: contractors, city inspectors, financiers, vendors, potential employees, food writers, and on and on. And with each one, we had some variation of this same conversation:

STRANGER: *So what's your business?*

ME: *We're opening a restaurant!*

STRANGER: *Oh, how great! What kind of food?*

ME: *Food from the former Soviet Union.*

STRANGER: [blank]

ME: *. . . like Russia, Belarus, Georgia, Latvia . . .*

STRANGER: [long pause] *Oh, is Belarus near Moscow?*

ME: *No, it's a country west of Russia.*

STRANGER: [confusion]

ME: *Anyway, it's basically Russian food with a lot of influence from countries surrounding it.*

STRANGER: *Huh. So what kind of food is that?*

ME: *Well, that would be like asking someone to explain what French or Italian food is in just one sentence. It's . . . well . . . I mean, there's lots of cabbage . . .*

STRANGER: [interjects] *Look at the time! I've got that thing I need to go do. Uh, good luck with your restaurant . . .*

Kachka opened its doors in April 2014. And although most diners were unfamiliar with Russian food, they gave us a shot—and keep coming back for more. Walking into Kachka is like walking into a party, pulling up a seat at the whole sprawling, eclectic, joyous table of the former Russian Empire. As Vladimir Vysotsky (aka Russian Bob Dylan) and post-Soviet rock alternate from the speakers, diners tear up over cabbage rolls that remind them of their long-departed grandmothers (be they from Ukraine, Poland, or Pittsburgh). Or they toast the night with spirituous cocktails and vodka infused with everything from sea buckthorn berries to dill flowers. Or they find themselves, to their great surprise, falling for beef tongue.

MY JOURNEY BACK TO RUSSIAN FOOD

Nowadays I can hold forth on the wonders of Russian cuisine for days and days, losing myself in Soviet-era culinary manuals and handwritten recipe cards. But growing up as a child of immigrants from the former Soviet Union, I didn't exactly extol the virtues of this food from the rooftops. I was born in suburban Chicago in 1981, a year after my parents immigrated. And like all good first-generation kids, I wanted nothing to do with my family's rich culinary legacy—I wanted to be *American*. I was embarrassed by the jars of pickles fermenting in the basement and cold hot dogs snuck into lunch boxes. I wished for the standardized perfection of Lunchables. I wanted to go out to White Castle, not White Nights, the glitzy Russian banquet hall of my Chicago youth. I'd warn visiting friends before they came to dinner, and pray that my mom not make anything too *foreign*. And then I went

through a period where I decided that Russian food was just broken—but I could fix it with healthy lashings of the French techniques I learned as an eager young culinary school graduate. Then I met my husband.

When I first took Israel home to meet my family during our early days, he wanted to make a good impression. And, in a Russian Jewish family, that means eating. It took a few family dinners before I realized he wasn't just cleaning his plate to be polite. Juicy-yet-crunchy sauerkraut, lively sorrel soup, and braised short ribs—they were exciting yet approachable, familiar but like nothing he'd ever tasted. And not just that—there was the ritual of the table, the series of toasts, and the family who came together over long, food-filled evenings.

And slowly, I began to see things anew through his eyes. This was more than just getting reacquainted with childhood dishes—as Israel asked my mother questions, she began to tell stories, call up recipes, and unearth dishes she hadn't made in decades. *Machanka* roasted in gravy, smoky-yet-lemony *solyanka* soup, little milk caramel *oreshki* cookies. At some point, it hit me: Russian food was never broken. Though I continued to work in professional kitchens, my long-term goal came into focus: reclaiming the food of my family.

As Israel and I fell in love with this food (and each other), we stayed up nights over satisfying bowls of Siberian dumplings, thinking about how to bring this cuisine—and this way of eating—to other people. And, with fingers crossed that even non-Russians could learn to love herring, we sketched out the menu and approach that would become our restaurant, made a business plan, and found financial backing. And after many awkward conversations with doubting strangers, we opened Kachka. It turned out that not only could non-Russians learn to love herring; they were clamoring for it. We struck a chord because Kachka is the story of my family, but also the experience of millions—told through food that is intoxicating, rich, and varied.

THE WAR, THE GENERATIONS, AND A LITTLE DUCK

Kachka's menu is firmly rooted in the Soviet era, with nods even further back to both czarist excess and traditional rustic foodways. But my own family's story—and the restaurant itself—owes its very existence to a singular moment seventy-five years ago. In October 1941, in a little town called Bobr in Belarus, the Jews were rounded up into the ghetto, and forced to dig a large hole. The next steps were pretty clear. So my grandmother Rakhil Altshuler layered on all of her warmest clothes. Bundled up her three-month-old baby, kissed her parents goodbye, and slipped out under the barbed wire fence. A day later, all of Bobr's 961 Jews were killed.

Photographs on opposite page, clockwise from top left: My dad and I sing Russian songs after dinner with friends; The Iron Curtain falls in the late eighties, and our relatives start emigrating. Our American family grows!; The American dream realized—our first car (I'm the bundle)!; Israel joins the family and joins in the fun.

My grandmother spent two months on foot, traveling through forests from village to village, begging for something to eat or a place to sleep. Her baby starved, and she dug a hole with her hands to bury him in a field. Finally, she was stopped by a *starosta*—one of the Nazi-appointed town wardens. My grandmother repeated the story she'd been carrying: she was a Ukrainian woman on her way to her husband's family. "If you're from Ukraine," he asked doubtfully, seeing the dark complexion of a Belarusian Jew, "How do you say '*ootka*' [duck] in Ukrainian?"

My grandmother didn't know Ukrainian. At home, she spoke Yiddish and Russian, a few words of Belarusian. So she crossed her fingers, took a deep breath, and pulled out the Belarusian/Yiddish word: *kachka.* And with this one little word, this little duck, the key slid in the lock and the gates fell open. My grandmother passed through, and went on to join the *partizan* resistance.

A generation later, her son—my father, Vyacheslav (Slava) Frumkin—would cross his fingers, take a deep breath, and say goodbye to his mother for the last time. He would leave the Soviet Union to move to Chicago with his wife, Lyubov, and young son, Simon, becoming part of the story of Soviet Jewish immigration to the New World. A year later, I was born. And when I took a deep breath and decided to open a Russian restaurant in Portland, there was no question what we would call it. The name Kachka is a shorthand for the courage of all of these journeys—my grandmother's perseverance through those life-or-death wartime years; my parents' chutzpah in leaving everything they knew to make a life in a new world that may as well have been a new planet; and my own mission to bring the food, stories, and feelings of all of these threads of the Russian experience to an entirely new table.

THIS IS NOT A RUSSIAN COOKBOOK

Yes, I know—I've just told the story of Russian food, my Russian family, and our Russian restaurant. But let me repeat: THIS IS NOT A RUSSIAN COOKBOOK.

When my parents emigrated in 1980, the word "Russia" was used interchangeably with "the Soviet Union." All fifteen republics were part of Mother Russia. But my parents are not Russian. Technically, they're Belarusian—although they never lived in a country called Belarus. Outside of a short-lived moment after the revolution, Belarus wasn't even an independent country until 1990, a decade after my family left. And on my parents' passports, their nationality was listed as "Jewish" (which is a whole other, far more loaded story).

But officially, on top of all of these identities, they spent their entire lives in the Soviet Union, which was very much its own thing—both culturally and culinarily. And that's just one experience, from a country that was relatively well appropriated into the Soviet Union. And so the food that I make is inspired by a place, the Soviet Union, that no longer exists. And as much as we shudder at the portrait of Lenin above the kitchen stove, the food on the table beneath it was a direct result of the forces he put into play.

So, yes, to call something Russian is a bit of a loaded gloss, a term I'm still working through (and perhaps will never pin down). But it's one that captures the wider picture of all of the regions, histories, and foods that spill out onto Kachka's tables (in addition to being less of a mouthful than "foods of the former Union of Soviet Socialist Republics"). Just know that whenever you see the word "Russian" from here on in, it comes with a big fat asterisk implied.

Through these pages, you'll find Latvian sprats and Georgian *khachapuri,* recipes inspired by both Soviet food ministers and beloved grandmothers. And, yes, vodka. And the very-much-alive souls of Chekhov and Dostoevsky, spilling out over silver samovars and folding tables. And the most heavenly yeasted blini, wrapped around caviar and cultured butter. Because this food, no matter how it's defined, is a soulful celebration in the face of harshness—be it government apparatchiks or punishing winters—where all you can do is seize the bounty and the moment, look around at your nearest and dearest, and raise your glass.

HOW TO USE THIS BOOK

In these pages you'll find not just Russian recipes, but a guide to the overall Russian way of eating—from showing proper hospitality with an epic spread of zakuski snacks (page 156), to preparing main dishes that range from slow-cooked humble homestyle staples (page 259) to czar-worthy creations (page 285). Learn what to stock your pantry with to be able to turn out a Russian meal on short notice (page 364), and have a handy guide should you choose to elbow a place on line amid the babushkas at your local Russian market (page 10).

Kachka tells the stories behind everything from filling your samovar (page 328) to raising your glass with a proper soul-baring toast (page 40), and why dumplings are so beloved that they merit their own chapter (page 193). Turning out a feast worthy of a tradition-bound babushka or a modern Muscovite can be easily accomplished with little more than supermarket staples and standard kitchen tools. Though we accept full blame if you end up obsessively seeking out sea buckthorn berries (page 32) or *pelmenitsa* molds (page 196)—not to mention shot glasses for your vodka.

A DISCLAIMER

Some of these recipes are (almost) straight from my mother's smudged and stained files, and some feature the results of my own deliciously inauthentic tinkering with the

ingredients of the region (Dungeness crab piroshki and beet-infused gin, I'm looking in your direction). I'd argue that both are equally authentic to the Russian experience. Invariably, it's the recipes I have barely changed that diners will admonish me are *not* traditional—by which they mean are different from the way their own babushka made them. This is not an encyclopedia or field study, capturing every regional variation. The recipes here are shaped by my background as both Russian and American, chef and home cook—and true believer in Russian cuisine and the fuller Russian experience of which food is just one (very, very critical) part.

A NOTE ABOUT SALT

Most of the recipes in this book (and really most cookbooks out there) call for "salting to taste"—this isn't meant to be a cop-out so much as a way of empowering you to respond to your own ingredients and palate. But seasoning food correctly is frankly *the most* important element to making it taste good. It is at once easy to attain and yet elusive. Properly salted food does not taste salty, but instead just has an amplified flavor. You'd be surprised how paying mindful attention to this one little step can take a dish from forgettable to phenomenal.

In cases where I do call for specific measurements (generally in marinades, meats, and doughs where you might not want to taste the unfinished product), recipe measurements have been developed using Diamond kosher salt, which I favor for its large flakes and clean, neutral taste. This is important to note because the shape and size of salt crystals can vary tremendously from brand to brand (for example, Morton kosher salt is at least *twice* as salty by volume as Diamond). If you are using any other salt (kosher or otherwise), adjust accordingly.

WHEN TO USE A SCALE

Most measurements are given by volume, but I have included weights in a few spots where useful for more consistent results. A digital scale is one of the handiest additions to any home kitchen, and worth the twenty-dollar-or-so investment. If you aren't in the mood, just ignore the weights and use the volume equivalents.

Photographs opposite page, top row: Lithuanian cured meats at a market in Vilnius; *plombir* sandwich. *Middle row:* slabs of cured *salo* at a market in Minsk; foraged porcini mushrooms, painstakingly hand-threaded together; kvas truck and attendant. *Bottom row:* hot-smoked mackerel at a beach-side smoke shack on the Baltic Sea; various herbal remedies; mountains and mountains of beautiful berries in Minsk.

Right: My mother's childhood home in Borisov, Belarus.

SMOKED FISH COUNTER

РЫБА

CURED MEAT CASE

МЯСО

THE HERRING COOLER

BOXED CHOCOLATES

ХЛЕБ

BREADS

RUSSIAN MARKET

CONDIMENTS

PICKLE AISLE

THE TVOROG
AND
SMETANA FRIDGE

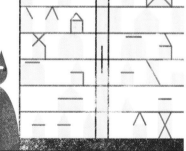

MINERAL
WATERS

THE PELMENI FREEZER

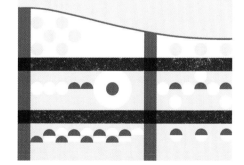

Even if you can source most ingredients at your local grocery store, it's still worth checking out the Russian markets for some inspiration (and surprising finds). Every market varies in its selection, quality (check labels!*), and use of English (be prepared to point and smile). Consult my guide to stocking your pantry (page 364) for more specific product details, but this overview should help orient you to the overall shopping experience.

Also note that in many smaller markets, the deli case is at the same counter as the register. In these setups, you're expected to pay for your entire basket after ordering from the case. If you plan to buy anything in the aisles, make the case your last stop.

HELPFUL PHRASES

PLEASE: пожалуйста (pa-ZHA-lu-sta)

THANK YOU: спасибо (spa-SI-ba)

CAN I TRY A PIECE?: можно мне попробовать кусочек?
(MO-zhna mnye pa-PRO-ba-vat ku-SO-chek?)

SLICE THINLY (AS A COMMAND): тонко порезать (TON-ka pa-REH-zat)

HALF A POUND: пол паунда (pol pOWn-da)

WHICH IS BEST?: какое лучше? (ka-KO-ye LUCH-shea?)

THE SMOKED FISH COUNTER

Not all cured fish deli cases are created equal—they vary depending upon the part of the country and makeup of the clientele, making it hard to predict the availability of specific products. If there's a robust selection, look for cold-smoked *syomga* (salmon) pieces (rather than slices), *kapitan* (a type of rich white-fleshed fish), or *ugor* (hot-smoked eel). If not, ask the clerk for recommendations, and look for smoked fish that are either vacuum-packed or sold whole, as they tend to be more *sochny* (juicy).

THE HERRING COOLER

Of course you would expect to find herring at a Russian market. But the sheer number of options can be a bit mind-numbing. There might be a few pickled varieties, but Russians aren't really into the sweet stuff (that's more Scandinavian)—salt-cured and stored in oil is what you're looking for. Gold Star and Haifa brands are typically good bets.

---

* Some translation apps will actually read labels and signs in other languages and translate them for you—try it on those mystery cans!

BREADS

To me, there is just no substitute for a good *chorni khleb* (black bread). And it is next to impossible to find a real loaf of black bread pretty much anywhere but a Russian store. Look for *Litkovsky* (dense, dark, and slightly sweet) or *Borodinsky* (similar, with coriander seeds), and pick up an extra loaf to stash in your freezer. These denser breads take to freezing particularly well, needing just a little wake-me-up in the oven before serving. Also check out Armenian lavash, *lepyoshki* (flatbreads), and all forms of lighter sour ryes.

THE CURED MEAT CASE

Holy moly—there are *a lot* of options here. But in general, you can't go too wrong, and you're totally allowed (encouraged, even) to ask for a taste before buying. Not all stores will automatically slice your meat for you, so be sure to ask—and watch that they remove any plastic casings before starting! I tend to stick with salamis made under the Alef label, which are consistently good. Try a sampling of styles:

- *Moskovskaya* (Moscow-style salami)
- *Yevreyskaya* (Jewish-style salami)
- *Basturma* (whole, air-dried beef loin)
- Hot-smoked *salo* (pork belly)
- Salt-cured *salo* (pork fatback—look for thick slabs, fully opaque)
- *Okhotnichya kolbasa* (skinny dried hunter's sausages)
- *Telyachiy rulet* (hot-smoked veal roll)

THE PICKLE AISLE

I'm not just talking cucumbers—everything from apples to squash to garlic scapes can be found on these shelves. In a good store, you'll find more species of mushrooms available than you probably knew existed. Larger markets may also have pickles fermented in-house available at the deli counter (sometimes with garlic cloves or scraps of horseradish leaves still bobbing in the brine).

THE PELMENI FREEZER

Making your own *pelmeni* is really worth tackling (pages 198–201). But buying a bag of these guys from the freezer section is nothing to shy away from. There will likely be several dozen options to choose from—pork, chicken, cheese, sauerkraut—and they make for an easy I'm-too-exhausted-to-cook dinner.

BOXED CHOCOLATES

DO NOT ACTUALLY BUY ANY OF THESE CHOCOLATES. They are generally stale and of poor quality (the chocolates available in bulk bins—see photo at right and pages 346–347—are usually a better bet). But *do* stare in awe of the size and variety of boxes available. This speaks to the importance Russians place on bringing gifts when visiting someone.

MINERAL WATERS

Glacier spring mineral waters from southern Russia and Georgia are a must-try. Full of many naturally occurring minerals (each with its own flavor profile), they make for a surprising sip. Narzan is a good starter water—the most subdued. Borjomi, from Georgia, has a nice fine bubble and a briny, mineral taste. Essentuki #4 is the most intense experience, like a glass of ocean spray.

CONDIMENTS

Satsebeli. Narsharab. Tkemali. Adjika. And so on. There's a wide range of interesting and tasty condiments to explore from all over the former Soviet Union. Quail egg mayo, anyone? Even the ketchups and mustards are a little different here. (PS: The good mustard is in the refrigerator—get the Zakuson brand.)

While we're on the subject, find the spice aisle and snag a few seasoning packets to experiment with the next time you roast a chicken. *Khmeli suneli*, *plov* mix, adjika spices, et cetera—all quick, easy ways to get familiar with the flavors of the cuisine.

THE TVOROG AND SMETANA FRIDGE

For a region of the world that loves its dairy (even the caramel is made from milk sugars!), there really isn't a tradition of Russian aged cheeses. Instead, you will find DOZENS of different brands and styles of *tvorog* (fresh farmer's cheese), kefirs, and *smetana* (sour cream). Spend some time poring over the options with the same gusto you would the cheese counter in Paris.

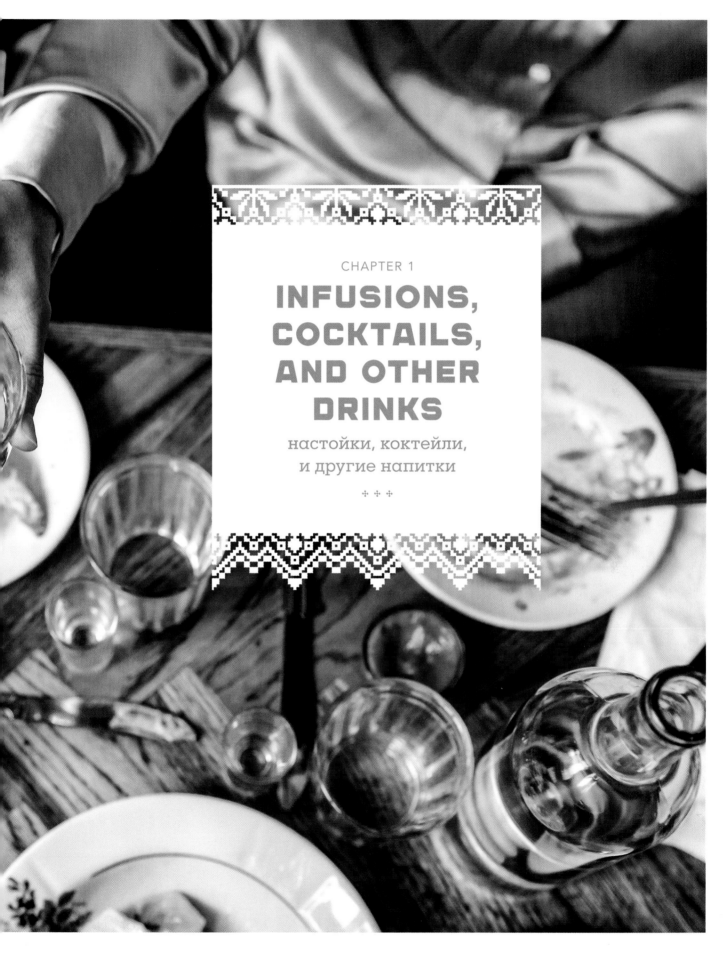

CHAPTER 1

INFUSIONS, COCKTAILS, AND OTHER DRINKS

настойки, коктейли,
и другие напитки

✣ ✣ ✣

I t's not an accident that beverages are at the front of this book. Drinking and eating are two sides of the same coin in Russia, so to prepare for a proper Russian feast, we must prepare the drinks.

Absolut Vodka first introduced the idea of flavored vodka to the American public in 1986, with their Absolut Peppar. But infusing vodkas (or, in many cases, *samogon*—moonshine) has been a regular part of life for millions of people all through the "vodka belt" of Russia, Ukraine, Belarus, and Northern Europe for hundreds of years. These started as medicinal tonics, or ways to process and preserve fleeting ingredients (or soften the blow of rough-around-the-edges samogon), but have evolved into complex, balanced libations.

Making a good infusion (marshmallow or cinnamon bun vodka aside) is a serious task, deeply rooted in geography and tradition. Alcohol is the perfect vehicle to both preserve and amplify delicate flavors—especially when done well. My husband, Israel, has taken on the task of creating a thoughtful infusion program at Kachka that gives a nod to this storied Slavic practice—but also reflects *our* geography and *our* traditions.

Though well-made infusions require little other than a few bites of *zakuski* (see "Slava's Guide to Drinking and the Pyanka," page 40) to accompany them, we also honor modern drinking convention by using them to craft cocktails—because while horseradish-infused vodka is stellar on its own, a horseradish-infused vodka Bloody Mary is not too shabby either.

A few general notes:

FOLLOW THE PRESCRIBED STEEPING TIMES
There is an almost parabolic curve to infusing, and you need to time things out depending on where on that curve you want to land. Sometimes you want to infuse well past the peak of flavor to let time mellow things out, while other ingredients require you to stop infusing before volatile or bitter compounds take over. In other words, longer does *not* always equal better—follow the infusion times provided.

CHEAP AND NEUTRAL ARE YOUR FRIENDS
Don't reach for that pricey you-can-really-taste-the-hand-harvested-wheat bottle of craft vodka if you're going to toss in a few aromatic heads of flowering dill. Clean, bottom-shelf brands, like Taaka or Gordon's, work best.

CONSIDER SHELF LIFE
No, an infused spirit will not go bad in a make-you-sick sort of way. However, you are introducing volatile compounds into an otherwise inert liquid. This means that the product will change as it sits, and not always in a tasty way. Infusions shouldn't typically hang out on your back bar for more than a few months, collecting dust—so drink up!

VODKA INFUSIONS AND COCKTAILS

Tarragon—Laika 21

Horseradish—Bloody Masha 22

Chamomile—Baba Yaga 25

Cacao Nib—Black/White Russian 27

Hunter's—Chervona Wine 29

Lime—Moscow Mule 30

Dill Flower 32

Sea Buckthorn Berry 32

Zubrovka—M. Bison 34

Cranberry—Kosmos-Politan 35

Strawberry 36

Rowanberry—Thor's Salvation 38

INFUSIONS AND COCKTAILS FROM OTHER SPIRITS

Orange Vermouth—From Russia with Love 45

Earl Grey Tea Brandy—Baba Sima's Tonic 46

Beet Gin—Red Heering 48

Grapefruit Gin—Pinko Commie Bastard 51

Lemon Aquavit—Nasha Dama 52

Caraway Rye Whiskey—Jewish Rye 55

OTHER DRINKS

Summer Kompot (Steeped Fresh Fruit Punch) 58

Blackberry Nalivka (Liqueur) 61

Kvas (Lightly Fermented Bread Soda) 62

Cranberry Mors (Juice) 64

Tarragon Soda 65

Slava's Guide to Drinking and the Pyanka 40

Babushka's Remedies 66

VODKA INFUSIONS AND COCKTAILS

TARRAGON VODKA

настойка из тархуне

+ + +

When you talk about tarragon in Russian cuisine, you're usually talking soda—bright green Georgian soda. But infuse the clean, anise-y flavor into vodka, and you get an herbaceous complement for fish-focused zakuski—and it also marries beautifully with grapefruit, making for an out-of-this-world greyhound cocktail. We call ours Laika, after the first dog in space (also an out-of-this-world dog).

4 sprigs fresh tarragon

1 750-milliliter bottle of vodka

1 teaspoon simple syrup

Place the tarragon sprigs in a quart-sized mason jar and pour the vodka over them. Reserve the vodka bottle for the finished product. Screw on the lid and let steep for 24 hours in a dark, cool place.

After steeping, carefully pour the simple syrup into the reserved bottle. Strain the vodka from the tarragon into the bottle using a fine-mesh strainer and funnel. Discard the tarragon. Close the bottle and shake to combine. Freeze for at least 1 hour before serving.

LAIKA

лайка

YIELDS 1 DRINK

1½ ounces tarragon vodka

1½ ounces fresh grapefruit juice

1 teaspoon simple syrup (optional—some grapefruits are sweet enough on their own)

Tonic water (we use Fentimans)

Grapefruit twist (use a vegetable peeler to take off one big strip)

Pour the vodka, grapefruit juice, and simple syrup (if using) into an ice-filled shaker, and shake to combine. Strain into an ice-filled double old-fashioned glass, and top off with tonic water. Squeeze the grapefruit twist over the drink to express the oils, and place the twist in the drink.

HORSERADISH VODKA

настойка из хреновуха

✦ ✦ ✦

So common is horseradish-infused alcohol that it has its own name—khren-a-VOO-kha. But often horseradish vodkas are too harsh, or just plain weak. On a trip to St. Petersburg in 2013, we tasted a horseradish vodka that was head and shoulders above the rest. So my dad charmed some tips out of our server, and when we got home, Israel got to work experimenting. The resulting infusion grew so quickly to cult status at Kachka that we've since started bottling it.

Amazingly, there is no Bloody Mary tradition in Russia—despite a well-demonstrated supply of vodka, hangovers, horseradish, and all sorts of pickled accoutrements. Clearly this was long overdue. In creating this Bloody Mary recipe, I turned to my brother, Simon, who is the king of Bloody Marys (and margaritas, but that's a different book).

1¼ ounces peeled horseradish root, cut into 2-inch chunks

1 750-milliliter bottle of vodka

1½ teaspoons honey

Place the horseradish root in a quart-sized mason jar and pour the vodka over it. Reserve the vodka bottle for the finished product. Screw on the lid and let steep for 1 week in a dark, cool place.

After steeping, carefully pour the honey into the reserved bottle. Strain the vodka from the horseradish into the bottle using a fine-mesh strainer and funnel. Discard the horseradish. Close the bottle and shake to combine. Freeze for at least 1 hour before serving.

BLOODY MASHA

YIELDS 1 PINT

1 teaspoon caraway seeds

1 teaspoon black peppercorns

1 teaspoon coriander seeds

1 teaspoon brown mustard seeds

6 ounces Campbell's tomato juice*

2¼ ounces horseradish vodka

2 teaspoons Worcestershire sauce

2 teaspoons fresh lemon juice

1 teaspoon chopped fresh dill

½ teaspoon prepared horseradish

½ teaspoon kosher salt

Garnishes of your choice†

Heat a small skillet over medium heat, and toast the caraway seeds, black peppercorns, coriander seeds, and mustard seeds, stirring until aromatic (a minute or two). Pulverize in a spice grinder and toss the ground spices into a mixing bowl along with the remaining ingredients. Whisk until combined, and taste to adjust seasonings.

Fill a glass (or two) with ice, and pour in the drink. Top with skewered garnishes of your choice.

---

* If using a different brand, you may need to add more salt.

†Pickles (green tomatoes and beets are especially nice), chunks or slices of cured meats, smoked fish, cheese, fresh herbs (dill, celery hearts, etc.)

CHAMOMILE VODKA

настойка на ромашке

✦ ✦ ✦

Russian grandmothers will administer chamomile infusions for ulcers, gas, and pretty much any complaint. Unlike chamomile tisane (which I've always found disappointingly one-note), an alcohol extraction pulls out different elements, leaving an infusion with strong honey and floral notes. Those flavors play nicely in the Baba Yaga cocktail.

Baba Yaga is a witchy grandma in Russian folklore, who lives in a house built on chicken legs and might occasionally eat a lost child or two. So what better to name a cocktail inspired by this medicinal grandma potion? Plus we slip in some Strega, a liqueur named for an Italian grandmotherly witch, so we couldn't resist. The resulting cocktail is basically a sour, but with a not-too-sweet floral element from the infusion.

½ cup loose-leaf chamomile tisane (flowers)*

1 750-milliliter bottle of vodka

1 teaspoon simple syrup

Place the chamomile in a quart-sized mason jar and pour the vodka over it. Reserve the vodka bottle for the finished product. Screw on the lid and let steep for 24 hours in a dark, cool place.

After steeping, carefully pour the simple syrup into the reserved bottle. Strain the vodka from the chamomile into the bottle using a fine-mesh strainer and funnel. Discard the chamomile. Close the bottle and shake to combine. Freeze for at least 1 hour before serving.

BABA YAGA

баба яга

YIELDS 1 DRINK

2 ounces chamomile vodka

¾ ounce fresh lemon juice

½ ounce simple syrup

¼ ounce Liquore Strega (if unavailable, substitute Yellow Chartreuse)

Lemon twist (use a vegetable peeler to take off one big strip)

Pour the vodka, lemon juice, simple syrup, and Liquore Strega into an ice-filled shaker, and shake to combine. Double strain into a coupe or martini glass. Squeeze the lemon twist over the drink to express the oils, and discard.

* Available in tea shops or natural-food markets

CACAO NIB VODKA

настойка на какао

✦ ✦ ✦

When you hear "chocolate vodka," you think sickly sweet kids' stuff. Which is why we initially resisted it. But we worked out a version that manages to be deep, rich, and bittersweetly balanced. Not surprisingly, it makes for a superior Black or White Russian.

2 tablespoons cacao nibs

1 750-milliliter bottle of vodka

1 tablespoon simple syrup

Preheat your oven to 375°F. Place the nibs on a rimmed baking sheet, and toast them for 5 minutes (they'll begin to smell delicious). Remove from the oven and let cool slightly, then place them in a quart-sized mason jar and pour the vodka over them. Reserve the vodka bottle for the finished product. Screw on the lid and let steep for 1 week in a dark, cool place.

After steeping, carefully pour the simple syrup into the reserved bottle. Strain the vodka from the nibs into the bottle using a fine-mesh strainer and funnel. Discard the nibs. Close the bottle and shake to combine. Freeze for at least 1 hour before serving.

BLACK/WHITE RUSSIAN

YIELDS 1 DRINK

1½ ounces cacao nib vodka

¾ ounce coffee liqueur (we use Portland's New Deal Coffee Liqueur)

5 drops Bittermens Xocolatl Mole Bitters (these are worth seeking out for the full effect)

FOR WHITE RUSSIAN ADD:

½ ounce simple syrup

2 ounces half-and-half

For Black Russian: Pour the vodka, coffee liqueur, and bitters into an ice-filled mixing glass, and stir for 5 seconds. Strain into an old-fashioned glass, then add ice. Serve with bar straws for stirring.

For White Russian: Follow directions above for Black Russian, but add the simple syrup to the stirred ingredients. After straining and adding ice, gently top with the half-and-half.

HUNTER'S VODKA

НАСТОЙКА ОХОТНИЧЬЯ

✢ ✢ ✢

Although the ingredients in this traditional infusion vary from house to house, you'll always find a mix of hard spices, creating a woodsy, wintery vibe. Which is why it works so well in the Chervona Wine cocktail.

The cocktail is based on a sangaree, basically a cold mulled wine (and a natural friend to these wintery spices). "Chervona" means red in Ukrainian (in addition to being the name of a great Portland band), and this cocktail is a perfect way to use up last night's red wine.

1½ teaspoons whole allspice berries

1½ teaspoons juniper berries

½ teaspoon whole black peppercorns

½ teaspoon whole coriander seeds

½ teaspoon whole fenugreek seeds

1 stick cinnamon

1 slice dried star anise

1 whole clove

1 750-milliliter bottle of vodka

1 tablespoon maple syrup

Heat a small skillet over medium heat, and toast the allspice and juniper berries, black peppercorns, coriander and fenugreek seeds, cinnamon, star anise, and clove, stirring until aromatic (a minute or two). Place the spices in a quart-sized mason jar and pour the vodka over them. Reserve the vodka bottle for the finished product. Screw on the lid and let steep for 4 days in a dark, cool place.

After steeping, carefully pour the maple syrup into the reserved bottle. Strain the vodka from the spices into the bottle using a fine-mesh strainer and funnel. Discard the spices. Close the bottle and shake to combine. Freeze for at least 1 hour before serving.

CHERVONA WINE

YIELDS 1 DRINK

1½ ounces hunter's vodka

1½ ounces dry red wine

½ ounce Dolin Rouge sweet vermouth

½ ounce simple syrup

Orange twist (use a vegetable peeler to take off one big strip)

Whole nutmeg

Pour the vodka, wine, vermouth, and simple syrup into an ice-filled shaker, and shake to combine. Strain into an ice-filled double old-fashioned glass. Squeeze the orange twist over the drink to express the oils, place the twist in the drink, and grate nutmeg over the top to finish.

LIME VODKA

настойка на лайме

✢ ✢ ✢

A Moscow mule is not a Russian cocktail. At all. But everyone expects us to make one—and so we've figured out how to make a pretty mean mule. The difference between ours and the standard bar offering? Lime-infused vodka. Infusing citrus carries deeper, more complex notes of lime than you can get from juice alone—it's got a nice snap on its own, and is strong enough to stand up to a stubborn mule's ginger and vodka.

2 whole limes

1 750-milliliter bottle of vodka

Place the limes in a quart-sized mason jar and pour the vodka over them. Reserve the vodka bottle for the finished product. Screw on the lid and let steep for 24 hours in a dark, cool place.

After steeping, remove and discard the limes. Using a funnel, transfer the vodka to the reserved bottle. Freeze for at least 1 hour before serving.

MOSCOW MULE

YIELDS 1 DRINK

2 ounces lime vodka

¾ ounce fresh lime juice

¼ ounce ginger syrup (we like Ginger People, or make your own by shaking together equal parts fresh ginger juice and granulated sugar)

Ginger beer (we use Fever-Tree)

Lime wheel

Pour the vodka, lime juice, and ginger syrup into an ice-filled shaker, and shake to combine. Strain into an ice-filled double old-fashioned glass (if you don't have a copper mug, that is), and top off with ginger beer. Garnish with a lime wheel.

DILL FLOWER VODKA

настойка на зонтиках укропа

✦ ✦ ✦

When you use dill flowers, you get so much more complexity than from the fronds alone. The clean, almost minty flavor is a natural fit for the zakuski table, especially paired with pickled green tomatoes (page 78).

1 fresh head flowering dill

1 750-milliliter bottle of vodka

1 teaspoon simple syrup

Place the dill in a quart-sized mason jar and pour the vodka over it. Reserve the vodka bottle for the finished product. Screw on the lid and let steep for 24 hours in a dark, cool place.

After steeping, carefully pour the simple syrup into the reserved bottle. Strain the vodka from the dill flowers into the bottle using a fine-mesh strainer and funnel. Discard the dill. Close the bottle and shake to combine. Freeze for at least 1 hour before serving.

SEA BUCKTHORN BERRY VODKA

настойка из облепихи

✦ ✦ ✦

Sea buckthorn is one of the common infusions you see steeping on a babushka's kitchen shelf. Usually taken as a get-your-vitamin-C tonic, these tiny Siberian berries are not just good for you—they carry an alluring mix of apricot, peach, and passionfruit flavors.

1 pound (about 3 cups) frozen sea buckthorn berries, thawed

4 ounces simple syrup

1 750-milliliter bottle of vodka

Toss the berries in a mixing bowl, and use a potato masher to smash them. Transfer to a quart-sized mason jar with the simple syrup. Add the vodka. Reserve the vodka bottle for the finished product. Screw on the lid and let steep for 1 month in a dark, cool place.

After steeping, line a fine-mesh strainer with several layers of cheesecloth or a coffee filter, and pour the vodka through the strainer and a funnel into the reserved bottle. Refrigerate before serving. Do not freeze.

ZUBROVKA VODKA

зубровка

✛ ✛ ✛

Zubrovka, also known as bison grass, is a sweet grass that grows throughout parts of Europe and North America. It has an intoxicating scent—like a clean whiff of hay mixed with vanilla. Commercially available zubrovka vodkas are made with an extract, which just doesn't capture the same heady harvest notes. Find braids of dried and cured zubrovka online, usually labeled sweetgrass, and infuse it for the real deal.

If you want to be like the cool kids in Belarus, mix zubrovka with Sprite or apple juice. If you want a more grown-up drink, make the M. Bison. Just like the Street Fighter video game character, it's bold yet light on its feet.

4 grams dried bison grass (this is strong stuff, so best to go by weight)

1 750-milliliter bottle of vodka

1 tablespoon simple syrup

Place the bison grass in a quart-sized mason jar and pour the vodka over it. Reserve the vodka bottle for the finished product. Screw on the lid and let steep for 24 hours in a dark, cool place.

After steeping, carefully pour the simple syrup into the reserved bottle. Strain the vodka from the bison grass into the bottle using a fine-mesh strainer and funnel. Discard the bison grass. Close the bottle and shake to combine. Freeze for at least 1 hour before serving.

M. BISON

YIELDS 1 DRINK

2 ounces zubrovka vodka

¾ ounce fresh lemon juice

½ ounce sour cherry syrup (available at Russian markets— you can substitute grenadine, or sour cherry juice plus some simple syrup)

½ ounce Bäska Snaps Med Malört (if unavailable, substitute Lillet Blanc or Cocchi Americano)

Club soda (use tonic water if substituting Lillet or Cocchi)

Amarena cherry

Pour the vodka, lemon juice, cherry syrup, and Bäska Snaps into an ice-filled shaker, and shake to combine. Strain into an ice-filled collins glass, top with club soda (tonic water if using Lillet or Cocchi), and garnish with an amarena cherry.

CRANBERRY VODKA

КЛЮКОВКА

✢ ✢ ✢

Many people think of cranberries as totally Thanksgiving-table America, but they are an important part of Russian cuisine year-round. *Klyukva* are a thinner-skinned and sweeter variety of cranberry, but the flavors are one and the same—and they happen to make for a lovely garnet vodka.

When it comes to vodka cocktails, the cosmopolitan is one of the classics. But why use cranberry juice when you can use cranberry vodka? Add some cranberry bitters, and the cranberry flavor is as big as the kosmos. Admittedly, this is a variation on the daisy cocktail rather than a true cosmo template—but really all that matters is it's out-of-this-world delicious.

12 ounces (about 3 cups) frozen cranberries, thawed

2 ounces simple syrup

1 750-milliliter bottle of vodka

Toss the berries in a mixing bowl and use a potato masher to smash them. Transfer to a quart-sized mason jar with the simple syrup, then add the vodka. Reserve the vodka bottle for the finished product. Screw on the lid and let steep for 2 weeks in a dark, cool place.

After steeping, line a fine-mesh strainer with several layers of cheesecloth or a coffee filter, and pour the vodka through the strainer and a funnel into the reserved bottle. Refrigerate before serving. Do not freeze.

KOSMOS-POLITAN

YIELDS 1 DRINK

1½ ounces cranberry vodka

¾ ounce fresh lime juice

½ ounce St. Germain

¼ ounce Giffard Crème de Pêche de Vigne

3 dashes Fee's cranberry bitters

1 ounce club soda

Pour the vodka, lime juice, St. Germain, Crème de Pêche, and bitters into an ice-filled shaker, and shake to combine. Double strain into a coupe or martini glass and top off with club soda.

STRAWBERRY VODKA

настойка на клубнике

✦ ✦ ✦

Strawberry vodka is like a time capsule in a shot glass, capturing a bowl of berries at their absolute peak ripeness. And somehow amplifying the flavors, making them even more than they are. One of our best regulars is so enamored of this infusion that he's been known to drop everything and come running when this highly seasonal infusion is ready. And he's not alone—it's something of a religious event around here.

1 cup whole strawberries (we use Oregon's Hood strawberries, but any peak-of-season variety will do)

1 750-milliliter bottle of vodka

2 tablespoons sugar

Thoroughly wash the strawberries and remove the stems. Place the whole strawberries in a quart-sized mason jar and pour the vodka over them. Reserve the vodka bottle for the finished product. Screw on the lid and let steep for 1 week in a dark, cool place.

After steeping, strain the vodka from the strawberries into the bottle using a fine-mesh strainer and funnel. Discard the strawberries. Add the sugar, close the bottle, and shake to combine. Freeze for at least 1 hour before serving.

ROWANBERRY VODKA

рябиновка

✧ ✧ ✧

Known as *ryabina*, rowanberry (or mountain ashberry) is a very traditional infusion. This tree is typically viewed as purely ornamental in the United States, which has led to some embarrassing grandma-stealing-from-the-neighbors moments (don't ask). Once you know what you're looking for, you'll find mountain ash shrubs everywhere you look. Rowanberries need to be picked after a frost for their full sweetness to develop—but you can fake it by tossing them in your freezer overnight.

In Norse mythology, the rowan is called "the salvation of Thor," because its branches saved the thunder god from drowning. Our play on a daiquiri is crisp and refreshing (while packing a wallop). We serve it with a large ice cube to symbolize Thor's hammer.

2 pounds frozen rowanberries, thawed

⅓ cup simple syrup

1 750-milliliter bottle of vodka

Toss the berries in a mixing bowl, and use a potato masher to smash them. Transfer into a half-gallon mason jar with the simple syrup, then add the vodka. Reserve the vodka bottle for the finished product. Screw on the lid and let steep for 1 month in a dark, cool place.

After steeping, line a fine-mesh strainer with several layers of cheesecloth or a coffee filter, and pour the vodka through the strainer and a funnel into the reserved bottle. Freeze for at least 1 hour before serving.

THOR'S SALVATION

YIELDS 1 DRINK

2 ounces rowanberry vodka

¾ ounce Falernum

½ ounce fresh lime juice

½ teaspoon Fernet-Branca

Pour all the ingredients into an ice-filled shaker, and shake to combine. Double strain into an old-fashioned glass with one big ice cube.

SLAVA'S GUIDE TO DRINKING AND THE PYANKA

There is a Russian word that has no English equivalent: **PYANKA** (пьянка)

A *pyanka* essentially translates as a party where drinking is the main objective. But it's not really about the alcohol—it's about the experience. About opening your heart when you open the bottle (and, of course, filling your plate as you fill your glass). At the center of a pyanka—of Russian drinking in general—are three guiding principles:

1. NEVER DRINK ALONE.
This doesn't just mean making sure you have a compatriot at your side (although that's part of it)—it means literally drinking in unison. Everyone fills up their shot glasses together, and then drinks their measure in tandem. At a pyanka, a *tamada* (host) serves as a sort of ringmaster for the unfolding group drinks and toasts.

2. ALWAYS DRINK FOR A REASON.
Each shot requires a reason—laid out in a toast. And a simple "cheers" just doesn't cut it. A drink requires some thoughtfulness. Raising a glass in honor of the host, reading a scrap of poetry for a loved one—this is why we drink.

3. NEVER DRINK WITHOUT EATING.
Eating means *EATING*. I'm talking breaking bread, not beer nuts. To a Russian, all parties are dinner parties—and having something in your stomach means you can keep toasting for the next several hours.

With these three guiding principles, a sort of cadence emerges. A toast to bring everyone together, the clinking of glasses, throwing back your drink, and eating a few zakuski. And this repeats itself over and over.

> Toast, clink, drink, eat, repeat.
>
> Toast, clink, drink, eat, repeat.

It's such a beautiful way to spend time together. And *that* is what a pyanka really is.

Didn't grow up pouring out your Soviet soul over shots of vodka? Here's a guide to the true Russian pyanka, according to my dad.

ON DRINKING IN GOOD COMPANY

"For me the drinking starts with the company. Great company is the key. As far as what does great company mean: obviously it's a conversation. I mean, if you sitting and keep quiet, this is not great company. You need to have respect for the people you are drinking with. Conversation is running like a *rechiyok*—how you say—a river?"

ON BEING AT THE READY

"Best parties happen spontaneous. No phones, people just show up. Pull out from refrigerator *salo* [cured fatback or pork belly], and *kapusta* [cabbage] from the *pogreb* [cellar]. Basically, you have to have at home permanent readiness. Always prepared for a party. We can't be caught with nothing to put on the table. If someone opens your door, you can hug your friend and start a party."

ON BEING IN THE MOMENT

"Americans need to understand. It's not just a long meal, it's a long process. Be prepared—*kak eto*—it's not a sprinter, it's a marathon. It's a whole-night event. Take your time. Enjoy yourself. Relax. Follow the crowd. You have a toast. You clink the glasses, drink, eat. And the next toast is not too far away."

ON THE TAMADA

"You elect a tamada—like a chairman of the drinking party. Tamada makes sure no one is passed over. Tamada is leading the conversation, unites all the individuals into one conversation and appoints the next toaster."

ON TOASTS

"Toasts are born. Toasts are like a punch line for what you are talking about. Like every time you go to a party, just in case, you should have something to say. Often people will write poems or speeches to prepare in advance for a party [or a] quick and sharp phrase."

ON FAUX PAS

"Never clink glass with your spouse (you will not have money). Never clink glasses when toasting to a departed. Always drink to the bottom—*do d'na*. Do not put down your shot glass after clinking without drinking—it's like you're ignoring the toast. To show respect, sometimes you get up and walk over to a specific person at the table to clink glasses."

ON COCKTAILING

"It's hard to change the habits in one night. Americans, they drink usually standing up before the meal, and then the dinner comes and that's it. This is not right. I would say to try it and see if you like it [the Russian way]. Try this system of sitting and eating and drinking instead of this standing up. Let me put it this way: I've seen some Americans in our parties, and it seems to me they enjoyed it. You should try. You know what, put my phone number—I will join the party."*

ON KNOWING HOW TO PACE YOURSELF

"Typically, I'm a good driver for a party. I know what's the menu and what rhythm or pace to take. In the beginning with the zakuski we are getting a little boom boom boom—more frequent. Slow down as the party progresses. Main and dessert. And by dessert the time is late. Comes to a natural end."

A NOTE ON DRINKING FROM THE AUTHOR

I find it helpful as the host of a party to set really small shot glasses to help control consumption (and allow more toasting before reaching capacity). And, of course, do drink responsibly: don't just elect a tamada; elect a designated driver, too!

If serving vodka, freeze it first. Also, know that you do not need to drink vodka—or really any alcohol—to "drink like a Russian." My babushka drinks Manischewitz. I often pour wine into my shot glass, and my six-year-old shoots with water (his favorite toast to give is "to the family!"). The important thing isn't what's in your glass—it's to give sincere toasts, and gather together around a bountiful spread.

---

* Much to my dad's disappointment, I chose *not* to list his phone number.

PYANKA CRIB SHEET

Use really small shot glasses (or don't fill larger ones all the way).

❖

You don't need to drink alcohol to "drink like a Russian." Pour juice or seltzer or anything you want in your shot glass.

❖

Don't cocktail first.

❖

Elect a tamada.

❖

Have enough food—and eat it!

❖

Drink in unison (and don't go rogue and drink alone between rounds).

❖

Toast, clink, drink, eat, repeat.

❖

Have a toast in your back pocket (see below).

❖

Don't keep drinking after dinner.

❖

Try a shot in the morning and some sauerkraut juice to cure a hangover.

SLAVA'S FALLBACK TOASTS
(if you're short on inspiration)

"For everything that joins us."

❖

"To the host and/or hostess."

❖

"To our friendship [or to the mothers, the wives, the children, the family, et cetera]."

❖

"To America." (Because it is a great country!)

❖

"Boodim [we will]."

❖

"Za dam [to the ladies]." (I don't like this toast, usually because you are getting in trouble with the ladies—happens a lot.)

❖

"Za oodachu [to good fortune]."

INFUSIONS AND COCKTAILS FROM OTHER SPIRITS

ORANGE VERMOUTH

настойка апельсиновая из вермута

✛ ✛ ✛

When you have a vodka list that's sixty deep, you're going to get calls for vodka martinis. This is known. So we set out to make a martini that 007 would be proud of (although we prefer ours stirred), with a classic ratio that pays as much attention to the vermouth as to the vodka. The pleasant bitterness of the orange infusion lends more complexity than the traditional dash of orange bitters. Be sure to use Russian Standard—there are few vodkas out there that make an equal martini.

1 whole orange

1 750-milliliter bottle of dry vermouth (we use Dolin)

Place the orange and vermouth in a container that's large enough to hold them. Reserve the vermouth bottle for the finished product. Cover the container with a lid or wrap it tightly, and let steep for 24 hours in a dark, cool place.

After steeping, remove and discard the orange. Using a funnel, transfer the vermouth to the reserved bottle. Refrigerate before serving. Do not freeze.

FROM RUSSIA WITH LOVE

из россии с любовью

YIELDS 1 DRINK

2 ounces Russian Standard vodka

½ ounce orange vermouth

Lemon twist (use a vegetable peeler to take off one big strip)

Olive (we use Alfonso olives)

Pour the vodka and orange vermouth into an ice-filled mixing glass, and stir for 10 seconds. Strain into a coupe or martini glass. Squeeze the lemon twist over the drink to express the oils, and discard. Garnish with an olive on a pick.

EARL GREY TEA BRANDY

чайная настойка на бренди

✢ ✢ ✢

If you get a cold, my babushka Sima insists that you drink black tea with vodka and raspberry jam all mixed up together into a sort of toddy. Her home remedy is the inspiration for making a tea infusion—though we've swapped out the vodka for brandy, as the caramel undertones play beautifully with tea leaves.

The resulting Baba Sima's Tonic is a striking drink (and you get to play with fire!). Verdict's still out on its cold-fighting properties, but just in case she's right, serve with a spoon of raspberry jam on the side.

¼ cup loose-leaf Earl Grey crème tea (if unavailable, standard Earl Grey will do)

1 750-milliliter bottle of brandy (we use Korbel)

1½ teaspoons maple syrup

Place the tea in a quart-sized mason jar and pour the brandy over it. Reserve the brandy bottle for the finished product. Screw on the lid and let steep for 24 hours in a dark, cool place.

After steeping, carefully pour the maple syrup into the reserved bottle. Strain the brandy from the tea into the bottle using a fine-mesh strainer and funnel. Discard the tea. Freeze for at least 1 hour before serving.

BABA SIMA'S TONIC

бабы симина микстура

YIELDS 1 DRINK

2 ounces Earl Grey tea brandy

¼ ounce simple syrup

1 sugar cube

¼ ounce overproof rum (we use Gosling's 151)

2 orange twists (use a vegetable peeler to take off nice big strips)

5 ounces (scant ⅔ cup) boiling water

Place the brandy and simple syrup in a warmed hot toddy glass. Balance a spoon over the top of the glass, and place the sugar cube on it. Carefully pour the rum over the cube, and then light it on fire. Flames! Carefully wave 1 orange twist over the flame for a few seconds, then squeeze the twist into the flame to express the oils. Fireworks! Carefully tip the flamey cube into the cup so that it ignites the liquid in the glass. Pour in the hot water, extinguishing the flames and stirring everything together. Squeeze the second orange twist over the drink to express the oils, and place the twist in the drink. Serve hot.

BEET GIN

свекольная настойка из джина

✦ ✦ ✦

The first infusion we ever made was a beet vodka (as contractually required for a Russian restaurant). And while it was good, we learned that beets are even better when paired with the astringency of juniper and other botanicals in gin—their velvety richness rounds out the sharper flavors (for a unique, remarkable infusion, try this exact recipe with Fernet-Branca).

The Red Heering cocktail pairs beet-y gin with other strong flavors (cherry Heering and absinthe, among others), letting the roots provide an earthy base note.

1 medium beet, peeled and coarsely grated

1 750-milliliter bottle of gin (we use Gordon's)

Place the grated beet in a quart-sized mason jar and pour the gin over it. Reserve the gin bottle for the finished product. Screw on the lid and let steep for 24 hours in a dark, cool place.

After steeping, strain the gin from the grated beet into the bottle using a fine-mesh strainer and funnel. Discard the beet. Refrigerate before serving. Do not freeze. Use within 1 week.

RED HEERING

YIELDS 1 DRINK

2 ounces beet gin

¾ ounce dry vermouth (we use Dolin)

¼ ounce cherry Heering

¼ teaspoon absinthe

Orange twist (use a vegetable peeler to take off one big strip)

Pour the gin, vermouth, cherry Heering, and absinthe into an ice-filled mixing glass, and stir for 10 seconds. Strain into a coupe or martini glass. Squeeze the orange twist over the drink to express the oils, and place the twist in the drink.

GRAPEFRUIT GIN

настойка из джина на грейпфрутах

✛ ✛ ✛

My dad used to feed me grapefruits when I was a little girl (we have a shared adoration for them). Since then, grapefruit has had a special place in my heart. The infused gin is clean and bracing on its own, and also makes for a fantastic base spirit in a cocktail—the Pinko Commie Bastard is fun, zippy, and, well, pink. We figured something this perky deserved a good slap-in-the-face name.

1 whole pink grapefruit

1 750-milliliter bottle of gin (we use Beefeater)

Place the grapefruit and gin in a container that's large enough to hold them. Reserve the gin bottle for the finished product. Cover the container with a lid or wrap it tightly, and let it steep for 24 hours in a dark, cool place.

After steeping, remove and discard the grapefruit. Using a funnel, transfer the gin to the reserved bottle. Freeze for at least 1 hour before serving.

PINKO COMMIE BASTARD

YIELDS 1 DRINK

1 ounce grapefruit gin

¾ ounce Combier Pamplemousse

¾ ounce fresh lime juice

½ ounce Aperol

2 dashes Peychaud's Bitters

Grapefruit twist (use a vegetable peeler to take off one big strip)

Pour the gin, Pamplemousse, lime juice, and Aperol into an ice-filled shaker, and shake to combine. Double strain into a coupe or martini glass. Squeeze the grapefruit twist over the drink to express the oils, and discard.

LEMON AQUAVIT

ЛИМОННЫЙ АКВАВИТ

✧ ✧ ✧

My favorite classic cocktail is a well-executed White Lady, but a good one is hard to come by. Knowing this, Israel insisted on having a version on Kachka's opening menu. And he outdid himself. This is better than any White Lady out there; it's "Our Lady"—Nasha Dama. The essential oils in the lemon that are absorbed by the aquavit make the infusion otherworldly.

1 whole lemon

1 750-milliliter bottle of aquavit (we use House Spirits Krogstad)

Place the lemon in a quart-sized mason jar and pour the aquavit over it. Reserve the aquavit bottle for the finished product. Screw on the lid and let steep for 24 hours in a dark, cool place.

After steeping, remove and discard the lemon. Using a funnel, transfer the aquavit to the reserved bottle. Freeze for at least 1 hour before serving.

NASHA DAMA

наша дама

YIELDS 1 DRINK

¾ ounce lemon aquavit

¾ ounce London dry gin (we use Gordon's)

¾ ounce fresh lemon juice

½ ounce Combier orange liqueur

¼ ounce simple syrup

1 large egg white

Lemon twist (use a vegetable peeler to take off one big strip)

Pour the aquavit, gin, lemon juice, orange liqueur, simple syrup, and egg white into a shaker. Shake vigorously (you are aerating the egg whites, so shake it like your life depends on it) for 10 to 15 seconds. Add ice to the shaker and briefly shake to get the drink cold. Double strain twice into a coupe or martini glass. Squeeze the lemon twist over the drink to express the oils, and discard.

CARAWAY RYE WHISKEY

НАСТОЙКА ИЗ ВИСКИ НА ТМИНЕ

✢ ✢ ✢

Caraway integrates seamlessly with the spiciness of rye—it makes sense in a loaf of rye bread, so why not in booze? The resulting Jewish Rye cocktail is based on an old-fashioned (and a delicious pun), with the orgeat and kümmel adding a rich texture to the whiskey.

¼ cup caraway seeds

1 750-milliliter bottle rye whiskey
(we use George Dickel)

Place the caraway seeds in a quart-sized mason jar and pour the rye over them. Reserve the rye bottle for the finished product. Screw on the lid and let steep for 48 hours in a dark, cool place.

After steeping, strain the rye from the caraway seeds into the bottle using a fine-mesh strainer and funnel. Discard the caraway seeds. Close the bottle and shake to combine. Refrigerate before serving. Do not freeze.

JEWISH RYE

YIELDS 1 DRINK

2 ounces caraway rye whiskey

½ teaspoon orgeat

¼ teaspoon kümmel (caraway liqueur—nice but optional)

2 dashes orange bitters (we use one dash of Regan's No. 6 and one dash of Angostura orange)

Orange twist (use a vegetable peeler to take off one big strip)

Pour the rye, orgeat, kümmel (if using), and orange bitters into an ice-filled mixing glass, and stir for 10 seconds. Strain into an old-fashioned glass. Add ice. Squeeze the orange twist over the drink to express the oils, and place the twist in the drink.

OTHER DRINKS

SUMMER KOMPOT

компот из свежих фруктов

✧ ✧ ✧

It's hard to classify this as strictly a beverage—because it's also a rather lovely heat-of-summer dessert, something between a punch and a fruit cocktail. My grandmother laments that fresh *kompot* in her childhood in Belarus contained only wild blueberries and strawberries (*chernika* and *zemlyanika*)—as stone fruits like peaches didn't grow that far north. That variation sounds delicious, but the kompot of my childhood in Chicago was much more varied. My mom would gather up all the various fruits that were ripening too fast and turn them into a refreshing summertime treat. Kompot can also be made with dried fruit any time of year, but the summer version is what makes me weak in the knees—especially when topped with a big scoop of vanilla ice cream and squirt of club soda.

In the true spirit of kompot, feel free to adjust the recipe to what you currently have in season.

YIELDS 1½ QUARTS

2 peaches, pitted and quartered

3 plums, pitted and quartered

3 apricots, pitted and quartered

1 cup strawberries, washed and hulled

¾ cup granulated sugar

1½ quarts water

Vanilla ice cream and club soda (optional)

Place the fruits, sugar, and water in a medium pot. Bring to a boil and stir to dissolve the sugar. Reduce the heat until it's just high enough to maintain a simmer, and simmer until the fruits soften and release their flavors, up to 5 minutes. Taste and add more sugar if desired, then remove the pot from the heat, and cool to room temperature. Refrigerate for about 4 hours, or overnight, to cool completely.

When the kompot is cold, ladle both the liquid and the fruit pieces into mugs, and serve with a spoon. To turn your kompot into a soda-fountain-inspired treat, add a scoop of vanilla ice cream and top with an ounce or two of club soda.

BLACKBERRY NALIVKA

наливка из ежевики

✛ ✛ ✛

Nalivka is a home-fermented fruit booze—at one time, it could be found on every windowsill in Russia. And it's something of an evolving, bottomless crock: Thirsty? Pour off some nalivka! Just come across a cache of wild blueberries? Toss them in with some sugar!

I take a still-flexible-but-somewhat-more-measured approach, using a basic formula to ferment whatever fruits have come in. Blackberries—which grow wild all over Oregon—yield a particularly rich, jammy cordial (a decided upgrade from grandma's Manischewitz stash).

Blackberries (or raspberries, plums, elderberries, etc.)

Granulated sugar

Everclear (optional)

Take a large glass or ceramic crock, and measure out your berries by volume (feel free to scale up or down according to the harvest—your finished product will be roughly half the volume of fruit you start with). Place the berries in the crock, and for every 2 parts berries, pour 1 part sugar over the top.

After you've layered in your fruit and sugar, cover the crock with several layers of cheesecloth secured with a string or band (or a lid with an airlock—available in brewing supply stores), and place on a sunny windowsill. After 2 weeks, give the mixture a stir—the sugar should be dissolving. Re-cover, and wait another 6 weeks. Check to see if the nalivka is ready—a mature brew will have stopped bubbling and will have a sweet, intense blackberry flavor.

Strain the mixture through cheesecloth into a clean container. You can add a few ounces of Everclear per quart if desired, to stop the fermentation (and give it a more adult taste), or leave as is. If you don't, just make sure you don't leave it sealed too long—pressure can build up from residual fermentation.

Serve nalivka on its own as a liqueur, or mix with seltzer for a low-proof cocktail.

KVAS

КВАС

✦ ✦ ✦

Kvas, a bread-based, mildly fermented drink, has been around for centuries—since back when drinking low-pH kvas was safer than drinking questionable water. Both of my parents have fond memories of lining up in summer for the kvas truck—a sort of tank on wheels serving ice-cold kvas for a few kopeks from a shared cup.

Unfortunately, most of the kvas in stores today is not the real deal. Instead of a live beverage made of heels of bread, yeast, and time, commercial kvas can be a disappointing mix of caramel coloring and far too much sugar. Do yourself a favor, and mix up a batch of real kvas.

YIELDS 2 QUARTS

¾ pound dark rye bread (the flavor of kvas comes from bread, so get yourself a good dense, hearty loaf)

3 quarts water, divided

¾ cup granulated sugar

1¼ teaspoons active dry yeast (half a standard packet, or 6 grams)

2 dozen raisins

NOTE Like kombucha, kvas is a fermented beverage that does contain small amounts of alcohol; the longer it ferments, the more alcohol it will contain.

Preheat your oven to 350°F.

Cut the bread into ¼-inch slices, and lay them out on a rimmed baking sheet. Toast in the oven until they're completely dry and have a little bit of color (but are not burnt)—about 20 minutes; the exact time will vary depending on how stale your bread was to start.

When the bread is toasted, place it in a large heatproof bowl or pot. Bring 1½ quarts of water to a boil, and pour the water over the bread. Let the mixture steep for 1 hour, and then strain, keeping both the bread and the water. Set aside the first steeping of water, and place the soggy bread back in the bowl. Bring another 1½ quarts of water to a boil, pour the water over the bread, and let the mixture steep another hour (the double steeping pulls more flavor out). Using a fine-mesh strainer, strain and discard the bread. Combine the steeped waters in a large container.

Add the sugar and yeast to the strained liquid, and stir to dissolve. Taste the liquid so you have a baseline to gauge the fermentation, then place a cheesecloth or clean dishtowel over the top. Let the mixture sit at room temperature for 8 to 10 hours (longer if the room is cool, shorter if it's warm), until it becomes slightly fizzy and less sweet (as the sugars are eaten by the yeast). It can sit out longer if you would like the finished product to be more dry than sweet. Continue to taste periodically until it gets to the desired flavor.

Add the raisins, cover, and transfer to the refrigerator. Chill thoroughly, popping the lid a few times to remove the pressure from residual fermentation.

CRANBERRY MORS

клюквенный морс

✦ ✦ ✦

Mors is a drink made from cooked rather than pressed fruit—think of a fruit stock. Especially when it's made with cranberries (the most common option), the fruit releases a lot of pectin in the pot, creating a drink with a pleasant bit of body to it. Mors is one of the classic staples of the Soviet era (more or less the fruit punch of state-run cafeterias), and continues to be popular even today.

YIELDS 2½ CUPS

1 quart cranberries, fresh or frozen

1 quart water

½ cup granulated sugar

Combine the cranberries, water, and sugar in a medium saucepan. Bring the mixture to a boil, give it a stir to dissolve the sugar, and reduce the heat until it's just high enough to maintain a very gentle simmer. Simmer for 15 minutes, then gently smush the softened berries with a potato masher to release their juices. Simmer another 10 minutes, then remove from the heat.

Pass the mixture through a fine-mesh strainer, discarding the solids. Line the strainer with a coffee filter, and strain again over a heatproof bowl. It may take a couple of hours for the liquid to pass through the coffee filter (you can let it sit, or gently stir every half hour or so to help things along). You can skip the filtering if you're tight on time, but the result will be a bit more rustic. Refrigerate the mors until chilled.

To serve, dilute the mors with club soda or ice water to taste, or use as a mixer.

TARRAGON SODA

тархун

✢ ✢ ✢

Walk into a Russian market, and you will see bottle after neon-green bottle of tarragon soda. As with kvas, what you'll find on the shelf is a pale imitation of the real thing (except for the color—that is far, far brighter than the herb garden intended). Luckily, making this classic licorice-y accompaniment to summery dishes is pretty easy and far more lovely.

YIELDS ¾ CUP SYRUP, OR 1¾ QUARTS SODA

½ cup granulated sugar

½ cup water

1 large handful fresh tarragon, coarsely chopped (both stems and leaves)

½ cup fresh lemon juice

1½ quarts club soda

Combine the sugar and water in a small saucepan. Bring to a boil, stir to dissolve the sugar, then remove from the heat. Let cool to room temperature, pour into a small container, and add the tarragon. Cover, and refrigerate overnight. The next day, strain through a fine-mesh strainer, and discard the tarragon. Tarragon syrup will keep for up to 2 weeks in the refrigerator.

To make a pitcher of soda: Mix the tarragon syrup with the lemon juice and club soda in a pitcher. Serve over ice.

To make a single serving: Mix 2 tablespoons tarragon syrup with 1 tablespoon lemon juice and 8 ounces club soda in a double old-fashioned glass. Add ice.

BABUSHKA'S REMEDIES

Many of us have had grandmothers foisting food upon us. Chicken soup for a cold, all manner of sweets because they're delicious, and second helpings of second helpings because food is love and don't you think you're looking a little thin? But Russian babushkas—well, they take it to new heights. Yes, food is love. But it's also medicine.

Most vodka infusions originated as babushka remedies, making the average grandma's kitchen counter look like an alchemist's studio—a tradition we draw on for Kachka's bar program. But there are also many remedies beyond the infusion. So I sat down with my very own babushka for some sound medical advice.*

MUSTARD PLASTERS (горчичники)
Mustard is not just for your *kholodetz*. Plasters—either homemade or available online—treat everything from muscle aches to the flu. You can't really deny that they bring the heat (so much so that you've got to be careful not to burn your skin). Don't want to deal with the old-school plasters? Just sprinkle mustard powder in your socks before bed to really kick a cold's butt.

BLACK RADISH AND HONEY (чёрная редька с мёдом)
Throat bothering you? Take a big black radish, slice off the top, and slightly hollow it out into a little bowl. Fill it halfway up with honey, place its lid adorably back on top, then let it sit overnight in a cup. The next morning, your magic root pot will have filled the cup with radish-honey cough syrup.

ROSEHIP (шиповник)
Walk through a Russian park in the fall, and you'll see the pensioners out picking rosehips to infuse into tea, vodka, or honey. Source of vitamin C, sure. But also for weight loss, improving kidney function, healthy pregnancy—and since you've probably destroyed your ovaries by sitting on that cold stone bench (don't ask), you really might need some.

BLACK CURRANT (чёрная смородина)
The raw berries are ground with sugar for a classic immunity booster. The leaves are a common home remedy to treat all kinds of illnesses—including tuberculosis. Efficacy emphatically not guaranteed there.

---

* Note: Babushka advice not vetted by medical professional. Heed (or ignore) at your own peril. At the very least, it's generally tasty. Also, success not guaranteed unless administered by a licensed housedress-wearing tough-as-nails Russian grandmother.

ACTIVATED CHARCOAL (активированный уголь)

Have an upset stomach? Don't reach for antacids—instead, it's activated charcoal, used to treat everything from a standard bellyache to food poisoning (and, in some circles, taken as a preemptive hangover cure before you start drinking—often with disastrous effects). In homegrown charcoal options, the smoke from a burning bread crust (*korka*) is thought to open your sinuses.

POTATO (картошка)

No need for a humidifier if you're feeling congested. Just boil some potatoes, drain, then lean over the steaming bowl and breathe deeply. (Tenting some sort of steam-containing *shmata* over your head optional but highly recommended.) The potatoes stay hot longer than water, with no potentially messy sloshing (and, if you don't sneeze over everything, you've also got dinner).

VODKA COMPRESS (водочный компресс)

Have a cold or flu? Soak a strip of cotton in vodka, then wrap it around the ~~victim's~~ patient's neck, which will feel like it's on fire. (According to my babushka, this is a good thing.)

BADGER FAT (барсучий жир)

Dip a couple of cotton balls in the badger fat and stick them in your ears to fight off ear infections. Shockingly, I have not as yet tried this one.

TEA (чай)

Well, of course it's good for everything. But if you're feeling an illness coming on, drink a cup with copious amounts of raspberry jam before getting into bed. But never, *ever* leave the house right after drinking this, as you will of course be in the process of sweating out impurities, and to go out into the cold would be very bad for you. Speaking of which, don't eat or drink anything cold when you have a sore throat. Do not even joke about this one. Actually, you probably shouldn't drink anything cold EVER. And speaking of the cold, NEVER EVER open more than one window in the house, car, or wherever you might be. Creating a cross-breeze is basically the kiss of death. You will blow your neck out and may not survive.

CHAPTER 2

PICKLES

соленья

✦ ✦ ✦

One crisp fall evening in Minsk, when my father was a young man, he walked into a phone booth (remember those?) to call a girl, and looked down to find a huge tub of fermenting sauerkraut. No, this is not the beginning of a man-walks-into-a-bar joke. This is a true story. What was that sauerkraut doing in a phone booth, you ask? Well, he never found out. But I love this little nugget of a story, which speaks to the importance of pickles to the Russian soul.

Preservation is obviously crucial in a country with such long, cold winters. But this is true of many parts of the world—Russia doesn't own the patent on cold weather (not to mention that some parts of the former Soviet Union are downright balmy). Whatever the reason, fermentation has found a particular and permanent place in the Russian palate. And the shortages of the Soviet era only reinforced the practice, as you couldn't necessarily go to the store and expect to find sauerkraut (or even cabbage)—hence the need to preserve by the barrelful whenever the getting was good. And if you happened to live in a communal three-room apartment with three or four other families—well, you might also find yourself sticking sauerkraut in a public phone booth to ferment.

MARINATED SHIITAKES

маринованные грибы

✦ ✦ ✦

One of the most amazing aisles in any Russian market is the one with shelves and shelves of marinated mushrooms. Yes, there are *that many* options. And it's not just different brands or flavorings—it's that there are dozens of different species of mushrooms, most of which you may not have ever heard of before. Those jars are handy in a pinch, but making your own is really quite easy and rewarding. After starting with shiitakes, I encourage you to travel the mushroom aisle (or your local farmers' market) for ideas on what variety to marinate next.

YIELDS ABOUT 1 QUART

1 pound small shiitake mushrooms, washed and trimmed (smaller mushrooms can be left whole, but remove stems from mushrooms over 1 inch in diameter—save the stems for mushroom broth, page 352)

1 cup white vinegar, plus more for finishing

½ cup water

¼ cup white wine

1 tablespoon kosher salt

1 teaspoon granulated sugar

2 bay leaves

3 black peppercorns

2 allspice berries

1 clove garlic, peeled

1 tablespoon refined sunflower or olive oil, plus more for finishing

Bring a large pot of salted water to a boil. Add the mushrooms and cook for 1 to 2 minutes, until they just soften.

Drain the mushrooms in a strainer (this will keep them from diluting the marinade, ensuring a flavorful result), and let them cool to room temperature. Transfer to a small container.

Pour the vinegar, water, and wine into a saucepan, and stir in the salt, sugar, and spices. Bring the mixture to a boil, then remove it from the heat and add the garlic. Let it cool to room temperature, then pour over the mushrooms. Pour the oil over the top, and refrigerate for at least 3 days, and up to 2 weeks.

To serve, strain the mushrooms from the liquid and dress with some oil and a splash of vinegar.

SALT-CURED CHANTERELLES

соленые лисички

+ + +

My mom's second cousin Lucik is an avid mushroom hunter (even more so than the average already-enthusiastic Belarusian), and he regularly preserves his finds with this recipe. This method of preservation has a lot going for it (beyond the fact that it's crazy simple): namely, it concentrates the chanterelles' delicious-yet-subtle flavors. Serve these little treasures with plenty of good-quality smetana and freshly sliced sweet onions for an unforgettable treat.

YIELDS 2 TO 2½ CUPS

2 pounds chanterelles

¼ cup kosher salt

Refined sunflower or olive oil for finishing

Sliced chives or sweet onion (optional) for finishing

Smetana (page 359) or European-style sour cream

Fill a large bowl or salad spinner with water, then thoroughly clean the chanterelles by dunking them in and vigorously swishing them around to shake loose any debris. Remove quickly, and repeat the process as needed until the chanterelles are clean.

Bring a large pot of water to a boil, and lay out some clean dish towels or paper towels. When the water boils, add the chanterelles, and blanch them for 15 seconds—you're sanitizing them, and also giving them a light cook, as chanterelles should not be eaten raw. After blanching, drain the chanterelles, and lay them out on the towels to absorb the excess water.

Transfer the chanterelles to a large nonreactive bowl, and mix them with the salt. Find a smaller bowl that fits within your bowl, and place it on top of the mushrooms to weigh them down. Grab some heavy weights (a few cans work well), and place them inside the bowl to compress the chanterelles. Refrigerate.

After a few days, the chanterelles will have released enough liquid that they should be fully submerged without weights. Transfer the chanterelles and liquid to a glass jar. Let the chanterelles continue to cure in the refrigerator for about 2 weeks—when they're done, the thickest part should taste salty when cut open. Store fully submerged in their own liquid—stored properly, chanterelles should keep for several months.

To serve, soak for up to 30 minutes in fresh water to remove the excess salt to your taste. With a clean dish towel, blot away the excess moisture, and toss the chanterelles with a bit of refined sunflower or olive oil, and sliced chives or sweet onion (if using). Serve with smetana or European-style sour cream.

MARINATED PEPPERS

маринованный перец

✦ ✦ ✦

As more and more of my family immigrated to Chicago throughout the eighties and nineties, each relative brought a new dish to the table. Zakuski spreads tend to be similar table to table, but there are always two or three personal touches. These marinated peppers were my grandmother's cousin Rya's recipe, which she brought when she came over in 1989—though her version featured quite a bit of celery (celery and I have a complicated relationship).

Really, any ordinary sweet bell pepper will work here, but if you can get your hands on Gogosari peppers (an heirloom Romanian variety) in the late summer, DO IT! This marinade captures their intense sweetness beautifully.

YIELDS 2 POUNDS

⅓ cup granulated sugar

2 teaspoons kosher salt

⅓ cup white vinegar

⅓ cup olive oil, plus more for finishing

1½ cups water

2 pounds red bell peppers

Pour the sugar, salt, vinegar, oil, and water into a large saucepan, and bring it to a boil over high heat.

While the mixture is heating, core and seed the peppers, and slice them into eighths. When the brine is boiling, add the sliced peppers (in batches, if needed), reduce the heat until it's just high enough to maintain a simmer, and simmer for 2 to 3 minutes—the peppers should soften and cook a bit, but you want to stop before they become totally limp and cooked through. Remove the pan from the heat, and cool the peppers in the brine.

The peppers are ready to use as soon as they're cooled, but if you'd like to store them for a while, pour in enough additional oil to cover the peppers. The oil will solidify in the refrigerator, creating a barrier that should keep the refrigerated peppers good for up to 1 month. Bring to room temperature before serving.

MARINATED STONE FRUITS

маринованные сливы

✦ ✦ ✦

Jams and jellies are good and all, but marinated fruit is so much more versatile—perfect for everything from perking up your pork to sweetening the farmer's cheese on your morning toast. Also, there's only so much jam one can eat (even if you're Russian). This recipe actually works for a whole host of fruits (pears, apples, peaches, apricots), but Italian prune plums or cherries develop the most character. The plums have a wonderful black-tea astringency that plays nicely with the subtle sweet-and-sour marinade, while the cherries are a magical addition to summer salads. Choose fruit that is ripe but still rather firm for the best results.

YIELDS 2 QUARTS

2 pounds Italian prune plums, or pears (peeled, halved, and cored), or cherries (on-stem is fine)

4 allspice berries (for plums only)

2 cloves (for plums only)

2 fresh bay leaves

4 cups water

⅔ cup granulated sugar

¾ cup white vinegar

Wash two quart-sized glass canning jars and lids, and sterilize them in boiling water.

Fill the cleaned jars full of the fruit (it will shrink a bit when the hot liquid hits, so don't be afraid to pack it in). Divide the allspice berries (if using), cloves (if using), and bay leaves between the two jars.

Pour the water into a large saucepan, add the sugar, and bring the mixture to a boil. When it boils, remove it from the heat, and stir in the vinegar. Pour the hot marinade over the fruit, filling the jars right to the bottom of the threads on the jar necks (give a little shake to make sure there aren't any big air bubbles).

Screw the lids on the jars, and seal in a boiling-water bath according to canning guidelines. Let plums marinate for at least 1 month, cherries and pears for 1 week. Be sure to use the liquid in the jars after opening! Try mixing it with seltzer for a zippy alternative to soda. Use within 1 year for best quality.

PICKLED GREEN TOMATOES

маринованные зелёные помидоры

✤ ✤ ✤

Every first-generation kid has a collection of memories of being forced to tag along while your weird immigrant parents do something mortifying. Top of that list for me was going to the local farm in suburban Chicago every fall to pick bushels and bushels of green tomatoes. To my Americanized eyes, they were literally picking and paying for trash. Why couldn't they be like everyone else and just pick out the red ones? And then they would always make a stink haggling over the price (haggling, in my childhood classification, was also very un-American). Green tomatoes are heavier, they reasoned—so they should be cheaper. We would schlep home hundreds of pounds, and spend all weekend pickling and jarring them.

And after all that drama, year after year, I refused to try them. Until I was much older—and sheepishly realized this is the best pickle in the world. Note that you want to make sure you pick tomatoes that are just on the about-to-think-about-turning-yellow side of green, and pickle them within a day or two of picking, before they begin to blush (yes, my parents were right to fuss).

YIELDS 1 GALLON

5 cloves garlic, peeled

A few fresh heads flowering dill

1 or 2 dried red chiles

4 to 5 pounds green tomatoes, thoroughly washed and picked through to remove bruised ones

¼ cup granulated sugar

¼ cup kosher salt

½ cup white vinegar

Wash a gallon-sized glass canning jar and lid, and sterilize it in boiling water. Add the garlic, dill, and dried chiles, then add the tomatoes (they'll shrink a bit when the hot liquid hits, so don't be afraid to pack them in).

Bring about ½ gallon of water to a boil. While it's heating, set a strainer over a large pot. Pour the boiling water over the tomatoes to the top of the jar, and let sit for 5 minutes. Pour the water out through the strainer into the pot. Take any chiles, garlic, or dill that have fallen out, and tuck them back in the jar.

Place the pot of water on the stove, and bring the liquid back to a boil. While it's heating, add the sugar, salt, and vinegar to the jar with the tomatoes.

When the water comes to a boil, pour it into the jar, coming as close to the top as you can without spilling over. Tightly screw on the lid. Lay out a clean dish towel on a dry surface, and invert the jar onto the towel. Leave the jar inverted overnight.

In the morning, check to make sure that the towel is still dry (a damp towel can indicate an unsealed jar). If the jar isn't sealed, repeat the process. If it is, bring the jar to your cellar or another cool, dark place, and store for at least 45 days before using. Use within 1 year for best quality.

PICKLED PATTYPAN SQUASH

маринованные патиссоны

✣ ✣ ✣

Pattypans are my son Noah's favorite pickle. When he was just learning to walk, these beautiful jars of little yellow squash were right at eye level at the local Russian market, and he reached for them. As any parent knows, you purchase any vegetable your child shows a vague interest in, so I happily bought them. And then, of course, I had to figure out how to make them. So many pickles turn drab or limp, but pattypans remain sunshiny and lively (plus they're just kind of adorable).

YIELDS 2 POUNDS

2 pounds pattypan squash (approximately 1½-to-2 inch diameter), washed and trimmed of stems/butts

3 sprigs dill (and/or flowers if you've got 'em)

2 sprigs parsley

1 sprig mint

2 cloves garlic, peeled

1 bay leaf

6 black peppercorns

1 quart water

3 tablespoons kosher salt

1½ tablespoons granulated sugar

⅓ cup white vinegar

Bring a large pot of salted water to a boil, and get a large bowl of ice water at the ready. Add the squash to the pot, simmer for 5 minutes, then drain and plunge them into the ice water to cool.

While the squash are cooling, add the fresh herbs, garlic, bay leaf, and peppercorns to a large nonreactive container. Drain the cooled squash, and place them on top.

Pour the quart of water into a pot, and add the salt and sugar. Bring the mixture to a boil, then remove it from the heat, and stir in the vinegar. Pour this hot brine over the squash. Place a weighted plate or plastic lid over the top to keep the squash submerged (they'll want to pop up). Leave the squash out at room temperature for 3 days, then place a lid on the container, and refrigerate for at least 1 week and up to 1 month.

UZBEK WATERMELON

арбуз маринованный по-узбекски

✤ ✤ ✤

A few summers ago I was invited to a party at my parents' friends' house. This pickled watermelon was featured as part of their Uzbek zakuski spread, so juicy and surprising that I requested the recipe. This isn't a sour pickle, but more of a salty-sweet-savory combination—and, like all watermelon, absolutely perfect on a hot summer day. Small, thin-skinned watermelons are best, but you can substitute full-sized if needed—just remove the very center, or "heart" of the melon, which would otherwise disintegrate in the brine. And do eat the whole thing—the rinds are the best part!

YIELDS ABOUT 3 POUNDS

1 quart water

¼ cup kosher salt

¼ cup granulated sugar

1 tablespoon white vinegar

1 teaspoon chile paste (I use a Calabrian chile paste, but you can substitute sambal oelek)

1 bay leaf

1 teaspoon whole black peppercorns

3 cloves garlic, peeled

4 sprigs dill (if you can find them, toss in 2 or 3 flowering heads as well)

2 sprigs mint

2 sprigs basil

2 chiles de árbol

1 small watermelon (approximately 3 pounds), sliced into 1-inch rounds, ends discarded

Bring the water to a boil, add the salt and sugar, and stir to dissolve. Turn off the heat, and stir in the vinegar and chile paste.

Place the bay leaf, peppercorns, garlic, fresh herbs, and chiles de árbol at the bottom of a very large nonreactive container or crock. Lay the sliced watermelon on top, then pour the hot brine over everything. If the melon bobs to the surface, you can weigh it down with a plate to keep it submerged. Let sit, covered, at room temperature for 24 hours, then place in the refrigerator. Let cure until the watermelon becomes darker, flavorful, and softens throughout, about 3 to 4 days. Slice into wedges and serve. Store any uneaten melon in the brine.

SAUERKRAUT

квашеная капуста

✛ ✛ ✛

I know my way around a kitchen, but when I was training our opening prep cooks at Kachka on how to make sauerkraut, I called in the experts: my parents. Making sauerkraut is not necessarily complicated, but I wanted to make sure our team really understood the gravity of making a good batch. It's serious business.

If you really get into making your own, invest in a *shinkovnitsa* (cabbage grater—basically a terrifyingly large industrial-scale mandoline). Or you can just thinly slice the cabbage by hand. But whatever you do, don't use a food processor, which will bruise up the cabbage pretty badly. If you've ever had mushy sauerkraut, that's usually the culprit. Proper sauerkraut is crunchy, juicy, and never bitter. Select a head of cabbage that is large and heavy for its size. In the fall, look for "kraut" cabbage at farm stands if you can—these late-harvest varieties are bred for the task.

YIELDS ABOUT 1 QUART

2½ pounds cabbage (after coring—about 1 good-sized head)

1 carrot

2 tablespoons kosher salt

1 teaspoon caraway seeds

Peel any dark or damaged outer leaves off the cabbage, and quarter and core it. Slice it into fine shreds, and place them in a large nonreactive container. Peel and grate the carrot on the large holes of a box grater, and mix it with the cabbage. Add the salt and caraway seeds and mix everything together with your hands, squeezing it as you go to work out some of the liquid (you're going more for loving massage than death grip; otherwise you risk bruising the cabbage).

After you've worked in the salt, find a plate or lid that fits inside your container. Place it over the cabbage, and add a good amount of weight (about 10 pounds) to press things down. Make sure whatever you use for a weight is clean and food-safe, as it will come in contact with the cabbage brine. Cover with cheesecloth, and leave out overnight.

The next day, enough liquid should have come out to cover all of the cabbage (it won't be swimming in brine, but it should be juicy). Remove the plate, and give the mixture a stir, making sure to scoop all the way to the bottom. Secure the cheesecloth over the container, and let the mixture ferment at room temperature for a few days. As it ferments, give it a good stir a few times each day—this both keeps the top of the sauerkraut from drying out and releases gases as the whole thing ferments. Dry sauerkraut can easily be contaminated.

Start tasting the kraut after 2 days of stirring. It is ready when it is juicy, translucent, and tangy without any hints of bitterness. Bitterness is a sign that the sauerkraut is not done fermenting, so let it sit for 1 to 2 days more. The exact timing will vary depending upon temperature, but in general it shouldn't go more than 4 days.

When the kraut has fermented enough, cover the container and transfer it to the refrigerator. It will keep for up to 1 month.

MALOSOL'NYE CUCUMBERS

маринованные огурцы

+ ‡ +

My father is obsessed with cucumbers. For a period of time, his office in Minsk was across from the building's cafeteria, and he had trouble concentrating when the first cucumbers of the season started coming in—he claims the smell carried across the hall.

When cucumbers start ripening on the vine every season, my father still eats as many fresh ones as he can. But they also meet this fate: salted and barely fermented, so they are somewhat preserved but remain light and refreshing. *Malosol'nye*—which literally translates to "lightly salted"—are nothing like kosher dill pickles. (That kind of heavily salted pickling happens at the end of harvest, when you're fermenting for the long haul of winter.)

This electrolyte-filled brine is surprisingly good for sipping (we use it for picklebacks at the bar). And though it sounds strange, you *must* try pickle soup: dice finished malosol'nye cucumbers into bite-sized pieces, toss them in a bowl with some brine, and stir in smetana (page 359) or European-style sour cream to taste (roughly 2 tablespoons per cup) and dill, for an ice-cold summertime snack.

YIELDS 5 QUARTS

5 pounds pickling or Persian cucumbers

A few fresh heads flowering dill

3 cloves garlic, peeled

2 quarts water

¼ cup kosher salt

2 tablespoons granulated sugar

Wash the cucumbers, and trim a sliver off each end. Place the cucumbers, dill, and garlic in a sterile, heatproof, nonreactive jar.

Bring the water, salt, and sugar to a boil, then pour the mixture over the cucumbers. Let it cool to room temperature and allow it to sit out overnight. Then cover with cheesecloth (or a clean dish towel) and refrigerate. Taste after a couple of days—when you cut the cucumbers open, they should no longer be opaque, and should still taste reminiscent of a fresh cucumber with a pleasant brininess. Eat within 1 month for best flavor.

QUICK PICKLED GARLIC SCAPES

маринованные стрелки чеснока

✦ ✦ ✦

Around here, garlic scapes seem to be a recent discovery, still confined to farmers' markets, in-the-know gardeners, and only the most well-stocked grocers. But in Russia—and in the Baltics—garlic is everywhere, and every part of the plant is important.

If you can't find garlic scapes, you can substitute green beans or chive scapes—because the latter are more delicate, they can be taken off the heat as soon as they're added to the brine. And while the garlic scape blooms are gorgeous, they do get a bit soggy—seek out scapes that are still tight little buds, or trim off any opening flowers.

YIELDS 1 QUART

1 quart water

1 cup white vinegar

¼ cup apple cider vinegar

1 cup white wine

½ cup kosher salt

½ cup granulated sugar

3 small dried red chiles

1 pound garlic scapes, starchy ends trimmed off (leave whole for a dramatic presentation, or cut to fit whichever jars you'll use)

Pour the water, vinegars, wine, salt, sugar, and chiles into a large pot. Bring the mixture to a boil, then add the scapes. Reduce the heat until it's just high enough to maintain a simmer, and simmer for 5 minutes. Remove the pot from the heat, and let cool to room temperature. Transfer the scapes and their pickling liquid to a covered container, and refrigerate for 24 hours.

PICKLED BEETS

маринованная свекла

✧ ✧ ✧

Beets are meant to be pickled. Well, they're meant for borsch. But pickling is a pretty close second. The punch of vinegar cuts through, balancing the beets' earthy sweetness. I use pickled beets to add some tang to Beet Caviar–Stuffed Eggs (page 108), but they're also lovely for snacking on their own, or diced up in a salad.

After making a batch of beets, be sure to save your brine to pickle chard stems—chop them into a ¼-inch dice, heat the brine to a boil, and pour it over the stems. By the time the liquid has cooled, they'll be done. These add a nice bit of pop to Kulebyaka (page 290) or Red Chard Pkhali (page 102).

YIELDS 1 PINT

1 cup water

½ cup red wine

½ cup apple cider vinegar

1 tablespoon kosher salt

1 teaspoon granulated sugar

8 black peppercorns

4 juniper berries

2 allspice berries

2 beets, cleaned, peeled, and quartered

Place all of the ingredients in a small saucepan. If the beets are not completely submerged, cut them smaller so that they are covered by the pickling liquid. Bring the mixture to a boil, then reduce the heat until it's just high enough to maintain a simmer. Continue to simmer until the beets are cooked through, about 40 minutes. Let the beets cool to room temperature in the pickling liquid—by the time they're cooled, they're infused enough to use. Store in the brine until using.

PO BLATU (FAVORS)

When the system fails to provide for its people, there's only one choice: cheat the system. My dad explains that every good Soviet woke up asking him- or herself, "What can I steal today?" And the tighter the government's record-keeping and audits got, the more creativity everyone applied to developing elaborate workarounds.

Several relatives of mine worked for O.P.C.—it stood for "**отдел рабочего снабжения**" (Department of Workers' Supply), but folks jokingly called it "**обеспечь раньше себя**" (Help Yourself First). My dad knows a guy who dressed up a slaughtered pig in a hat and trenchcoat and drove it home in the front seat of his car after lifting it from the slaughterhouse floor (think *Weekend at Bernie's*).The women who tended kvas and mineral water carts were said to have "built dachas on [mineral] water" by systematically underserving and pocketing the difference. I learned that you could steal sugar, and then place a pail of water next to the bag (so that the remaining scant sugar absorbed the extra moisture and became heavier just in time for inventory). There was a common joke about one clerk leaving a note to the next between shifts: "Don't add water to the smetana. I already did it." But this wasn't an each-man-for-himself scenario: all of these schemes involved cooperation, networks of people helping each other out.

The term *po blatu* refers to things done "by favors"—the name for the informal, collaborative (and wholly illegal) economy that emerged. Just as the Soviet state had its official system of production, so the workers within that system had their own, with stops and measures and *blat* at every stage of the process. And it was *everywhere*—even in something as humble as, say, sauerkraut (see opposite page).

And that is why the smetana was always watery, the *kotleti* (meat patties) full of bread, and the glass of kvas half filled with foam.

A DAY IN THE LIFE OF SAUERKRAUT IN THE SOVIET UNION

START HERE

GET SOME CABBAGE

You drive to the collective farm to pick up some cabbage to make sauerkraut at your factory. The farmworker gives you 11 tons of cabbage, but he invoices for only 10 tons.

LET'S MAKE A DEAL

You make sauerkraut from the extra ton of freebie cabbage you were "gifted" from the collective farm. You send the extra product (*lyevi*) to the store for free. The store then sells the extra sauerkraut and splits the unaccounted profits with the factory.

BONUS

DETOUR!

On your way back to the factory, you stop at the farmers' market to buy a nominal amount of cabbage (just so that there is a record that you were there).

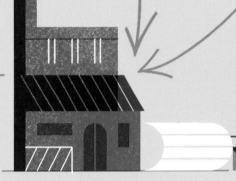

FUDGE SOME NUMBERS

You drive back to the factory and falsify your expense ledger (*zakupochnaya vedomost'*) to say that you purchased 1 ton of cabbage at the farmers' market. You pocket the inflated reimbursement, minus the kickbacks you give to the collective farmer and the market seller.

GAME OVER

JUST ADD WATER

The store adds extra brine to the sauerkraut to make it heavier and to dilute it. The store pockets the unaccounted-for profits (but lines the pockets of the auditor, just in case the math doesn't add up).

CHAPTER 3
COLD ZAKUSKI
холодные закуски

✦ ✦ ✦

A dinner party in the Frumkin household starts with a nightlong planning session. My dad gets out the steno pad, and he and my mother start drafting out a menu. The most important matter to discuss? The zakuski (appetizers). Between eight and twelve guests, you need about a dozen different recipes. A larger party of about twenty requires at least sixteen. Then they run down the proposed list, to make sure there's an equilibrium among meat, fish, and vegetable dishes. And how many of each would be enough?

If you answer "enough to feed your guests," you have clearly not been to a Russian party. My mom, like most Russian hosts, lives in fear of running out of a zakuska (this is something I have never actually witnessed). Because a good Russian host must lay out a spread so big that nobody ever has to worry about holding back, or taking the last bite.

The word *zakuska* (plural: *zakuski*) comes from the word *zakusit'*, which basically translates as "to bite after." Bite after what? Vodka, of course. Zakuski are dishes meant to accompany drinking. But that doesn't capture the half of it. Zakuski aren't the pregame—they are the event itself. A good host will spend *days* planning and preparing an expansive spread, covering every square inch of the dinner table (see "How to Tetris Your Table," page 156). But the spirit of hospitality doesn't have to handcuff you to the kitchen. Proper curation (see page 116) of store-bought charcuterie, cheeses, pickles, et cetera, is commonly enlisted to round out the spread.

LOBIO

лобио

✦ ✦ ✦

Lobio is the Georgian word for beans. And Georgia loves its beans—dried beans, green beans, braised beans, breads filled with beans, et cetera. And the most well-known lobio dish (especially outside of Georgia) is this cold kidney bean salad.

Georgian touches really elevate the humble bean—especially the cinnamon, pomegranate, and marigold petals, which give a flavor profile seldom found in bean salads. It's an easy addition to the zakuski table, but equally well suited to cookouts (or really anything from chapter 7), and it travels well for picnics and potlucks.

YIELDS ABOUT 6 CUPS

¼ cup olive oil

Juice of ½ lemon

1 small clove garlic, minced

1 tablespoon pomegranate molasses

2 teaspoons Turkish hot pepper paste (you can substitute harissa, but you might want to start with a smaller amount, as heat levels can vary)

¼ teaspoon ground cinnamon

½ teaspoon dried marigold/calendula petals, crumbled (optional)*

1 quart cooked kidney beans (or 2 15-ounce cans, drained and rinsed)

¼ sweet onion, thinly sliced

½ bunch cilantro, coarsely chopped

½ bunch parsley, coarsely chopped

½ cup coarsely chopped toasted walnuts

Kosher salt

½ cup crumbled feta, preferably sheep's milk

¼ cup pomegranate seeds

Handful fresh marigold petals (optional)

In a large bowl, whisk together the oil, lemon juice, garlic, pomegranate molasses, pepper paste, cinnamon, and marigold petals (if using). Add all of the remaining ingredients except for the feta and pomegranate seeds, and stir to combine. Taste, and adjust for seasoning (the feta will contribute some salt, so err on the side of undersalting). Gently stir in the feta, and top with the pomegranate seeds and marigold petals (if using). Serve right away, or refrigerate. If you're making this a day ahead, add the feta, fresh herbs, and lemon juice just before serving.

---

* Available in Middle Eastern markets or well-stocked natural food stores

DACHA SALAD

салат из помидоров и огурцов со сметаной

✦ ✦ ✦

Winters in Belarus are no joke. And so when the summer harvest finally rolls around, tomatoes and cucumbers from the dacha garden are diced and mixed with smetana and herbs in a salad that's eaten every day. Every. Single. Day. Because you know that winter is coming. My mother spent ten rubles (three days' pay) to buy a kilo of Armenian tomatoes in May 1978— because a taste of summer was worth that much.

But once my parents arrived at the bountiful supermarkets of Chicago, they were amazed to find you could buy cucumbers and tomatoes all year round. And they did—to make this salad (dressed up a bit here). Of course, it's best in the fresh-from-the-garden height of summer, as a side for your cookout. But I still crave it alongside weeknight dinners throughout the year.

YIELDS ABOUT 6 CUPS

SALAD:

1 pint cherry tomatoes, halved (heirloom local varieties if possible)

3 pickling cucumbers, or 1 large English cucumber, peeled, quartered, and sliced into ½-inch pieces (1½ cups)

1 bunch radishes, quartered and sliced into ¼-inch pieces (about 1 cup)

½ cup pickled onions (page 121), drained and minced

½ cup scallions, cut into ¼-inch slices

½ cup loosely packed dill, chopped

Freshly ground black pepper

Kosher salt

DRESSING:

½ cup smetana (page 359) or European-style sour cream

2 teaspoons fresh lemon juice

2 teaspoons refined sunflower or olive oil

1 tablespoon minced parsley

1 tablespoon minced dill

1 teaspoon kosher salt

Mix all of the salad ingredients together in a mixing bowl.

In a food processor, pulse together all of the dressing ingredients (you can also whisk together in a bowl, if you mince the herbs very finely first).

Pour the dressing over the salad, toss, and season with additional salt and pepper as needed to taste. Serve immediately.

PKHALI TRIO

пхали

✢ ✢ ✢

To wrap your head around Georgian *pkhali*, think of pesto. Now switch out the pine nuts for walnuts. Swap basil for cilantro. Get rid of the cheese and add a vegetable to beef things up. The resulting rich and flavorful mixture can be rolled into balls, stuffed inside vegetables, or served in a bowl with some fresh bread or crackers.

I've seen pkhali play well with everything from beets to cabbage to spinach. Try serving the variations below together as an assortment, or just pick one based on what's in season. And once you get the hang of the method, try your hand at turning whatever is in your CSA box into a pkhali!

EGGPLANT PKHALI ROLLS

рулетики из баклажан

YIELDS ABOUT 18 ROLLS

2 eggplants, preferably on the skinny side

¼ cup olive oil, divided, plus more for pan-frying

½ bunch cilantro, large stems removed (reserve a few sprigs for garnish)

Juice of ½ to 1 lemon

1 clove garlic, chopped or pressed

1 cup walnuts

Kosher salt

Pomegranate seeds

Trim off the eggplant caps and bottoms, and slice top-to-bottom into ¼-inch-thick planks (a mandoline makes this easy, but you can do this with a sharp knife and some care). Set aside. Take the peel-covered end slices, and any center cuts that are too seedy to form nice slices, and roughly chop them.

Heat 1 tablespoon of the oil in a heavy skillet or griddle over medium heat, and sauté the chopped eggplant trimmings until cooked through, 5 to 7 minutes. Transfer the trimmings to a food processor, along with the remaining 3 tablespoons oil, the cilantro, lemon juice (start with the smaller amount), garlic, and walnuts. Process until it comes together in a rough paste—the nuts should still be identifiable, but with no large chunks remaining. Add salt and additional lemon juice as needed to taste. Set aside.

In the same skillet or griddle, cook the eggplant slices until fully softened and golden, a few minutes per side. When cooked, remove from the skillet, and season with a sprinkling of salt. Repeat with the remaining eggplant slices.

(continued page 102)

When all of your eggplant has been cooked, assemble the rolls. Place 1 tablespoon of filling at the large end of the cooked eggplant slice, and roll the strip up around it to form a snug little roll. Repeat with remaining eggplant slices and filling. Before serving, squeeze a little additional lemon juice over the top, and garnish with pomegranate seeds and the reserved cilantro sprigs.

RED CHARD PKHALI

пхали из красного мангольда

YIELDS ABOUT 12 PKHALI

1 bunch red chard

⅓ cup walnuts

1 clove garlic, coarsely chopped

2 tablespoons olive oil

½ bunch cilantro, stems removed

Juice of ½ lemon

½ teaspoon freshly ground black pepper

Kosher salt

2 very small beets, cleaned and very thinly sliced (optional)

¼ cup pickled chard stems (optional)

Bring a large pot of salted water to a boil. Remove tough stems from the chard and set aside for pickling (see headnote page 88). Roughly chop the chard leaves.

Fill a large bowl with ice water. Place the chopped chard in the boiling water, and blanch until just cooked through (about 30 seconds). Drain the chard into a colander, and immediately transfer it to the waiting ice water bath. When completely cooled, remove the chard from the bath, squeezing out as much water as you can.

In a food processor, pulse together the walnuts, garlic, oil, cilantro, lemon juice, pepper, and salt. Pulse until the mixture is fairly uniform, but slightly chunky. Add the cooked chard to the walnut mixture. Pulse to combine. Taste, and add more lemon juice and/or salt as needed.

Scoop out bite-sized spoonfuls of the mixture—about 1 scant tablespoon—and roll into balls, placing 1 ball on top of each beet slice (if using). Dip your hands in water as needed to keep things from sticking. Arrange the balls on a serving dish. Alternatively, spoon into a bowl and serve as a dip. Garnish balls or bowl of dip with pickled chard stems if desired.

STUFFED PEPPER PKHALI

пхали из перца

YIELDS 12 TO 18 PKHALI, DEPENDING ON PEPPER SIZE

1½ pounds mini sweet peppers

¼ cup olive oil, plus more for roasting mini peppers

Kosher salt

2 cups roasted, peeled, seeded red peppers (if using jarred, drain well)

½ bunch cilantro, roughly chopped

Juice of 1 lemon

1 clove garlic, coarsely chopped

1 cup walnuts

½ teaspoon smoked paprika

Preheat the oven to 400°F.

Cut the tops off the mini peppers and discard them, and scoop out any ribs and seeds (being careful not to break the peppers in the process). Toss them with a bit of oil and salt, and place on a rimmed baking sheet. Roast until just barely cooked, 6 to 8 minutes—they should hold their shape, but just be starting to soften. Set the mini peppers aside to cool while you prepare the pkhali filling.

Place the 2 cups roasted red peppers (not the little peppers you just cooked) in a food processor, and pulse a few times to form a chunky puree. Transfer to a bowl lined with cheesecloth. Gather the cheesecloth into a ball and gently squeeze out any excess moisture.

Place the drained pepper puree back in the food processor, add the ¼ cup oil, cilantro, lemon juice, garlic, walnuts, paprika, and salt, and pulse to form a puree—you should still be able to identify the walnuts, but not see any large chunks. Taste, and adjust the seasoning as needed.

Fill the mini peppers with the pkhali mixture and serve.

VINEGRET SALAD

винегрет

✛ ✛ ✛

This hearty salad is so ubiquitous that my relations will likely laugh to see a recipe for it. It is a quintessential standard of the Russian canon—but without the pomp and circumstance of something like Kulebyaka (page 290) or the stature of salat Olivier (page 152).

The caramelized onions are my mother's touch, which (in my humble opinion) elevates our family's version. And though it's named for the classic vinaigrette, this salad doesn't feature any actual vinegar—the zip comes instead from pickles and sauerkraut.

SERVES 8 TO 10 AS PART OF A LARGER ZAKUSKI SPREAD

6 medium beets

2 tablespoons cooking oil (I use refined sunflower)

1½ yellow onions, cut into a ½-inch dice

2 large Yukon Gold potatoes, peeled and cut into a ⅓-inch dice

1 carrot, peeled

½ sweet onion, cut into a ¼-inch dice

4 Israeli pickles, diced into ¼-inch cubes (you can substitute kosher dills)

1 cup sauerkraut (page 84, or store-bought)

1 tablespoon unrefined sunflower oil (you can substitute olive oil)

2 tablespoons kosher salt

Preheat the oven to 350°F. Give the beets a quick scrub (but don't peel), wrap them in foil, and bake until they're fully tender so a knife slides easily through the center (about 1½ hours, depending upon size). Remove the beets from the oven, and as soon as they're cool enough to handle, rub off the skins, using a paring knife or your hands. Let the peeled beets cool to room temperature, then dice into ⅓-inch cubes.

While the beets are roasting, heat a large skillet over medium heat. Add the cooking oil and the yellow onions, sautéing until they're fully softened and starting to caramelize, about 20 minutes. Adjust the heat as needed if they color before they're softened. Let cool.

While the yellow onions are cooking, place the potatoes and carrot in a saucepan, and add water to cover by an inch or two. Bring to a boil over high heat, then reduce the heat until it's just high enough to maintain a simmer. Cook until the vegetables are tender when pierced with a knife—5 to 10 minutes, depending upon size. You want the carrot to be fully tender, offering little resistance, but the potatoes to be just barely tender (they will likely take different times, so remove as needed). Drain and cool. When the carrot is cool enough to handle, grate it on the large holes of a box grater.

Mix the cooked ingredients together with the sweet onion, pickles, sauerkraut, sunflower oil, and salt, and adjust the seasoning to taste. This salad is best served the day it's made.

(see photograph on page 277)

BRINDZA PASHTET

паштет из брынзы

✦ ✦ ✦

Brindza is a type of cheese very similar to feta, but it is almost impossible to find real brindza in the States (and if you do find something labeled as brindza, it still might actually just be feta). But luckily, the difference doesn't matter too much—especially if you get a creamy sheep's milk feta. To make things even creamier, I've added enough butter to smooth things out, and a bit of smoked paprika (rather than the more traditional Hungarian) to liven things up.

The result is what I like to think of as the gateway drug to Eastern European food—a creamy, addictive spread that would feel just as at home at my babushka's house as it would at your next Super Bowl party. Because the recipe is simple, and it really comes down to patience—make sure everything is fully warmed to room temperature for a smooth, luscious spread.

YIELDS 2 CUPS

½ pound sheep's milk feta, brought to room temperature

2 sticks (1 cup) unsalted butter, softened to room temperature

1 tablespoon smoked paprika, plus extra for garnish

Kosher salt (as needed)

2 to 3 scallions, thinly sliced

Lepyoshki (252), bread, or crackers for serving

Before beginning, be very sure that the feta and butter are fully softened—no shortcuts! Place the feta, butter, and paprika in a food processor, and run them together for 1 to 2 minutes, until uniformly combined and very, very smooth. Taste and add salt if needed—it most likely won't be necessary, but all fetas are different.

Scrape the *pashtet* into a bowl, and garnish with scallions and a sprinkle of paprika for pop. Serve with lepyoshki, bread, or crackers. If you make the pashtet in advance or have leftovers to refrigerate, make sure the pashtet comes to room temperature for at least 2 hours before serving, to ensure it is fully softened. Give it a good stir before serving.

BEET CAVIAR–STUFFED EGGS

яйца фаршированные свекольной икрой

❖ ❖ ❖

In Russia, caviar doesn't just mean fish eggs. There's a whole tradition of vegetable caviars—beets, eggplants, or mushrooms, all finely minced. The beet version usually has prunes, walnuts, and mayo. And though beet caviar is very good on its own, I especially love what happens when you stuff it into hard-boiled eggs (a mash-up of another tradition involving eggs as vessels for all sorts of stuff—Russians have this deviled thing on lockdown).

Because beets can be a bit sweet and rich, I spike the filling with some that have been pickled, to make the whole thing a bit lighter on its feet (so you can then eat a little more of it). Beet caviar filling can be made a day ahead, and the egg cups can be prepared a few hours in advance—but don't assemble until shortly before serving to avoid bleeding. And if you're not setting up for a party, you can also just make the filling sans eggs, for a lunchtime spread or salad.

YIELDS 24 STUFFED EGG HALVES

FILLING:

1 medium beet

1 large or 2 small pickled beets (page 88), grated on the large holes of a box grater

1 clove garlic, minced

⅓ cup finely chopped walnuts

¼ cup pitted prunes, finely chopped

½ cup parsley mayonnaise (page 357)

Juice of ½ lemon

Kosher salt (beets can stand up to quite a bit of salt, so don't be shy)

TO FINISH:

12 large hard-boiled eggs

3 very small chioggia or red beets, scrubbed and sliced as thinly as possible with a mandoline or knife (optional)

Young celery leaves (from the heart of a head of celery) for garnish (optional)

Preheat the oven to 350°F.

Give the beet a quick scrub (but don't peel it), wrap it in foil, and bake until it's fully tender so a knife slides easily through the center (1 hour or more, depending upon size). Remove the beet from the oven, and as soon as it's cool enough to handle, rub off the skin, using a paring knife or your hands. Let the peeled beet cool to room temperature, then grate on the large holes of a box grater.

Place the grated beet in a small bowl, and mix it with the pickled beets, garlic, walnuts, prunes, parsley mayonnaise, lemon juice, and salt. Taste, and adjust the seasoning as needed. Transfer the mixture to a piping bag fitted with a ½-inch tip, or a plastic bag with the corner snipped off.

Now to fill the eggs: I cut them in a bit of a weird way, but it lets you stuff more inside. Peel the eggs, and make 3 cuts in each: slice a small bit off the very bottom and top, to allow each end to sit flat on the plate, and then cut each egg in half width-wise, right down the center. Pop out the yolk (the removed yolks and trimmed whites can be used to garnish Herring Under a Fur Coat [page 119] or a caviar plate).

Place the 24 egg cups on a serving plate. Fill each with a substantial portion of piped-in beet caviar filling, mounded generously, and top with a slice of the raw chioggia or red beet and celery leaves (if using).

PERLOVKA SALAD WITH PEARS, MUSHROOMS, HAZELNUTS, AND SORREL

салат из перловки с грушами, грибами, фундуком, и щавелем

† † †

It wasn't until a 2015 road trip through Belarus that I realized just how much barley grows there. Field after field of it rolled between Brest and Grodno—and as we drove, we talked about barley. My dad evidently ate so much of it growing up that he can't even stomach the stuff anymore.

This salad was inspired by those fields, still young and flowering in the early summer. It's dressed with a lively sorrel pistou, and the pears, hazelnuts, and mushrooms round things out with a harvesty feel—and, like all grain salads, it holds up well as a packed or picnic lunch.

YIELDS 1½ QUARTS

5½ cups water, divided

Kosher salt

2 cups pearl barley

DRESSING:

1 small bunch sorrel (or spinach with fresh lemon juice)

1 bunch fresh dill

1 clove garlic, peeled

½ cup hazelnuts, toasted

¾ cup olive oil, plus more for sautéing

2 tablespoons white wine vinegar

1 tablespoon kosher salt, plus more for seasoning

TO FINISH:

6 king oyster mushrooms, cut into a ½-inch dice (you can substitute maitakes or shiitake caps)

¾ cup diced pears cut into a ⅓-inch dice (fresh or marinated, page 76)

⅓ cup chopped toasted hazelnuts

Sorrel leaves

A few sprigs dill

Salt 5 cups of water, bring to a boil, and add the barley. Reduce the heat until it's just high enough to maintain a simmer, cover, and cook until the liquid is absorbed and the barley is tender, about 30 minutes.

While the barley is cooking, remove any tough sorrel and dill stems, and give the herbs a rough chop. Transfer to a food processor, along with the garlic, and process for a minute, scraping down the bowl as needed. Add the hazelnuts, pulse a few times until ground, then slowly drizzle in the oil while the motor is running to create a smooth emulsion. Add the vinegar and salt. Set aside.

Next, heat a large saucepan over medium-high heat, and add the mushrooms and ½ cup water. Braise until the water cooks away, about 10 minutes, then increase the heat to high and add a glug of oil to coat the bottom of the pan, and sauté, stirring occasionally, until the mushrooms color to a nice golden brown (a few minutes per side). Season with salt. Set aside.

When the barley has cooked, and while it is still warm (but not hot), toss it with the dressing—it'll drink it in. Stir in the mushrooms. Right before serving, add the diced pears and hazelnuts. Garnish with herbs and serve.

MOLDOVAN EGGPLANT SALAD

баклажанный салат по-молдавски

✛ ✛ ✛

This recipe is inspired by a jarred eggplant salad that my mom buys all of the time. You know how that goes—you express interest in something once, and before you know it, the pantry is three deep with the stuff and it has been worked into the weekly dinner rotation. And if I don't eat any, I get the "Why you don't eat? This is that eggplant you like!"

While I don't want it as often as my mother might think, I will concede that the jarred stuff is pretty good—that is, pretty good for jarred stuff. But this recipe is better—fresh, balanced, and vibrant. Serve it as a salad on its own, or lay a thick swipe on a (lamb) burger, a veggie wrap, or a grilled chicken pita.

YIELDS ABOUT 1 QUART

¼ cup olive oil, plus more to coat the eggplant

1 onion, diced into ½-inch cubes

2 cloves garlic, minced

1 16-ounce can tomato puree

½ cup pitted prunes, finely minced

Kosher salt

3 medium eggplants (2 pounds total), cut into 1½-inch cubes

¼ cup white wine vinegar

2 tablespoons honey

2 tablespoons Turkish hot pepper paste (you can substitute harissa, but you might want to start with a smaller amount, as heat levels can vary)

1 bunch parsley, coarsely chopped (1 cup), reserve some for garnish

½ bunch mint, coarsely chopped (½ cup)

¼ cup pine nuts, toasted

Crusty bread or lavash for serving

Heat the oil in a large sauté pan over medium-high heat, and add the onion. Sauté, adjusting the heat as needed, until the onion is soft and translucent but not colored, about 10 minutes. Add the garlic and cook for 1 minute more. Then add the tomato puree, prunes, and a pinch of salt. Let the mixture bubble, then reduce the heat to maintain a gentle simmer. Cook for 1 hour, stirring occasionally, as the flavors deepen and combine. Remove from the heat and set aside.

While the tomato mixture is cooking, preheat your oven to 400°F. Toss the eggplants with enough oil to coat, and a generous sprinkling of salt. Roast, checking and turning the pieces as needed to cook evenly, until they're browned to a nice golden hue with a little char here and there (about 45 minutes—the more color the more flavor, so give it time).

While the eggplants are roasting, whisk together the vinegar, honey, and pepper paste in a large bowl, then stir in the herbs.

When the eggplants are done, let them cool for 1 to 2 minutes, and then transfer from the tray into the bowl with the dressing. Toss everything well. Let it sit for half an hour, then mix in the tomato-prune mixture. Taste for seasoning, and let cool. Top with pine nuts and reserved parsley. Serve with a crusty bread or lavash. The salad can be made a few days in advance and will keep for up to 1 week. Warm to room temperature before serving.

BUCKWHEAT HONEY BUTTER

масло с гречишным мёдом

✢ ✢ ✢

The first time I tasted buckwheat honey was at a Portland farmers' market—but this amazing variety has been produced in buckwheat-growing regions for centuries. It has a robust and haunting flavor that I just love, though it can be a bit overwhelming on its own. Mixing it with high-quality butter and a touch of mustard both tempers and amplifies it at the same time.

The resulting butter makes the best accompaniment to fresh vegetables (in addition to adding a complex note to your pancakes). I like assembling a platter of different radish varieties, and serving it with a swipe of the butter on the side. Just dress the radishes with a kiss of oil and a sprinkle of sea salt, and be sure to bring the butter to room temperature before serving. Serve this combination on its own, or with some dark bread, or a batch of buckwheat blini (page 182) for the full buckwheat-on-buckwheat effect. Dot your radishes with springy blossoms like borage or mustard, if available, for a truly Instagram-worthy snack.

YIELDS 1 GENEROUS CUP

1 cup smetana butter (page 359), or cultured European-style salted butter, softened to room temperature

1½ tablespoons buckwheat honey

1 teaspoon kosher salt

1 teaspoon Russian mustard (page 355, or store-bought)

Mix all the ingredients together with a spoon or mixer to form a smooth spread. Store in the refrigerator, but bring to room temperature before serving.

THE ART OF CURATION

Making a proper table-groaning spread can be a bit daunting. But don't worry—it's not all on you. Any good Russian host relies on curation—picking up a few prepared items to round out the homemade options. My mom points out, for example, that her close friend Zhenya rarely prepares any of her zakuski, relying almost exclusively on expert curation. And this is not meant as a slam—Zhenya's zakuski spreads are at the top of my mom's list.

This is easily (and enjoyably) done at home. Lay out a board of charcuterie (bonus points for Armenian basturma or Moskovskaya salami), or a platter of smoked and cured fish. Does your Eastern European deli sell some prepared salads? Give them a try! Don't have pickles fermenting in the pantry? Pick some up!

Pick two or three recipes from this chapter that sound the most exciting to you, and shop around them to create a balanced, bountiful (and low-stress) zakuski experience.

SOME QUICK ZAKUSKI IDEAS (No Recipe Required)

❖ Jarred marinated mushrooms, drained, tossed with a good-quality oil and sliced sweet onions

❖ Meat board with spicy mustard

❖ Herring fillets with boiled potatoes and herbs

❖ Caviar with challah and butter

❖ Jarred eggplant caviar with flatbreads

❖ Pickle plate

❖ Olives

❖ Sprats with mayo on toast

❖ *Ajvar* (pepper spread) and crackers

❖ Hot-smoked salo (pork belly) with sliced pickles and honey on black bread

❖ Bread rusks with melted cheese and tomato

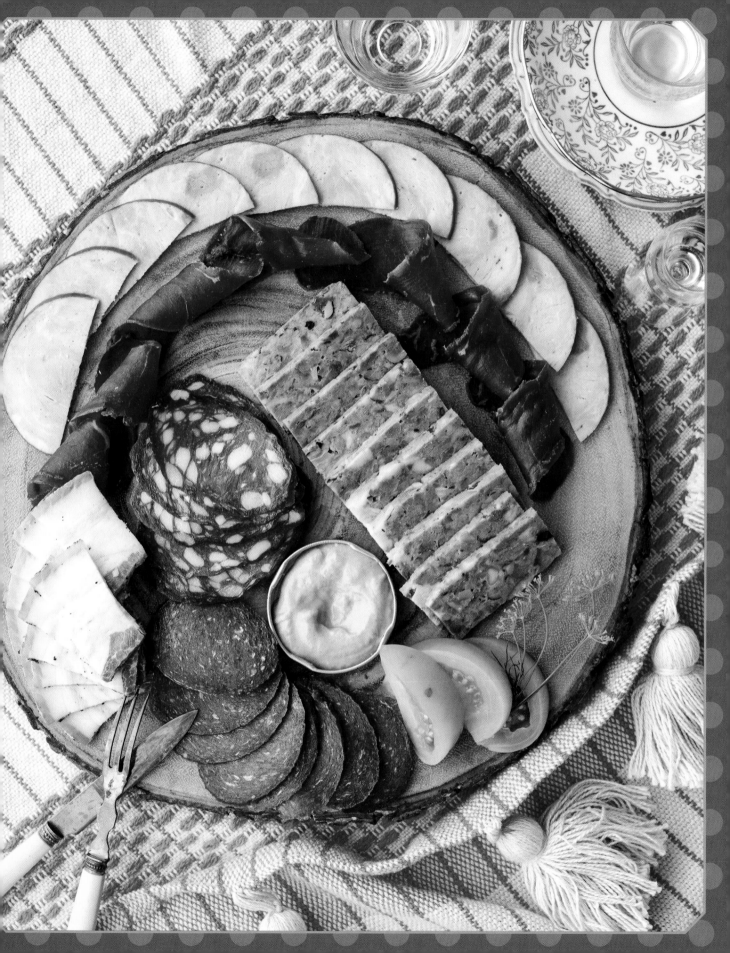

HERRING UNDER A FUR COAT

селедка под шубой

✦ ✦ ✦

This is the dish I was initially afraid to put on the menu—with its beets-herring-mayo triple punch, perhaps it's *too* Russian? But the combination of briny oil-cured herring, sweet beets, and grated potatoes (and, yes, that pink mayo) won people over—and now there would be riots if I ever took it off. It's a stunning first course and, with the combination of fish, veg, and potatoes, can serve as an all-in-one lunch. Make sure you make this in a glass-sided dish (or a ring mold, if you're feeling fancy) to show off the full layered effect.

YIELDS 4 FOUR-INCH TERRINES, OR 1 LARGE BOWL

2 medium beets

2 large or 3 medium Yukon Gold potatoes

2 carrots, peeled

2 fillets salted herring in oil (pickled herring can be substituted, but it's sweeter and a bit less decadent—seek out the oil-packed stuff in your local Russian market if possible)

¼ cup finely chopped onion

2 tablespoons roughly chopped fresh dill, plus a few sprigs for garnish

½ cup mayonnaise (preferably homemade, page 357)

Kosher salt

2 large hard-boiled eggs*

* If your zakuski table includes stuffed eggs (page 108) or buterbrodi (page 121), you can use the excess bits of hard-boiled whites and yolks here, instead of preparing additional eggs.

Preheat the oven to 350°F.

Give the beets a quick scrub (but don't peel), wrap them in foil, and bake until they're fully tender so a knife slides easily through the center (about 1½ hours, depending upon size). Remove the beets from the oven, and as soon as they're cool enough to handle, rub off the skins, using a paring knife or your hands. Let the peeled beets cool to room temperature.

While the beets are roasting, place the potatoes and carrots in a saucepan, and add water to cover by 1 to 2 inches. Bring to a boil over high heat, then reduce the heat until it's just high enough to maintain a simmer. Cook until the vegetables are tender when pierced with a knife, 5 to 10 minutes, depending upon size. The vegetables may not be done at the same time, so remove as needed—you want to be sure that the potatoes aren't overcooked, lest they fall apart, but that the carrots are cooked until soft all the way through, with no resistance. Drain the cooked vegetables, and let them cool to room temperature.

While the vegetables are cooking and cooling, make the herring mixture: Remove the herring fillets from their package, reserving the oil. Give a taste— if they're too salty, soak until they're to your taste. Dice the fillets into ¼-inch pieces. Place the diced herring in a small dish with the onion, dill, and 3 tablespoons of the oil the fillets were packed in (if you're using pickled herring fillets, drain them first, soak them for ½ hour in cold water to draw down the pickled flavor, and add 3 tablespoons sunflower or vegetable oil). Mix to combine, and set aside.

(continued page 120)

When the vegetables have cooled, peel the skin off the potatoes, and grate them on the large holes of a box grater. Rinse the grater, and grate the carrots into a separate pile. Rinse the grater again, and grate the beets, being careful to keep them from bleeding onto the other vegetables.

In a small dish, mix the mayonnaise with 2 tablespoons of the grated beet, turning it a brilliant pink.

To assemble, take a large clear glass bowl or pie plate, and lay down a layer of potatoes. Smooth with the back of your spoon to roughly even things out (but don't tamp them down), and season with salt. Add the herring mixture. Smooth this layer as well, then add the carrots, and smooth them too. Add the grated beet—to avoid making a purple mess, place a mound of beets in the center, and then smooth outward. Season with salt, then top with the beet mayonnaise, smoothing out from the center as well.

Remove the egg whites from the yolks, and, using the back of a spoon, press them through a sieve to garnish the top of the mixture (you can also finely chop the whites by hand instead, and sprinkle them on). Repeat with the yolks. Garnish with the reserved dill sprigs and serve. If you're making the dish in advance, wait until serving to garnish with the egg and dill.

If you want more of a showstopper, Herring Under a Fur Coat can be prepared in 4-inch ring molds: Place each ring mold on a plate, and then follow the instructions as given, using one-quarter of each mixture in each mold. When your individual herring towers have been constructed, gently slide the ring molds up and off. If you have only one ring mold and are reusing it, make sure to rinse and dry the mold between uses, so that you get nice clean stacks.

SPRAT BUTERBRODI

бутербродики со шпротами

✤ ✤ ✤

What I am about to share might start a family feud: I credit these little party-sized fish, egg, and mayo toasts to my aunt Asya—they've been a staple in her zakuski rotation for decades. This is known. My mother, as far back as I can remember, never made them. That is, until my mother noticed the gusto with which my now-husband-then-boyfriend enjoyed Asya's buterbrodi (this was back when he was still new to the family, and everyone was trying to win him over with food). Sure enough, they started appearing on my mom's zakuski table. And not only appearing—my mother maintained, vehemently, that they were her recipe from the outset, and Asya stole them from her.

Far be it from me to get between two Soviet women and their signature zakuska. But the joke in all of this is that sprat buterbrodi are a bit of an archetypal dish—like B.L.T.s, or bagels with lox and cream cheese. Although, of course, I've made a few tweaks to the standard combination (whoever's it may be).

YIELDS 12 SMALL TOASTS

PICKLED ONIONS:

½ large onion, sliced into ⅛-inch-thick half-moons

½ cup red wine

¼ cup distilled white vinegar

¼ cup apple cider vinegar

1 tablespoon kosher salt

2 teaspoons granulated sugar

TOASTS:

12 slices pumpernickel cocktail bread (Rubschlager brand, if available)

⅓ cup smetana butter (page 359) or cultured European-style salted butter, softened to room temperature

To make the pickled onions: Place the onions in a heatproof bowl. Pour the wine, vinegars, salt, and sugar into a small saucepan, and bring to a boil (run the fan—hot vinegar packs a punch). Remove from heat, and pour over the onions. Let the mixture cool to room temperature, then use, or refrigerate for up to 1 week.

To make the pumpernickel toasts: Generously spread the bread with butter on both sides. Heat a griddle or skillet over medium heat, and toast the bread for a few minutes, until it starts to darken (but not burn—adjust heat as needed). When the first side is toasted, flip the bread over, and cook the second side. Remove from the pan when the toasts are crunchy on the outside but slightly soft in the middle, and set aside. Toasts can be made 1 to 2 hours in advance—if you need to make them much farther in advance, toast the bread a few minutes more, until it's crisp throughout (it'll keep better).

(continued page 122)

HERB SALAD:

2 tablespoons dill sprigs, torn or picked into feathery fronds

2 tablespoons radish sprouts (optional)

2 tablespoons parsley leaves (use the smallest leaves available)

2 tablespoons chives, sliced into 1-inch batons

1 teaspoon refined sunflower or olive oil

Kosher salt

TO ASSEMBLE:

½ cup parsley mayonnaise (page 357)

3 large hard-boiled eggs

12 smoked sprats, drained (Riga Gold brand, if available; about ½ of 1 jar/tin)

Shortly before serving, make the herb salad: Mix together the dill, radish sprouts (if using), parsley, chives, oil, and salt. Be gentle—the herbs are delicate!

TO ASSEMBLE THE BUTERBRODI:

Place the toasts on a serving plate, and top each one with a spoonful of the parsley mayo. Using an egg slicer or a sharp knife, slice the eggs, and top each blob of mayo with an egg slice (leftover egg whites and yolks can be used to garnish Herring Under a Fur Coat [page 119] or Salat Mimoza [page 130]). Press down gently on each egg slice, so that the mayo spreads beneath it to form a nice egg-framing halo. Top each toast with a sprat, a few slices of pickled onion, and a generous pinch of herb salad. Serve.

COD LIVER PASHTET

паштет из печени трески

✛ ✛ ✛

There was a time during the Soviet shortages of the seventies when the most prized food item was a can of cod liver—so valuable that it was used as currency. Luckily the market has calmed down since then, and cod liver is again readily available at Russian markets. In addition to being fashionable, cod liver also happens to be quite delicious. Mixed with a little onion and hard-boiled egg and spread on pumpernickel toasts or butter crackers, it's like the most rich and decadent tuna fish salad you'll ever try. The pashtet will keep a few days, but it's best enjoyed the same day it's made.

YIELDS 1 GENEROUS CUP

1 300-gram can of cod liver, drained (available at Russian markets—cod liver from Norway is generally the best quality)

½ sweet onion, roughly chopped

1 large hard-boiled egg

½ teaspoon kosher salt

Pumpernickel toasts, crackers, or challah for serving

Place the cod liver, onion, egg, and salt in a food processor, and process 1 to 2 minutes until smooth, scraping down the bowl as needed. Serve with pumpernickel toasts, crackers, or challah.

CURED MACKEREL

скумбрия маринованная

＋ ＋ ＋

Mackerel—rarely seen here outside of izakayas and sushi joints—is common in Russia (where it's known as *skumbriya*). My parents, however, never came across it in the old country. Instead, they were introduced in Italy, where they awaited entry to America for several months. Mackerel was the cheapest option in the Roman markets—and they'd heard through the Soviet refugee grapevine that it made for a satisfying meal (especially paired with some boiled new potatoes and sorrel soup, page 220). And since then, hardly a family party has passed without some form of it on the table.

When my sister-in-law first introduced my five-year-old nephew (who can eat his weight in maki rolls) to this dish, she described it as Russian sushi. And it's not too far off—just swap the rice and soy sauce for fingerling potatoes and smetana.

SERVES 6 TO 8 AS PART OF A LARGER ZAKUSKI SPREAD

4 cups water, plus more to cook potatoes

⅓ cup kosher salt

2 tablespoons granulated sugar

1 bay leaf (fresh, if possible)

2 teaspoons whole black peppercorns

2 allspice berries

1 whole mackerel (1 to 2 pounds), cut into fillets*

1 pound new potatoes

Handful of dill sprigs for garnish

1 tablespoon unrefined sunflower oil

¼ cup smetana (page 359) or European-style sour cream

¼ sweet onion, thinly sliced

1 tablespoon coarse kosher salt for finishing

Combine 4 cups of water, the salt, sugar, bay leaf, peppercorns, and allspice berries in a pot. Bring to a boil, stir to dissolve the salt and sugar, then turn off the heat and let the brine cool to room temperature. Pour over the mackerel fillets, and refrigerate for 4 days, until the flesh firms up. The water will get murky, but don't worry, that's normal.

To serve the mackerel: Place the potatoes in a pot and cover with cold, salted water. Bring to a boil and simmer until the potatoes are knife-tender.

While the potatoes are cooking, clean the mackerel. Remove the fillets from the brine. If the outer clear membrane is firm, peel it away. Cut each fillet into 1- or 2-inch pieces, and place on a serving plate.

When the potatoes are ready, drain and place in a serving bowl. Garnish with dill sprigs and drizzle with sunflower oil.

Serve the mackerel and potatoes with a bowl of smetana and sliced onion. Store any leftover mackerel in the brine for up to 1 week.

---

* Note that the fish will be cured, not cooked, so start with a piece of fish you'd be comfortable eating raw.

BEET AND HORSERADISH—CURED BLACK COD

угольная рыба засоленная в свекле с хреном

❖ ❖ ❖

This cure is inspired by my culinary school days, a not-so-Russian recipe involving some oh-so-Russian ingredients. The beet and horseradish add not only a brilliant color, but also strong flavors that pair well with fattier fish. I especially like this with black cod (aka sablefish), where the scarlet cure makes for an especially striking contrast to the rich white flesh. While it's designed for the zakuski table, this also does an admirable job of bringing your Sunday bagel brunch over the top.

YIELDS ENOUGH CURE FOR UP TO 2 POUNDS FISH

1 8-ounce jar prepared beet horseradish

1 large beet, unpeeled but well scrubbed, grated on the coarse holes of a box grater

2 cups kosher salt

1 cup granulated sugar

Up to 2 pounds skin-on fillet of black cod, pin bones removed (or other fish of your choosing, like steelhead, salmon, etc.)*

Black bread, fingerling potatoes, or yeasted blini (page 139) and smetana (page 359) or European-style sour cream for serving.

In a medium bowl, mix together the horseradish, beet, salt, and sugar. Grab a casserole dish that's large enough for your fillet. Place one-third of the cure mixture on the bottom of the container. Top with the fish, skin side down, and then spread the remaining cure mixture on top. Cover the container with plastic wrap, and place in the refrigerator.

The fish cure time will vary—8 to 12 hours for thinner fillets, 16 to 18 hours for a whole side (start checking for doneness earlier rather than later). As the fish cures, the salt and sugar will melt away somewhat—you can pile some back on if desired, but don't worry.

When you think the fish might be cured, give it a poke with a clean finger—the fish will feel somewhat firm on the outside, in a way that's different from raw fish, with a bit of give on the inside. The narrower tail end of the fillet will feel almost entirely firm. If you cut through, the fish will look cured, not raw—kind of like lox—and taste salty and seasoned throughout.

When the fish is cured, wash off the fillets, and pat dry. Place the cured fish on a rack over a rimmed tray, and return to the refrigerator for 12 hours to dry the outside of the fish a touch (you're not looking for it to form a skin, just to remove any residual moisture). After drying, wrap tightly. Cured fish keeps best whole, so only slice as needed.

To serve, take a sharp knife and slice as thinly as possible on the bias, keeping your knife as

* Note that the fish will be cured, not cooked, so start with a piece of fish you'd be comfortable eating raw.

horizontal as possible to create wide, thin slices that best showcase the color of the cure, leaving the skin behind. If you don't have a sharp enough knife, don't worry about the thin bias cuts. Simply remove the skin entirely, and make vertical slices as thin as you can.

Serve the sliced fish with butter on black bread, or with fingerling potatoes, or with yeasted blini and smetana or European-style sour cream or butter.

SALAT MIMOZA

салат мимоза

✦ ✦ ✦

Mimoza is named after the yellow pom-pom mimosa blossoms, which grow in Russia's warmer regions (and are especially popular for the requisite flower-giving on International Women's Day). But the only mimosas in this layered salad are the "flowers" created from sieved egg yolk, blossoming on top (have I mentioned Russia's love of baroque salad art?). I add a luxurious textural component using both hot- and cold-smoked salmon—salad art still strongly recommended.

YIELDS 1 LARGE DISH

2 large or 3 medium Yukon Gold potatoes

2 carrots, peeled

¾ cup mayonnaise (page 357, or store-bought)

Zest and juice of 1 lemon

¼ cup smetana (page 359) or crème fraîche

1 tablespoon fresh dill, finely chopped, plus a few sprigs for garnish

1 tablespoon parsley, finely chopped

½ pound cold-smoked salmon, cut into a ½-inch dice (go to a Jewish deli or Russian market to find an unsliced piece of fish)

½ pound hot-smoked salmon, cut into a ½-inch dice

Kosher salt

1 large hard-boiled egg yolk, sieved

Place the potatoes and carrots in a saucepan, and add water to cover by 1 to 2 inches. Bring to a boil over high heat, then reduce the heat until it's just high enough to maintain a simmer. Cook until the vegetables are just tender when pierced with a knife, 5 to 10 minutes, depending upon size. The vegetables may not be done at the same time, so remove as needed—you want to be sure that the potato isn't overcooked, lest it fall apart, but you want the carrot cooked until soft all the way through, with no resistance. Drain the cooked vegetables, and let them cool to room temperature.

Mix together the mayonnaise and lemon zest and juice in a small bowl. Transfer two-thirds of the mixture to a larger bowl and stir in the smetana and fresh herbs. Gently fold in the hot- and cold-smoked salmon, and season to taste.

When the vegetables have cooled, peel the skin off the potatoes, and grate them on the large holes of a box grater. Rinse the grater, and grate the carrots into a separate pile.

To assemble, take a glass pie plate, and lay down a layer of potatoes (if you want to be fancy, you can also build these individually in ring molds or small glass dishes). Smooth with the back of your spoon to roughly even things out (but don't tamp them down). Add the salmon mixture, then the grated carrot, evening out each layer before adding the next. Spread on the reserved lemon mayo. Fashion your best mimosa tree from dill sprigs and sieved yolk. Serve as is, or with some crackers. (Leftovers make a delicious tuna melt alternative.)

CAVIAR
DEMYSTIFIED

When I was growing up, a common childhood snack was a slice of Wonder Bread, spread thick with butter and just paved with caviar. The sheer joy of eating it is difficult to convey. Caviar was cheaper than it is now—maybe a hundred dollars a pound—though it was still expensive, especially for a new immigrant family. But treating your guests—or your children—was what money was *for*. There was no thought to rarity, or price, or the proper way to serve or enjoy—just soft bread, rich butter, and the briny pop of those eggs.

These grown-up days, the whole affair can be a bit more fraught, with hospitality and enjoyment lost amid terrifying price points and in-the-know lingo. But it doesn't need to be. Here's my guide to understanding the good, the bad, and the overpriced of caviar, and how to shop for and serve up your own bit of indulgence.

Carp Roe
Cyprinus carpio
$

Whitefish Roe
Coregonus clupeaformis
$

Trout Roe
Several species
$$

Salmon Roe
Several species
$$

Bowfin Roe
Amia calva
$

Paddlefish Roe
Polyodon spathula
$$–$$$

Siberian Sturgeon Caviar
Acipenser baerii
$$–$$$

White Sturgeon Caviar
Acipenser transmontanus
$$–$$$$

Russian Sturgeon Caviar
aka Osetra
Acipenser gueldenstaedtii
$$$–$$$$

Persian Sturgeon Caviar
Acipenser persicus
$$$$

ALL FISH EGGS ARE CAVIAR

False! Caviar *only* refers to the cured eggs of certain species of sturgeon. That's it. Salmon, tobiko, trout, paddlefish—those are technically roe, *not* caviar. Note that this is not a regulated term: buyer beware!

CAVIAR IS EXPENSIVE BECAUSE IT'S A LUXURY ITEM THAT GETS MARKED UP A BAJILLION TIMES

False. Well, also true. Yes, it's a fashionable luxury item. But, like wine, true caviar is made from a single ingredient that takes a long time to mature—for some of these fish, I'm talking a decade, or more, before they're ready. Not to mention caviar is perishable. Don't try to find a bargain on the real stuff. But good quality *roe* (salmon or trout) can be found for reasonable prices—or made yourself for next to nothing (page 136).

ONLY WILD BELUGA CAVIAR FROM THE CASPIAN IS GOOD

False. False. False. Actually, I will never buy any caviar purporting to be wild—there's a significant chance it's counterfeit, or black market, or both (especially when you're talking about the Caspian Sea). There are fantastic sturgeon farms all over the world that are producing some of the most delicious caviar that I've tasted. And *none* of it is beluga (in the United States, at least, which currently bans all imports of this critically endangered species).

CAVIAR <u>MUST</u> BE SERVED ON ICE WITH A MOTHER-OF-PEARL SPOON

False (and a big eye roll). Serving food ice-cold masks a lot of flavors. You're shelling out big bucks to enjoy some caviar—don't you want to actually taste it?

The whole mother-of-pearl spoon thing is grounded in some science, but it's a bit dated. Actual silver is reactive and will create off flavors (for both caviar and roe), but stainless steel (which is what most silverware is made from these days) is nonreactive. If you're still worried, you can always use plastic (if your hand-carved tortoiseshell spoons are in the dishwasher).

WHAT TO LOOK FOR

Read the label. You want to see a far-off expiration date (most jars get at least two months from the time of packing), a lot number/harvest date to show tracking, and the scientific species, country of origin, and farm to know you're getting what you're paying for. Be wary of:

❖ the words "beluga," "Caspian," or "wild" (with caviar—for other roes it's okay)

❖ "osetra" that is not specifically *Acipenser gueldenstaedtii*

❖ sodium tetraborate—a preservative that's not necessarily terrible, but is often used to obscure/mask off flavors

Look in the jar. You should see individual, taut spheres—nothing smashed or deflated, no liquid pooling.

Smell the jar. Caviar should be buttery and briny, with a hint of fresh fish. No strong fishy or soapy smells—and don't hesitate to return a jar that smells off.

SERVING SUGGESTIONS

Once you've got a quality product, you want to treat it well. Store the caviar in the coldest part of your fridge (i.e., not the doors), pull it out about ten minutes before serving, and plan for roughly an ounce per person. Beyond that, keep it simple: this is not the time for your strong-flavored Russian rye. Good caviar needs nothing more than a buttery bread (brioche or challah), crepes, or yeasted blini (page 139). Lay out an assortment of snipped chives, minced shallots, and sieved hard-boiled egg. Crème fraîche is often recommended as a good accompaniment, but I think it obscures the caviar too much—just go for some good-quality softened butter. And skip the champagne—ice-cold vodka or sake is a much better companion.

HOW TO MAKE ROE

как засолить икру

✛ ✛ ✛

Yes, caviar is a storied product, shorthand for the very idea of czarist luxury. But here's a dirty secret: cured roe is shockingly cheap and easy to make. Really. Once you've found your fish eggs, you're more than halfway there.

Whether you're curing trout, salmon, or sturgeon, the method is the same. I'm talking old technology here—just salt—so this mostly comes down to finding a good skein of eggs. Look for a thin membrane that's peeling back to let the eggs blossom out like a flower (immature skeins are tighter, and entail both more fussing and lower yields). In addition to maturity, you're also looking for freshness: eggs that are clear and plump, not weeping any liquid. Needless to say, this is an uncooked product, so seek out a reputable source (a fisherman or fish supplier that deals directly with fishermen). From there, it's more formula than recipe.

YIELDS ABOUT 1 PINT

1 skein of King Salmon eggs (or any other roe skein)

1 quart water, plus more for cleaning roe

¼ cup kosher salt

To clean the roe (once you've found a good skein of eggs): Fill a large pot with hot water (as hot as it comes out of the tap), and put the skein in. Let the skein sit for 5 minutes, to contract the membrane and release the eggs more easily. You'll feel like you're cooking these delicate eggs, but they can handle the hot water (don't be afraid!). The eggs may pick up a slight cloudiness, but that's fine—they'll clear up as soon as they hit the salt.

While the skein is soaking, prepare your station: Take a casserole dish or bowl, and set something over it to help free your eggs. You need anything with openings slightly larger than the eggs themselves—you can use a cooling rack with a wire grid, or even a clean tennis racket.

Take your soaked roe and lay it over the grate, with the membrane on top. Gently press on the membrane and massage the sac in small circles, carefully pushing the roe sac into the grate, until the eggs begin to separate from the membrane and fall into the container below. Some eggs may rupture in the process, but for the most part you should be able to gently work them through. Continue until all the eggs have been worked out (you may need to pluck the last few eggs from the membrane by hand). Discard the membrane, and transfer the eggs to a bowl or container that's taller than it is wide.

Fill the container with enough cold water to cover the eggs by a few inches. With your hand, scoop the eggs from the bottom a few times, then let them settle (bits of membrane and broken eggs will float to the top). Pour off the water with detritus, and repeat several times, until the water is clear (this may take half a dozen rinses, depending on how easily your eggs released from the membrane). When the water is clear, pour it off completely through a strainer. Rinse out the container, and return the cleaned eggs to it.

To brine the roe: Once your eggs are clean, it's time to cure them. Pour 1 quart of water mixed with ¼ cup kosher salt into your drained eggs. Use your hand to gently mix the salt water with the eggs. Watch your eggs go from cloudy to clear (magic!), and let the mixture sit for 20 minutes.

After 20 minutes, fish out a few eggs and take a taste, making sure you're tasting the eggs, not the brine on their surface (you can rinse the eggs before tasting if you're not sure). You want to taste a pleasant level of saltiness, which flavors (and preserves) the eggs, but doesn't entirely mask their taste. If it's not to your desired taste, let the mixture soak a little more, tasting every few minutes until it's to your liking. If you prefer a much saltier roe, you can always add more salt to the brine, too.

When the eggs have cured to your taste, strain and discard the brine. Leave the eggs in the strainer, and place in the refrigerator overnight, uncovered, to let any remaining brine drip off and allow the surface of the eggs to dry to a slight tackiness.

The next day, transfer the roe to a sterile container, cover, and refrigerate. They're ready to eat at this point, but the flavor improves—at first they have a fresh fish flavor, but then it transforms over a few days to more of a caviar flavor. I think they're at their peak at around 3 to 5 days, and start to go downhill after 7 (and please don't eat them after 10 days). Good-quality cured roe can also be frozen for up to 4 months. Serve with challah bread or yeasted blini and softened butter.

YEASTED BLINI

блины дрожжевые

✦ ✦ ✦

I'm going to take this opportunity to get two things out of the way: (1) Blini do not and should not contain potatoes. (2) The singular form of the word in question is *blin*. *Blini* is the plural form. There is no such thing as blinis.

Now that the vocabulary's established, let's talk shop. There are larger, thicker blini, the size of dinner plates, appetizer-sized blini for the fancier zakuski tables, and thinner, crepe-like versions to fold around savory fillings. But most important, there are "fast" and "slow" blini.

Fast blini are made from a straight batter, like I use for my *blinchiki* crepes (page 177). They're easy to mix up and fire off, and totally delicious—especially when wrapped around a filling. But it's the slow ones I crave—with a bit of bubbly loft from yeast, and a nice long rise in the refrigerator overnight. These blini are what pancakes want to be. They've got a delicious complexity from the slow fermentation, managing to be simultaneously both rich and light.

Blini are delicious on their own, with some smetana and sugar, or served with syrup instead of your usual flapjacks. Or go savory—fold them around smoked salmon, or (need it be said?) top with caviar. Beyond some advance planning, they're no more difficult than any other pancake. Just better.

YIELDS ABOUT 48 LARGE BLINI, OR 72 ZAKUSKI-SIZED BLINI

SPONGE:

1 cup water, warmed to body temperature

½ cup all-purpose flour

2 teaspoons active dry yeast

2 teaspoons sugar

BATTER:

1¼ cups heavy cream

1¼ cups whole milk (to make large, slightly thinner blini, omit heavy cream and increase to 3¼ cups milk)

½ stick (¼ cup) melted butter

2 large egg yolks (you'll use the whites later)

2⅓ cups (300 grams) all-purpose flour

The day before you're going to cook, take a large container (large enough to hold the full batter, and then some), and whisk together the sponge ingredients. Let the mixture sit out at room temperature until doubled in size, about 1 hour.

When the sponge has doubled, whisk in all of the batter ingredients. Cover the container, and refrigerate overnight. BE FOREWARNED: this will expand. Much, much more than you might think. Contain accordingly, or scrub the batter off your refrigerator shelves the next day (I know from whence I speak).

The next day, take the batter out of the refrigerator, and let it sit out for 1 to 2 hours to come to room temperature. Whisk the egg whites to soft peaks, and gently fold them in.

To cook the blini: Grab a well-seasoned pan, and heat it over medium-high heat. Melt some butter in the pan.

(continued page 140)

2 tablespoons granulated sugar

2 teaspoons kosher salt

TO FINISH:

2 large egg whites

Butter for frying

Caviar and butter, smetana
(page 359) and sugar,
machanka (page 287),
cured fish, etc., for serving

For smaller blini, spoon out 2-inch circles (this batter will be thicker than pancake batter, but should spread more readily—you'll need about a tablespoon). If you want to make things easier, a squeeze bottle is handy. Cook until bubbles form and pop and the top dries out, while the bottom cooks to a nice golden color (just a few minutes). Flip, and cook the other side. Add more butter and adjust the heat as necessary. Unlike pancakes, which are best hot from the griddle, blini are actually better if they set for a few minutes—cover and hold in a warm spot in your kitchen for up to 1 hour or so.

For larger blini, ladle out ¼ cup of batter, and spread it out to form a 6-inch circle. You want it spread fairly thin so as to be pliable (it'll puff up a bit). Cook until bubbles form and pop and the top dries out, while the bottom cooks to a nice golden color (just a few minutes). Flip, and cook the other side. Add more butter and adjust the heat as necessary. If the batter is too thick, add more milk as needed. As with small blini, let them set for a few minutes after they come off the heat, and hold covered, in a warm spot in your kitchen for up to 1 hour.

Serve blini (of any size) with caviar and butter, smetana and sugar, dipping into machanka, alongside cured fish, for your kid's after-school snack, etc.

SMOKED TROUT SALAD

салат из копченой форели

✛ ✛ ✛

Jewish deli–style whitefish salad is something I grew up eating a whole lot of, and was looking to re-create at Kachka. But obtaining a whole whitefish proved surprisingly difficult on the West Coast. Instead of smuggling some of Lake Superior's finest in my luggage during midwestern visits, I started hot-smoking local trout instead. I love adding little bits of crunch and sweetness with apples, cucumbers, and mustard seeds. Spread it on a bagel, add it to a bed of lettuce, or serve it with toast points.

YIELDS 1 PINT

1 pound smoked trout fillets

1 apple (tart or sweet), peeled, cored, and cut into a ¼-inch dice

1 pickling or Persian cucumber (or ½ English cucumber, seeded), peeled and cut into a ¼-inch dice

½ cup smetana (page 359) or crème fraîche

¼ cup thinly sliced scallions

¼ cup minced fresh dill

¼ cup dijon mustard

2 tablespoons pickled mustard seeds (page 356—optional, but gives a nice little pop)

Juice of ½ lemon

Kosher salt (as needed)

Remove the skin and pin bones from the smoked trout, and flake it into bite-sized pieces. Add the remaining ingredients and mix to form a cohesive spread. Taste, and add salt if needed (it might not be necessary, depending upon the saltiness of the trout).

SALTISON WITH HAZELNUTS

сальтисон с фундуком

✛ ✛ ✛

Saltison is a type of head cheese. Somewhere along the way, Olga, my chef de cuisine, started adding butter and hazelnuts to it, as a sort of mash-up of saltison and another Russian dish that resembles rillettes. The result is something akin to a richer, porkier country pâté. I think this is a fantastic entry into charcuterie production—saltison doesn't require any special equipment, curing salts, aging, or temperature control (and, if you want to move beyond the charcuterie spread, it makes for a nifty Russian fusion banh mi base). All you need is a big enough stockpot and a bit of cheesecloth. Plus it looks pretty badass to leave the butcher shop with a whole pig's head. Remember to save the resulting liquid to make fancy broth.

**YIELDS ONE
13-X-9-INCH PAN**

1 pig's head

1 cup toasted hazelnuts, roughly chopped

2 sticks (1 cup) unsalted butter, softened to room temperature

4 cloves garlic, minced

4 teaspoons kosher salt, plus (optionally) more as needed

Black bread, spicy mustard, and pickles for serving

Place the pig's head in a large stockpot, and cover with water. Bring the pot to a boil over high heat, then discard the water (keeping the head!), and add fresh water and start again (this will help remove surface impurities). Once the second round of water comes to a boil, reduce the heat to a gentle simmer, and cook until the meat is very tender and falling off the bones (about 4 hours). Remove the head and let it cool until you can handle it, saving the liquid to make fancy broth (page 351).

When the head is cool enough to handle, pick through and reserve all the meaty bits and collagen. Discard the bones, gristle, and any undesirable parts, but the rest should all be edible—ears, tongue, etc. Finely mince the meaty bits, and transfer the mince to a large mixing bowl. Add the hazelnuts, butter, garlic, and salt, and mix until well combined. Taste, and add more salt if needed.

Line a 13 x 9-inch casserole dish with cheesecloth, overhanging it on all sides by several inches, and pack the meat mixture inside. Fold the cheesecloth over the top, and place a weight on top (another casserole dish filled with cans or other heavy objects works really well). Refrigerate overnight. After pressing, unwrap the cheesecloth, then slice and serve with black bread, spicy mustard, and pickles. Store any leftovers for up to 1 week, tightly wrapped to prevent oxidation.

BUZHENINA WITH SHAVED CELERY SALAD AND TOASTED CARAWAY VINAIGRETTE

буженина с салатом из сельдерея с тмином

✛ ✛ ✛

Buzhenina refers to a roasted pork loin or ham typically served cold. This particular preparation was inspired by an old recipe that called for boiling a pork loin in kvas—but instead of boiling, I give it a low-and-slow poaching, to infuse the lean meat with kvas's savory, malty richness without risking overcooking. For a satisfying lunch (or impressive cold zakuski platter), make sure to prepare the accompanying celery salad—or build it up as an entrée salad, on a bed of greens. The toasted caraway vinaigrette doubles as a dressing for both the loin and the salad.

SERVES 8 TO 10 AS PART OF A LARGER ZAKUSKI SPREAD

1 tablespoon caraway seeds

1 pork tenderloin (about 2 pounds)

Kosher salt

2 tablespoons cooking oil (I use refined sunflower oil)

2 to 3 cups kvas (either homemade [page 62], or a drier store-bought variety, such as Nash Kvas, or substitute a Baltic-style porter)

2 tablespoons apple cider vinegar

Shaved celery salad and toasted caraway vinaigrette (page 146)

Heat a large Dutch oven over medium heat. Add the caraway seeds to the dry pot and toast, stirring frequently, until they become fragrant and darken (just 1 to 2 minutes). Pour out into a small dish and set aside.

Season the pork tenderloin on all sides with salt. Add oil to the Dutch oven and heat until just shy of smoking. Add the loin and quickly brown on all sides. Remove the tenderloin.

Pour the kvas, vinegar, toasted caraway seeds, and 2 tablespoons salt into the Dutch oven. Bring the pot to a boil, and then immediately drop it to the lowest setting—you want it to be just under a simmer. Place the tenderloin into the poaching liquid, making sure it is completely submerged (add a bit of water if needed to cover). Stick a meat thermometer in the thickest portion, and cover with foil, being careful to work around the thermometer. Poach until the thermometer reads 135°F, about 40 minutes.

Remove the pot from the heat, uncover, and allow the loin to continue to cook in the residual heat of the liquid. When it's cooled to room temperature, place the pot in the refrigerator to cool completely—at least 4 hours, or overnight.

When you're ready to serve, remove the chilled loin from the poaching liquid. Slice into ¼-inch slices, and serve with shaved celery salad and toasted caraway vinaigrette.

(continued page 146)

CONTINUED
*buzhenina with shaved celery
salad and toasted caraway
vinaigrette*

SHAVED CELERY SALAD AND TOASTED CARAWAY VINAIGRETTE

1 tablespoon caraway seeds

½ cup refined sunflower or olive oil

8 stalks celery

2 tablespoons apple cider vinegar

2 teaspoons white vinegar

Kosher salt

2 apricots, halved, pitted, and thinly sliced (or 6 dried apricots, thinly sliced)

Heat a small skillet over medium heat. Add the caraway seeds to the dry skillet and toast, stirring frequently, until they become fragrant (just 1 to 2 minutes). Pour out into a small bowl, add the sunflower oil, and set aside to steep for 1 hour.

Use a vegetable peeler to remove the tough outer strings on the stalks of celery, then use the peeler or a mandoline to shave the stalks into very long, thin ribbons. Place the shaved celery in a bowl of ice water and refrigerate until it firms up and curls, about 20 minutes.

To make the vinaigrette, pour the vinegars into a small mixing bowl. Slowly whisk in the caraway oil. Season to taste.

When you're ready to serve, drain and dry the celery well on a paper towel. Give the dressing another whisk, lightly dress the celery with it (you won't need all of it), and add the apricot slices. Serve with the buzhenina, with the additional dressing on the side.

SLICED VEAL TONGUE WITH DAIKON RADISH SALAD AND PICKLED CRANBERRIES

телячий язык с редиской и маринованной клюквой

✛ ✛ ✛

Salat Tashkent is a famous Russian dish—a mixture of shredded beef, grated green radish, and mayonnaise. I love the meat-heat-mayo flavor combination, but not the homogenous mixture, so I've separated out the elements. Green radishes are a spicier variety hard to come by here, but you can punch up the more mild daikon with a horseradish dressing, and toss in some pickled cranberries to cut through the richness. And instead of beef, I like to use veal tongue, another popular zakuska option, which is particularly supple when properly cooked. It's not exactly Salat Tashkent, but it is delicious.

SERVES 6 TO 8 AS PART OF A LARGER ZAKUSKI SPREAD

PICKLED CRANBERRIES:

¼ cup red wine

2 tablespoons white vinegar

2 tablespoons apple cider vinegar

2 teaspoons granulated sugar

1 teaspoon kosher salt

¼ cup fresh cranberries (frozen are totally okay)

TONGUE:

1 veal tongue

2 quarts fancy broth (page 351), or beef or veal stock, seasoned to taste

HORSERADISH SAUCE:

¼ cup prepared horseradish

1 tablespoon dijon mustard

1 teaspoon fresh lemon juice

¼ cup mayonnaise (page 357, or store-bought)

¼ cup smetana (page 359) or crème fraîche

At least 1 day (and up to 1 month) before you're going to serve, pickle the cranberries: Combine the wine, vinegars, sugar, and salt in a small saucepan. Bring the mixture to a boil, and stir to dissolve the sugar and salt. Remove the pot from the heat, and stir in the cranberries. Cool to room temperature, transfer to a storage container, and refrigerate. The cranberries will be ready in 24 hours and will keep refrigerated, in their pickling liquid, for up to 1 month.

The day before you're going to serve: Place the tongue in a medium-sized Dutch oven (one that just fits it, nice and snug), and add the broth to cover by about 1 inch. Bring the broth to a boil, then reduce the heat until it's just high enough to maintain a gentle simmer. Simmer for 3 to 4 hours, covered, until the tongue is tender to the touch and a knife poked through the skin slides through the meat (alternatively, you can stick it in the oven at 250°F instead of on the stovetop for the same amount of time).

When the tongue is tender, pull it out of the liquid, and let it cool until it's just cool enough to handle (don't let it get too cold, or the skin will be hard to peel). Carefully peel off and discard the skin, then place the tongue in a covered container and

(continued page 149)

CONTINUED
*sliced veal tongue with daikon
radish salad and pickled cranberries*

TO FINISH:

1 daikon radish (or an equivalent
amount of black radish)

Celery leaves (optional)

refrigerate until fully chilled (ideally overnight—a
warm tongue doesn't slice easily!). Save the
braising liquid for any other recipes that call for
meat stock—short rib borsch (page 221), floating
your pelmeni (chapter 5), etc. It's free flavor!

The day you plan to serve, make the horseradish
sauce: Mix together the prepared horseradish, dijon
mustard, and lemon juice in a bowl. Let the mixture sit
at room temperature for 1 hour so the flavors mellow
and infuse.

Stir in the mayonnaise and smetana. Taste for
seasoning, and add more horseradish and/or salt if
needed.

To serve: Cut the pickled cranberries into thick
slices (maybe 3 per berry), and set aside. Peel and
grate the radish—you can use a food processor,
the large holes of a box grater, or julienne it with a
mandoline. Place the radish shreds in a colander
in the sink, and press out any excess liquid (be
especially firm if you've used a box grater, or if
it's sat for a bit and starts to weep). Mix the grated
radish with enough of the horseradish sauce to
make it creamy, and add additional salt to taste.

Take the chilled tongue from the refrigerator, grab
your sharpest slicing knife, and cut it as thinly
as possible. Serve the tongue with the pile of the
dressed radish salad in the center of a plate and
the slices of tongue fanned around it. Sprinkle
sliced cranberries and celery leaves (if using) over
everything, and serve. For a more casual take, this
is also fabulous layered on rye for an alternative to
the usual roast beef sandwich.

WHIPPED SALO WITH ROASTED GARLIC AND CORIANDER

взбитое сало с жареным чесноком и кориандром

✛ ✛ ✛

Whipping salt-cured salo (pork fatback) into a spread is something I first encountered at Taras Bulba, a Ukrainian restaurant in Moscow. Traditionally, salo is served in thick chunks, alongside slabs of brown bread, pickles, and vodka. But for the uninitiated, a whipped spread makes for a less imposing intro to this porky treat—just think of it as Ukrainian butter.

We never had salo during my pork-free childhood, but now that the fam has rediscovered it, my uncle Misha requests we bring slabs back whenever we return to Chicago (as it is next to impossible to find it in the kosher-style delis in Russian Jewish neighborhoods there).

Note: Not all salo is created equal. Look for a piece that is at least three fingers thick, and cured to an opaque, snowy white, with very little meat.

YIELDS 1 POUND

4 cloves garlic, peeled

Olive oil

Kosher salt

½ pound salt-cured salo (pork fatback)

1 tablespoon Russian mustard (page 355, or store-bought)

1 teaspoon ground coriander (freshly ground is always best, but you can also just revive your preground with a quick dry toast in a pan)

Black bread for serving

Preheat oven (or a toaster oven) to 350°F.

Place the garlic cloves on a square of foil, drizzle them with a bit of the oil and salt, and wrap the package up to seal it. Roast until golden and fragrant, 20 to 30 minutes. Remove and let cool.

Wash the excess salt off the salo. Remove the skin, and trim off any meat and discard, or freeze and save for shkvarky (page 180) or solyanka (page 224), and roughly chop the fat. If you have a meat grinder, run the salo and garlic cloves through on fine first, and then transfer to a food processor. Otherwise place in the food processor, and add the mustard and coriander. Whip, using short pulses (you don't want this to heat up too much), until everything is incorporated and the mixture is smooth and fluffy (this should just take a few minutes). Due to the saltiness of the salo, it likely won't need any additional salt. Serve with black bread.

SALAT OLIVIER

салат оливье

✛ ✛ ✛

Olivier is all about status. In its original incarnation, this prerevolutionary indulgence featured czar-worthy ingredients ranging from grouse to crayfish to caviar. And in the Soviet era, the most coveted ingredient? Peas. To be exact, *canned* peas. Of course, during Soviet times, you could only get canned peas if you knew the right people. And so you would save that high-status luxury can for the most special of occasions: New Year's Eve.

Beyond the peas, anything is fair game. You can make Olivier with ham, *doktorskaya* bologna, or chicken (if you don't happen to have grouse and crayfish, that is). And each ingredient has its devotees. But the Frumkin clan stands squarely with poultry. And so what you have here is a recipe for the best chicken salad you'll ever make. Make sure to take the time to dice all of your vegetables nice and small—as a general rule, everything should be about the size of a pea.

YIELDS 3 QUARTS

1 large roaster chicken

Kosher salt

6 large Yukon Gold potatoes, peeled and cut into a ⅓-inch dice

2 cups fresh peas (my seasonal choice, although frozen peas are an acceptable substitute—and if you really want to be authentically Soviet, go for canned)

1 large sweet onion, cut into a ⅓-inch dice

7 Israeli pickles, cut into a ⅓-inch dice

5 large hard-boiled eggs, cut into a ⅓-inch dice

1 cup mayonnaise (page 357, or store-bought)

Freshly ground black pepper

Handful of pea shoots for garnish (optional)

Place the chicken in a large pot, cover with cold water, and add in a generous amount of salt. Bring to a boil, then reduce the heat until it's just high enough to maintain a gentle simmer. Simmer, skimming off anything that comes to the top, until the chicken is cooked and you can easily pull the joints apart—begin checking after about 30 minutes, but if you've got the heat nice and gentle, you shouldn't have to worry about overcooking things. When the chicken is cooked, remove from the pot and let it cool until you can handle it (reserve the poaching broth for another use). Discard the skin, pull the meat from the bones, and cut into a ⅓-inch dice.

While the chicken is cooking, place the potatoes in a pot, cover with water, salt generously, and bring to a boil. Reduce the heat until it's just high enough to maintain a simmer, and cook until the potatoes are tender, about 5 minutes. Remove the potatoes with a slotted spoon, and set them aside to cool. Prepare a bowl of ice water and bring the water in the pot back up to a boil, add the peas and cook for 30 seconds, then drain and shock them in the ice water.

In a large bowl, mix all of the remaining ingredients (except the pea shoots) together with the chicken, potatoes, and peas, and season to taste. Serve right away, garnished with the pea shoots (if using)—if you're making this in advance, refrigerate, but let it come to room temperature before garnishing and serving.

KHOLODETZ

холодец

❖ ❖ ❖

Let's not beat around the bush—*kholodetz* is meat Jell-O.* And it's good. If it were French,
you'd call it an aspic terrine, and pay sixteen dollars for a skinny slice at a fancy restaurant.
But luckily you can make it yourself for far less, to round out your zakuski table or charcuterie
spread—or just to serve with some bread and mustard for lunch.

Prerefrigeration, kholodetz was only made in the wintertime, and left out in the snow to set.
When my father was a kid, he was responsible for chilling this dish. One time he went to
retrieve it before a party—only to find an empty tray, its contents likely devoured by a stray
cat (or drunk neighbor, perhaps?). From then on, he was required to dutifully stand guard,
shivering, over the kholodetz for an hour (or three) in the dead of winter until it would set.

YIELDS 1 LOAF

1 pound veal feet (or beef feet)

1 pound veal shank (osso bucco)

6 cups water

Kosher salt

1 clove garlic, minced

2 or 3 large hard-boiled eggs,
peeled

Russian mustard (page 355), brown
bread, and pickles for serving

* Before you wrinkle your nose at
that, remember that all Jell-O is made
from the collagen of pigs and cows.
Really, it's the lemon-lime stuff that's an
abomination.

Preheat the oven to 425°F.

Place the veal feet and shank on a rimmed baking
sheet, and roast until the bones turn golden (a
few spots of char are fine) and your kitchen smells
amazing, 30 to 40 minutes. Turn halfway through.

Transfer the bones and shank to a pot that's just
big enough to hold them, add the water, and salt
to taste. Bring to a boil, skimming off any foam
that rises, and then lower the heat until it's just
high enough to maintain a gentle simmer. Simmer,
uncovered, until the meat is fork-tender, about
4 hours. Strain, reserving the liquid.

Pick through the shank and bones, pulling off any
usable meaty bits. Discard the bones, and finely chop
all of the meat. Mix with the garlic, and season to taste
with salt. Skim the fat off the cooking liquid, then pour
the liquid on top of the meat (if you're super fussy
about presentation, you can fully chill the stock, so
that the fat will be easy to separate out cleanly, and
then heat it back up, but this isn't really required).

If you want a fancy molded version, à la French
style: Take a terrine mold, place half the meat at the
bottom, line up whole eggs, then scatter the rest of
the meat over everything, and add stock to cover. For
a more homestyle Russian approach, take any old
casserole dish, add the meat and pour the stock over
it. Slice the eggs and gently lay egg slices on top.

Carefully move the dish to the refrigerator, and chill until it's completely set and firm, about half a day. For French-style, fill a large bowl with hot water, set your terrine in it for a minute to melt the outer layer (being careful not to get any water inside), then run a knife along the edge and unmold. For Russian-style, cut the terrine into slices (while still in the dish), and grab a cake server. Either way, serve with spicy mustard, brown bread, and pickles.

HOW TO TETRIS YOUR TABLE

It's no surprise the Russians invented Tetris—they've had years of practice trying to fit far, far too many dishes on the zakuski table. To put on a proper Russian-style spread, pick a handful of recipes from this chapter, hit the market for some good-to-go items, and consult this guide for pulling it all together.

Centerpiece? Schmenterpiece. Don't even try. If you have room for a centerpiece, you don't have enough food.

Give yourself some time. All the food should be out just before guests arrive. For us Russians, it's status quo, but it makes quite an impact on the uninitiated. To keep delicate items from drying out, cover in plastic wrap until just before sitting down.

Let those dishes cozy up to one another. They should be touching—negative space is nice for Martha Stewart magazine spreads, not for zakuski tables. A proper Russian host is embarrassed if any tablecloth is showing. You do have a tablecloth, don't you?

PRO MOVE: Lift and tuck! Use a riser to lift a plate, then tuck bordering plates underneath. Three dimensional zakuski!

Unless you're serving eight or fewer guests, don't even think about a single serving plate for each item. Break it up! Dishes should repeat every six seats or so—more small plates rather than one large platter. This is crucial for not spending all of your time passing items, in addition to being practical: one large platter is far less forgiving than several small plates when you're Tetris-ing.

Get a side table for bread and backup beverages (make sure there is room on the table for in-use bottles, though).

Keep glassware options minimal. A larger glass for water or soda and a shot glass for whatever you are toasting with. That's it! If you insist on wineglasses, don't set the table with them—keep them on the side just for the people who need them.

Just like football, this is a game of inches: move the plates so that the lip hangs off the edge of the table by a bit—not so much they can tip off, though!

There's valuable real estate between place settings! Put silverware and napkins ON the plate rather than alongside.

CHAPTER 4

HOT ZAKUSKI

горячие закуски

✛ ✛ ✛

As people start slowing down on the spread of cold zakuski, usually one or two hot zakuski are brought to the table. Hot zakuski are the iconic items, the heavy hitters—your piroshki, your blinchiki (in other words, lots of Things Wrapped in Dough (page 190). In addition to being a part of a bigger spread for special occasions, many hot zakuski also double as lunch options, especially when paired with a small salad.

Dishes in this category are both crowd-pleasers and impressive to make. If you are trying to feed both your finicky eight-year-old nephew and your judgy Russian mother-in-law, this chapter's for you!

MUSHROOMS JULIENNE

грибной жульен

✦ ✦ ✦

Sometimes it seems like French words are just thrown in Russian culinary creations to make them sound fancy, like you've got your own czarist-era French chef—but there's little regard for the actual meaning. Take Mushrooms Julienne. There are no matchstick-cut vegetables (the actual meaning of the French word) to be found. Instead, it's creamy braised mushrooms, topped with cheese and broiled.

My experience with julienne dates back to the Russian banquet halls of my Chicago childhood, where it was served as a mid-meal hot zakuska—but only if you sprang for the premium banquet package. The course would be brought to the table in individual metal dishes, which only served to further elevate its fancy status (at least in my childhood understanding). The adjika and smoked paprika I add at Kachka aren't traditional, but they give a nice bit of depth and spice that cut through the richness (so that you can keep eating more of it).

SERVES 8 AS AN APPETIZER, OR 4 AS A MAIN DISH (PAIRED WITH SOME NICE CRUSTY BREAD AND A SALAD)

2½ pounds mixed mushrooms (make sure to include plenty of flavorful varieties—shiitakes, oysters, king trumpets, porcini, maitake, chanterelles)

1 stick (½ cup) unsalted butter

½ cup all-purpose flour

2 cups mushroom broth (page 352, or store-bought)

Kosher salt

¾ cup smetana (page 359) or crème fraîche

¼ cup adjika (page 358), or 2 tablespoons prepared harissa (optional)

1½ teaspoons smoked paprika

½ pound grated Litkovsky cheese (sold at Russian markets—if not available, substitute a mild, semisoft cheese like Monterey Jack)

Fill a large bowl or salad spinner with water, then thoroughly clean the mushrooms by dunking them in and vigorously swishing them around to shake loose any debris. Remove quickly, and repeat the process as needed until the mushrooms are clean, changing out the water each time. Spread the mushrooms out on clean dish towels to dry. Remove any tough ends, or stems if you're using shiitakes (save these scraps for making mushroom broth, page 352), and cut or tear the mushrooms into bite-sized pieces.

Heat a large pot over medium heat, and add the mushrooms. Once the liquid comes out, let the mushrooms braise, stirring occasionally and adjusting the heat as needed to keep everything cooking gently. The mushrooms are done when they are fully tender (not chewy), and most of the liquid has been cooked off, about 30 minutes.

While the mushrooms are cooking down, start the gravy: Heat the butter in a medium saucepan over a medium-low heat. As soon as it melts, add the flour, and whisk well to incorporate and remove any lumps. Keep stirring the roux until it cooks to a golden peanut color and any grittiness disappears, about 10 minutes. When the roux has reached this stage, slowly whisk in the mushroom broth, increase

(continued page 163)

the heat to bring it to a boil, and then reduce the heat until it's just high enough to maintain a gentle simmer. The mixture will be thick, somewhere between a gravy and a loose pudding. Simmer for 10 minutes, whisking periodically, then season with salt to taste.

When the gravy is done, whisk in the smetana, adjika (if using), and paprika. Stir this spiced gravy into the cooked mushrooms, and adjust the seasoning to taste—it should be rich, smoky, and slightly spicy. If you're making it in advance, you can refrigerate the mixture at this point.

To serve, transfer the mushrooms to an oven-proof skillet or casserole dish (or individual ramekins, if you're feeling fancy). If the mushroom mixture was made in advance, place it in a preheated 350°F oven for 30 minutes, until it's nice and warm (if you didn't chill the mixture, skip this step). Top the mushrooms with the cheese, switch your oven to broil, and adjust the rack so it's just below the broiler. Broil for a few minutes, until the mixture is bubbling and the cheese is starting to brown. Serve hot, on its own or with some crusty bread and a salad.

CABBAGE PIROG

пирог с капустой

❖ ❖ ❖

Although I grew up eating all sorts of savory pies, I didn't truly fall in love until I walked into Stolle, a chain of Russian cafés specializing in ornately pimped-out pirogi that are almost too beautiful to eat. I know what you're thinking—cabbage pie doesn't exactly jump out as a drool-worthy dish. But I feel compelled to make the case for cabbage—and this pirog shows how dynamic it can be.

At Kachka, we give the cabbage a nice hard sear to get some caramelization going, dress it up with pickled raisins and mustard seeds, and throw in some gooey cheese for good measure. The dough can be frozen for up to a month ahead of time, and the filling can be made up to three days in advance—making this a very easy, low-fuss project with just a little planning.

SERVES 8 TO 12 AS PART OF A LARGER ZAKUSKI SPREAD

DOUGH:

4 cups (515 grams) all-purpose flour, plus more for rolling

4 teaspoons kosher salt

3 sticks (1½ cups) unsalted butter, frozen

Up to 1 cup ice water

FILLING:

High-heat oil (I use canola or peanut)

1 small green cabbage, quartered, cored, and shredded

Kosher salt

1 batch pickled mustard seeds and raisins (page 356)

½ pound shredded Gouda

¼ cup all-purpose flour

TO FINISH:

1 large egg, beaten with a splash of milk or cream to make a wash

Make the dough: Stir together the flour and salt in a large bowl. With a box grater, grate in the frozen butter, and gently toss to coat the butter shreds with the flour. Sprinkle in up to 1 cup ice water—the amount you need will vary based upon humidity, flour, room temperature, etc., so start with about ½ cup. Toss the mixture to distribute, and continue adding and mixing in water until the mixture holds together when you squeeze it. Form the dough into a rough ball, give it a knead or two, and then wrap it in plastic wrap and refrigerate for at least 1 hour.

While the dough is resting in the refrigerator, prepare the filling: Heat a large pan over high heat. Add enough oil to coat the bottom, then add half the cabbage. Give it a sprinkle of salt, and sauté hard for a few minutes, until the cabbage softens and begins to caramelize. Transfer the cooked cabbage to a large bowl, and repeat with the remaining raw cabbage. When it's all cooked, let the cabbage cool slightly, then add the mustard seeds and raisins, the Gouda, and more salt to taste. Stir in the flour and let the mixture cool to room temperature.

When you're ready to bake the pirog, preheat your oven to 375°F, and line a rimmed baking sheet with parchment paper. If you've made the filling in advance, take it out a few hours before baking to warm to room temperature. Grab a rolling pin, and lightly flour a clean countertop.

(continued page 166)

Take the dough out of the refrigerator, and divide it in two roughly equal pieces, with one slightly larger than the other. Leaving the larger piece covered, take the smaller piece of dough on a floured countertop, and roll it out to an 8-by-4-inch rectangle. Transfer the rolled-out dough to the baking sheet.

Mound the cabbage filling onto the dough, leaving about 1 inch of dough exposed along each edge.

Roll out the remaining dough so it is about 1 inch longer and wider than the first piece. Brush the egg wash along the exposed edges of the smaller piece of dough, then drape the larger piece of dough over the top. Smooth the top piece of dough over the filling, and use a fork to crimp the edges together. Trim away any uneven edges (if you want, you can save these bits of trimmed dough, cut them in decorative shapes, and affix them to the top for a bit of flair). Brush the egg wash over the entire pirog, and cut some vent holes through the top layer of dough to allow the filling to release steam as it cooks. If you've reserved trimmed bits of dough to decorate the top, add them now, and give them a brush with the egg wash as well.

Transfer the pirog to the oven, and bake until well browned and bubbling, about 40 minutes. Let cool slightly, then serve.

KHACHAPURI IMERETIAN

хачапури по-имеретински

+ + +

We've heard of the S&P 500 and the Consumer Price Index. But I'd argue the tastiest financial metric is Tbilisi's little-known yet delicious Khachapuri Index—the cost of the ingredients (flour, cheese, yeast, eggs, and butter) and energy (gas and electricity) required to make one unit of this beloved Georgian cheese-filled bread. Any time a food item becomes an economic measure, you know it's important.

And the reason for khachapuri's prominence is simple: it is addictively good. Khachapuri is found throughout Georgia, with huge variation—from the Adjarian cheese boat topped with a pat of butter and raw egg yolk (just in case, you know, melted cheese isn't rich enough), to the Rachian bean-stuffed variety. I'm partial to Imeretian style, which at Kachka we playfully describe as the love child of a crunchwrap and a calzone. Chopped cilantro and a smoky version of the requisite *sulguni* cheese add a little extra interest.

YIELDS 8 KHACHAPURI

DOUGH:

2 cups whole milk

1 cup water

¼ stick (2 tablespoons) unsalted butter

¾ teaspoon active dry yeast

5⅔ cups (720 grams) all-purpose flour, plus more for rolling

1 tablespoon kosher salt

FILLING:

1 pound smoked sulguni, grated (available at Russian markets—if unavailable, substitute mozzarella)

½ pound crumbled feta, preferably sheep's milk

1 bunch cilantro, coarsely chopped

TO FINISH:

Butter for frying

Adjika (page 358)

Tkemali (page 361)

Make the dough: In a saucepan, warm the milk, water, and butter to body temperature (too hot and you'll kill the yeast, so let it cool back down if needed). Add the yeast, and let it sit for 5 to 10 minutes for the yeast to wake up.

Pour the liquid into the bowl of a stand mixer fitted with a dough hook, add the flour and salt, and knead on low speed for 5 to 10 minutes, until the dough comes together to form a smooth (albeit sticky), elastic mass.

Oil a large bowl (large enough for the dough to double), and scrape in your dough. Cover, and let sit at room temperature until doubled in size (about 1 hour, depending upon the temperature). Punch the dough down, re-cover, and refrigerate overnight.

When you're ready to make the khachapuri the next day, take the dough out of the refrigerator, and let it sit for 1 to 2 hours to come to room temperature. Divide into 8 equal balls on a floured countertop, and let them rest, covered with a dish towel so they don't dry out while you prepare the filling.

Mix the filling ingredients together in a large bowl.

(continued page 168)

To assemble: Roll out one of the portioned balls of dough on a lightly floured surface to form a circle 6 inches in diameter (if it resists, let it sit for a few minutes to relax, then try again). Place a generous ½ cup of filling in the center, then bring the dough in to cover it in overlapping sections. Flip the bundle over, then roll it out to a 7-inch-diameter circle (which will both flatten the khachapuri and seal the overlapping dough on the underside). Place the finished khachapuri aside (rimmed baking sheets are helpful here), cover with a dish towel, and let rest for 30 minutes (or freeze on a parchment-lined baking sheet for later*). Repeat with the remaining dough and filling.

After the khachapuri have rested, melt a generous amount of butter in a skillet over medium/medium-low heat (enough to come halfway up the side of the khachapuri). Fry the khachapuri until golden brown, about 7 minutes, then flip and fry for a few minutes until golden on the other side. Serve hot, with adjika and tkemali. If you're making for a crowd, keep them warm in a low oven.

If you have leftover filling: Georgian nachos!

---

* Frozen khachapuri should thaw at room temperature for about 1 hour, then be cooked as above.

KORUSHKA WITH
KOREAN CARROT SALAD

корюшка с морковью по-корейски

⁜ ⁜ ⁜

At the end of every school year, my mother would be sent off to stay with her grandmother in Leningrad. And the end of May also happens to coincide with the running of the *korushka*, aka smelts. My mother says that the whole Neva River—the whole city, in fact—would smell of them, heralding the coming of summer. This is a good thing.

Korushka have a seductive smell—clean and briny, like oysters and freshly cut cucumbers. If you're getting good fresh fish, they should still have a whiff of that smell about them (though they'll lose it after a few days, or after being frozen). And, as a bonus, small smelts can be eaten bones, head, and all—aquatic french fries!

SERVES 5 TO 6

2 cups all-purpose flour

2 tablespoons paprika

1 tablespoon turmeric

1 tablespoon kosher salt, plus more for sprinkling

1½ pounds smelt (fresh if possible, no more than 5 inches long)

High-heat oil for frying (I use canola or peanut)

Parsley mayonnaise (page 357) for serving

Korean carrot salad (page 172) for serving

In a shallow dish, stir together the flour, paprika, turmeric, and salt. Set aside.

If your fishmonger hasn't gutted the smelt, clean them out: Take a small knife, and cut a ventral (aka bottom) slit from the tail end to the gills. Scoop out the entrails, and rinse the cavity under water. There's no need to debone the fish—everything will fry up crisp. When the fish are clean, pat them dry, and then dredge them in the seasoned flour mixture.

Pour a few inches of oil into a heavy pot, and heat it to 375°F (if you toss in a pinch of flour, it should sizzle but not brown immediately). Alternatively, if you favor shallow-frying over deep-frying, you can just pour oil to about halfway up the side of the fish, and heat to the same temperature.

When the oil is hot, gently add some of the dredged smelts—enough so that the pan is full, but not crowded. Let them cook (turning once if you're shallow-frying) until they're golden brown and crispy, about 5 minutes total. While the fish are cooking, take out a cooling rack, and line a plate with a paper towel.

(continued page 172)

When the smelts are cooked, remove with a skimmer or slotted spoon, give them a shake, and place them on the paper towel. Give them a shimmy to shake off the excess oil, then gently tip them out on the rack, and sprinkle them with salt. Repeat with the remaining fish. Serve hot, with parsley mayo and Korean carrot salad.

KOREAN CARROT SALAD

This salad didn't come from Korea. It's a creation strictly of the *Koryo-Saram*, ethnic Koreans in Russia (especially in Kazakhstan and Central Asia). Over the years, it's become very popular throughout the former Soviet Union—and even made its way back to Korea.

This slaw is fresh and punchy, with a good bit of kick from the garlic and chiles (which I've ramped up even further). Pair with korushka or other fried fish, *chebureki* (page 187), grilled items, or really anytime you want a refreshing bit of crunch.

YIELDS ABOUT 1 QUART

½ cup refined sunflower oil

1 clove garlic, minced

½ tablespoon onion powder

½ teaspoon paprika

¼ teaspoon freshly ground black pepper

¼ teaspoon ground coriander

¼ cup white vinegar

2 teaspoons Calabrian chile paste (or sambal oelek)

½ tablespoon kosher salt

½ teaspoon granulated sugar

2 pounds carrots, peeled and coarsely grated

Pour the oil into a large pan, and warm it over medium-high heat until you can just smell it, but it hasn't started smoking or shimmering, about 2 minutes. Turn off the heat, and whisk in the garlic, onion powder, paprika, pepper, and coriander. Let the mixture cool for a few minutes, then whisk in the vinegar, chile paste, salt, and sugar. Taste and adjust the seasonings—the dressing should be flavorful, aromatic, slightly spicy, and pungent from the vinegar. Let cool to room temperature.

Pour the dressing over the carrots, and toss to combine. Let the salad sit at least a few hours (or overnight) to marinate—it is best the second day, but it'll start to get soggy if it sits for more than 3 days. Stir before serving.

DUNGENESS CRAB PIROSHKI

пирожки с крабами

+ + +

Piroshki are Russia's street food. They are soft, pillowy buns stuffed with all sorts of fillings, both sweet and savory. You can find some form of piroshki in every bus station, corner kiosk, and café the country over. In the winters, they're served with an accompanying cup of broth made from the poaching liquid of whatever meat was used in the filling—sort of like Russia's soup-and-sandwich combo meal.

Piroshki are often filled with chicken, beef, or cabbage, but I'm particularly fond of the humble hard-boiled egg and scallion. And while egg and scallion are already pretty damn delicious, adding in a little Dungeness crab takes it to eleven. If using whole crab, simmer up some stock from the shells. Otherwise, serve the piroshki with garlic broth (page 353), or on their own.

YIELDS 16 PIROSHKI

DOUGH:

1¼ cups whole milk, warmed to body temperature

¼ cup vodka

1½ teaspoons active dry yeast

2 tablespoons granulated sugar

1 teaspoon kosher salt

1 large egg

1 large egg yolk

3½ cups (450 grams) all-purpose flour, plus more for rolling

½ stick (4 tablespoons) unsalted butter, softened to room temperature

FILLING:

¾ pound cooked Dungeness crab meat

5 hard-boiled eggs, coarsely chopped

Zest and juice of 1 to 2 lemons

⅓ cup thinly sliced scallions

⅓ cup coarsely chopped fresh dill

¾ cup mayonnaise (preferably homemade, page 357)

Kosher salt

Make the dough: Pour the milk and vodka in the bowl of a stand mixer fitted with a whisk attachment, and sprinkle in the yeast. Let the mixture sit for a few minutes to allow the yeast to wake up. Add the sugar, salt, egg, and yolk, and whisk to combine. Add the flour gradually, eventually switching over to a dough hook.

When the flour has all been incorporated, add the butter, pat by pat, adding more after each previous pat has been incorporated. Once the mixture comes together, knead for an additional 5 minutes. It will be quite sticky, not clearing the sides of the mixer.

Use a bowl scraper or spatula to transfer the dough to an oiled container, and cover with a lid or plastic wrap. Let the dough rise until doubled, either overnight in the refrigerator, or about 2 hours at room temperature. When it's risen, punch it down, and then let it proof another 45 minutes. While the dough is proofing, prepare the filling.

Check the crab meat very carefully and remove any shells. Then check again! In a large bowl, gently fold all of the filling ingredients together, starting with the zest and juice from just 1 lemon. Add salt to taste, and add additional lemon zest/juice as needed. Set aside.

(continued page 175)

CONTINUED
dungeness crab piroshki

TO FINISH:

1 large egg, beaten with a splash of milk to make a wash

3 tablespoons unsalted butter

After the dough has risen and the filling is prepared, line a few rimmed baking sheets with parchment, and generously flour a clean countertop (this is a fairly soft dough). Divide the dough into 16 equal balls, and fill a small dish with water.

Roll out a dough ball (keeping the remaining dough covered so that it doesn't dry out) into a 5-inch round (it'll be not quite ¼-inch thick). Place a scant ¼ cup of filling in the center, and either spray or brush the edges of the dough with water. Bring up the sides, and pinch together to form a football shape. Flip it over, seam side down, and round off the pointed edges to form more of a blunt-edged oval (this will help it cook more evenly). Place the piroshki on a prepared baking sheet, and repeat with the remaining dough and filling.

Let the piroshki puff up for 20 to 30 minutes, while the oven preheats to 375°F. When the oven is preheated, brush the piroshki gently with the egg wash, and bake until golden brown, about 20 minutes.

While the piroshki are baking, melt the butter in a small pot. As soon as they come out of the oven, brush them with melted butter. Serve warm.

CHICKEN BLINCHIKI

блинчики с курицей

✛ ✛ ✛

Blinchiki (blintzes, if you're American) are to Russia what burgers are to America. Russia even boasts several popular fast-food chains that serve only blinchiki, filled with everything from smoked salmon to farmer's cheese to Caesar salad (Moscow is inexplicably in the throes of a Caesar salad obsession).

Back in the nineties, sparked by this popularity in the motherland, my parents and their good friends Bronya and Anatoly had visions of turning blinchiki into the next craze here in the United States. Our home was turned into a test kitchen, with all three of our refrigerators (yes, three refrigerators for a family of four) packed full of trials. The plan quickly dissolved upon the discovery that making blinchiki en masse is a huge pain in the ass. Thankfully, this home-scaled version is way more manageable.

YIELDS 12 BLINCHIKI

CREPES:

1½ cups milk

2 large eggs

¼ stick (2 tablespoons) unsalted butter, melted

1 cup all-purpose flour

½ teaspoon granulated sugar

½ teaspoon kosher salt

FILLING:

2 tablespoons cooking oil (I use refined sunflower)

1½ pounds boneless, skinless chicken thighs

Kosher salt

1 medium onion, cut into a ¼-inch dice

3 to 4 cups chicken stock

3 tablespoons unsalted butter, plus more for cooking the blinchiki

3 tablespoons all-purpose flour

¼ teaspoon freshly ground black pepper

Make the crepe batter: Place all the crepe ingredients into a blender, and blend on high for 1 to 2 minutes until uniform (or you can place in a bowl and whisk). Let the crepe batter rest for 20 to 30 minutes while you make the filling (or refrigerate up to 2 days).

Make the filling: Heat a sauté pan over medium-high heat, and add the oil. Season the chicken thighs with a generous sprinkling of salt, and sear them until golden brown (just a few minutes per side). Remove the thighs from the pan and set aside, and reduce the heat to medium.

Add the onion to the pan, and sauté until it is translucent with bits of caramelization (and even a bit of char) in spots, about 7 minutes. Pour in 3 cups of the chicken stock, give a stir to loosen up any bits sticking to the bottom, and then place the thighs back in the pan. If the chicken isn't covered, you can add a bit more stock. Bring the mixture to a gentle simmer. Taste the liquid, and season as needed. Braise at a simmer, uncovered, until the thighs are tender, about 45 minutes, turning the pieces once to braise evenly.

When the chicken thighs are cooked, remove them with a slotted spoon, and set them aside on a cutting board to cool. Pour the broth and onions from the pan into a measuring cup—you want to have 2 cups of liquid (if you're short, add additional chicken stock).

(continued page 178)

In the now-empty pan (no need to clean it out), melt the butter over medium-low heat. When it's melted, whisk in the flour. Continue to whisk for a few minutes, letting the roux color slightly to a golden brown. Bring the heat up to medium, and add the broth-onion mixture while whisking. Continue to whisk until the mixture thickens and is uniform, about 2 minutes. Reduce the heat to low, so that the broth is just simmering, and cook for another 5 minutes for the mixture to come together. Remove from the heat.

When the chicken is cool enough to handle, cut it into a ½-inch dice. Add the chicken back into the sauce, mix everything together, and set aside to cool. Mix in the pepper, and taste for seasoning, adding more salt if needed. If assembling the the crepes later, refrigerate.

Cook the crepes: Heat an 8-inch nonstick sauté pan over medium-low heat. When the pan is hot, swirl in a scant ¼ cup (3 tablespoons) of batter so that it makes a thin, even circle. Work on your wrist skills by swirling the batter out quickly before it sets. Cook the crepe for about 2 minutes, until it just begins to get some golden color on the underside— it can be a bit crispy on the perimeter, but overall it should be soft and pliable. Slide the finished crepe onto a dinner plate, cooked side down. Continue to cook off the remaining batter in this fashion, stacking the finished crepes directly on top of each other. You should end up with about 12 crepes.

If you're not filling immediately, wrap tightly and refrigerate. The crepes can be cooked up to 2 days ahead.

To assemble the blinchiki: Lay the crepes out on a clean work surface, with the pale side down. Place ¼ cup of filling in the center of each one. Use your fingers or a spoon to shape the filling into a rectangular mass, and roll up each one like a small 4-by-1-inch burrito. If not serving immediately, move the wrapped blinchiki to a container, and store in the refrigerator for up to 12 hours, or in the freezer for up to 2 months (frozen blinchiki can be fried up straight from the freezer—just add a few minutes to the cook time).

To serve: Heat a large skillet over medium heat, and melt a few spoonfuls of butter. When the butter starts to foam, place the blinchiki in the pan, seam side down. Let sizzle until golden and crispy on both sides and hot in the middle, about 3 to 4 minutes per side. Season the finished blinchiki with salt, and serve warm (or hold in a warm oven). Repeat with the remaining blinchiki.

SHKVARKY WITH BUCKWHEAT BLINI AND LINGONBERRY MUSTARD

гречневые блины со шкварками и брусничной горчицей

✦ ✦ ✦

My parents came to the United States as refugees through HIAS (Hebrew Immigrant Aid Society) in 1980. Part of the deal was that my then-eight-year-old brother, Simon, would enroll in Solomon Schechter, a Jewish elementary school. Full of fervor for his newly realized religious identity, he came home one day and declared that he was no longer eating pork. My parents, feeling guilty, also denounced swine. From then on, the Frumkin household was a bacon no-fly zone.

These days, we are all happily back on the pork wagon, and my parents are reacquainting themselves with dishes they haven't prepared since the great pork ban of 1980. Including shkvarky. That's "shk-VAR-key": once you get the hang of pronouncing it, you won't want to stop; it's rather satisfying to say. And eat.

Shkvarky are, essentially, rendered lardons of salt-cured salo (pork fatback)—cooked low and slow with a whole mess of onions. For a rich-earthy-tart combination, spread the meaty mixture on buckwheat blini, and top with lingonberry mustard. Besides being a zakuska in its own right, shkvarky paired with blini or draniki (potato pancakes) (page 268) makes for a memorable brunch.

SERVES 8 TO 10 AS AN APPETIZER

1 pound salt-cured salo (pork fatback), as meaty as possible (you can swap in bacon for a smokier take), skinned and cut into a ¼-inch dice

1 large onion, cut into a ¼-inch dice

1 recipe buckwheat blini, (page 182)

½ cup pickled mustard seeds (page 356)

½ cup lingonberry jam (available at Russian markets, well-stocked grocery stores, and, surprisingly, IKEA)

Leaves from a few sprigs of fresh thyme

In a large skillet or sauté pan, cook the salo over a very low heat—you want to render the fat out without burning things. After some of the fat comes out, about 15 minutes in, add the onion, and increase the heat to medium-low. Once the onion is sweating and more liquid comes out, you can increase the heat to medium. Continue to cook until the salo has rendered as much as it can (the remaining bits aren't getting any smaller), and the onion is well caramelized, about 45 minutes. Reduce the heat as needed to keep things from burning, and stir regularly so that it cooks evenly.

While the salo and onion are cooking, you can cook your blini (see page 182). In a small dish, mix together the mustard seeds and lingonberry jam, and set aside.

When the salo has rendered and the onion is caramelized, strain the salo and onion bits out of the rendered fat. Set the fat aside for another purpose (pan-frying some dumplings, perhaps?),

(continued page 182)

reserving the cup or so yield of intensely flavored pork and onion.

To serve, fan out the warm blini on a platter. Evenly distribute the shkvarky over the blini, and drizzle on some of the lingonberry mixture. Finish with a few fresh thyme leaves.

BUCKWHEAT BLINI

These blini were actually inspired by an old recipe from the Russian Tea Room. But buckwheat itself is a common flour in Russia. I love the toothsome texture and satisfying earthiness. These aren't delicate blini to accent your spendy caviar—these are blini that can stand up to big flavors, perfect for some rendered lardons, or a dip in your breakfast gravy or machanka (page 287). At the restaurant, we pair buckwheat blini with buckwheat honey butter (page 115) for a buckwheat-on-buckwheat play. But they also make for a perfect simple snack, especially with a generous swipe of butter and gooseberry jam.

YIELDS ABOUT 3 DOZEN 3-INCH BLINI

1⅓ cups milk

½ stick (4 tablespoons) unsalted butter, sliced into pats

1 teaspoon active dry yeast

2 large eggs

¾ cup all-purpose flour

¾ cup buckwheat flour

2 tablespoons sugar

1 teaspoon kosher salt

Butter for pan-frying

Heat the milk and butter together in a saucepan until the butter just melts. Transfer the mixture to a large bowl, and let cool to body temperature. Stir in the yeast, and let the mixture sit for a few minutes to allow the yeast to wake up.

After the yeast has softened, whisk in the eggs, then add the flours, sugar, and salt. Whisk until combined. Cover the batter with a lid or plastic wrap, and place in the fridge overnight. The mixture will double in size—make sure your container is big enough! (I've learned this the hard way.)

The next day, take the batter out of the refrigerator, let it come to room temperature, and give it a good stir. The batter will be slightly thicker than pancake batter. Heat a griddle or a couple of pans over medium heat, and melt a few pats of butter in each. When the pans are hot, ladle in your batter to form 3-inch pancakes (this will take somewhere between 1 and 2 tablespoons per blin). Let the blini cook a few minutes, until the bubbles in the batter rise and pop, the top dries slightly, and the underside is golden. Flip, and cook until the other side is golden as well, then transfer the cooked blini to a plate. Repeat with the remaining batter, adding more butter to the pan and adjusting the heat as needed.

Serve warm.

BEEF TONGUE CONFIT WITH WHOLE SATSUMA PUREE, PARSLEY, AND OLIVES

язык говяжий с мандаринами, петрушкой и маслинами

✤ ✤ ✤

When I was growing up, tongue was on the dinner table about once a week. It was boiled and served with mashed potatoes and pickles, and it required a knife. A very sharp knife.

I break down tongue's toughness by giving it a long, slow cook in beef fat. By the end of the confit it's nearly molten, requiring little more than a look to fall apart (and a quick sear to give a nice contrasting bit of crust on the surface). I dress it up with seasonal elements—from lemon balm and cherries to this mandarin puree and parsley root chips—but honestly it's still delicious with good old mashed potatoes and a kosher dill. To break down the steps, render out the fat for confiting the first day, cook the tongue the second, chill and serve the third.

SERVES 10 AS AN APPETIZER, OR 5 TO 6 AS A MAIN DISH

5 pounds beef suet (available at butcher shops) or 8 cups rendered beef fat

1 beef tongue

Kosher salt

TO SERVE:

Whole satsuma puree (page 186)

¼ cup olives, pitted and quartered (I use Alfonso olives)

2 oranges, supremed

1 handful parsley leaves

If you're rendering the beef fat: Cut the suet into chunks, and place them in a large saucepan over medium heat. Add about 1 inch of water and cover. At first you'll need to stir every 10 minutes or so, until the fat starts to melt. Then reduce the heat to low, and stir every 30 minutes until it renders, about 4 hours, removing the lid halfway through. After 4 hours the fat should have come out, and the rendered chunks won't be getting any smaller. Strain the fat to remove any big solids. If you make this in advance, it can be refrigerated for up to 1 month or frozen for up to 6 months.

A few hours (and up to a day) before you'd like to confit the tongue, place it in a container or Ziploc bag, and salt it generously on all sides. Refrigerate for several hours, or overnight.

When you're ready to confit, preheat the oven to 225°F. Place the tongue in an oven-proof pot or casserole dish—whatever's small enough to just fit. If you've rendered your fat in advance, melt it, and pour it over the tongue to cover. Place the entire thing on a rimmed baking sheet (the liquid in the tongue will come out and raise the level slightly as it cooks, so you don't want to risk an overflow).

(continued page 185)

CONTINUED
*beef tongue confit with whole
satsuma puree, parsley, and olives*

Place the tongue in the oven, and confit 13 to 14 hours, until a knife slides in with no resistance (you're looking for nice and soft, like braised short ribs). This seems like a ridiculously long time, but it's necessary to get the tongue tender—you've got no business peeking until at least 12 hours. Note: Some newer ovens have an auto-off function that keeps you from inadvertently leaving the oven on for too many hours on end. If yours is one of these, make sure that it doesn't turn itself off midway through this long cook time.

When the tongue is tender, pull it out of the fat, and let it cool until it's just cool enough to handle (don't let it get too cold, or the skin will be hard to peel). Peel off and discard the skin, starting from the base, being careful not to tear the meat—it should come apart easily. Place the peeled tongue in the fridge, and refrigerate until completely cool (and up to 3 days).

Take the fat, and separate off any liquid—this can be incorporated into fancy broth (page 351), or saved for floating your pelmeni (page 211). Reserve about ¼ cup of fat for finishing the tongue—the rest can either be discarded, or strained and reused for confiting future tongues (or short ribs, or anything else you desire).

When you're ready to serve, slice the cold tongue against the grain into 1½-inch slices (that'll give you a nice ratio of crispy outside to tender inside). Heat a large skillet over medium-high heat, and add a nice slick of fat. When the pan is hot, add the tongue slices, and pan-fry on each side until the sides are bubbling and golden brown, and the center is warmed through, about 2 minutes per side. Serve hot with whole satsuma puree and garnish with the olives, orange segments, and parsley (or omit them all, and serve with mashed potatoes and pickles).

(continued page 186)

CONTINUED
*beef tongue confit with whole
satsuma puree, parsley, and olives*

WHOLE SATSUMA PUREE

This bright and pleasantly bitter sauce is a nice counterpoint to the richness of tongue confit. Blitzing whole citrus feels a bit strange, but thin-skinned mandarins yield a sauce that's just sharp enough to offset the rich tongue.

YIELDS 1 CUP

4 satsuma mandarins, washed well

¼ cup granulated sugar

2 teaspoons kosher salt

2 tablespoons olive oil

Roughly chop mandarins, removing and discarding any seeds, and place them in a blender. Add the sugar and salt, and run the blender, gradually increasing the speed to high, until the mixture is completely pureed and starting to heat up from the friction. Drizzle in the oil in a thin stream to form an emulsified sauce.

Strain the mixture through a fine-mesh strainer, and season with additional salt and sugar as needed to create a pleasantly astringent, balanced sauce. Serve immediately.

CHEBUREKI

чебуреки

✛ ✛ ✛

I'm in love with mid-twentieth-century Soviet design. The problem, for shopping purposes, is that the concept of "vintage" doesn't really exist in Russia. Sure, there are flea markets—full of old munitions and socks. There are antiques galleries—with Fabergé eggs and relics. Trying to explain to Russians that I am looking for polka-dotted enamelware and dinged-up old metal caviar tins yields puzzled looks. But during a trip to Moscow a few years back, I got a tip about a weekly market that catered to my "strange" tastes. We schlepped out across town early in the morning to find the market (Moscow is huge—every errand is an epic endeavor), only to learn that it had been canceled due to lack of interest just the week before.

But all was not lost—because as we turned the corner, a sign for a *cheburechnaya* came into view. We ducked in, and salvaged an otherwise failed mission with some nice cold beer and freshly fried *chebureki*. These half-moon-shaped lamb pies are Crimean in origin but served at little hole-in-the-wall spots all over the former Soviet Union. Generally they're more suited for a midday snack than a breakfast, but either way the lamb pick-me-up works some restorative magic.

YIELDS 8 PIES

DOUGH:

Scant 4 cups (500 grams) all-purpose flour, plus more for rolling

2 teaspoons kosher salt

1 cup water

1 large egg yolk

1½ tablespoons refined sunflower or canola oil

FILLING:

1¼ pounds ground lamb

½ yellow onion, grated on the large holes of a box grater (include liquid)

⅔ cup ice water

½ bunch cilantro, coarsely chopped

1 tablespoon kosher salt

TO FINISH:

High-heat oil for frying (I use canola or peanut)

Kosher salt

Make the dough: In a stand mixer fitted with a dough hook or in a large bowl, knead together the flour, salt, water, and egg yolk until it binds. Add the oil, and then knead for another 5 minutes (longer if you're doing it by hand), until the dough is smooth, uniform, and elastic. Cover the bowl with plastic wrap or a dish towel, and let it rest at room temperature for at least 30 minutes. While the dough is resting, prepare the filling.

Make the filling: Place the lamb, onion, ice water, cilantro, and salt in a stand mixer fitted with a paddle attachment or in a large bowl. Mix on low (or with your hands), until the mixture comes together—you're basically looking for the fat to emulsify, which will coat everything with a nice fat-smeared sheen, and incorporate all of the water into the meat. If you stop and grab a pinch of the mixture, it will stick to your fingers. Under- or over-processing will lead to dry meat, so try to hit this nice sticky sweet spot—stop and check. The entire process should take 1 to 2 minutes tops with the paddle attachment (longer by hand).

(continued page 188)

When your filling is ready and the dough has rested, divide the dough into 8 equal balls (these should weigh about 100 grams each). Lightly flour a clean countertop, and grab a rolling pin, a small dish of water, and a pastry brush (or spray bottle if you've got one), and a fork.

Place one of the balls of dough on a lightly floured surface (keep the rest of the dough covered while you're not working with it). Roll the ball of dough into an 8-inch circle—it will be somewhat thinner than a pie crust. With a spray bottle or a pastry brush (or your fingers), give the outer edge of your dough circle a light brush of water. Take ⅛ of the filling (a heaping ⅓ cup), and spread it evenly over half of the dough circle (the back of a spoon works nicely for this), leaving a ½-inch border. Fold the dough into a half moon, and use a fork to crimp the edges down tightly (at Kachka we roll a little fluted wheel to clean up the edges all pretty, but that's optional). Make sure you seal them well—unsealed chebureki will turn into a sputtery mess in the fryer (although they will still be delicious). Repeat with remaining dough. If you want, you can freeze them at this point. *

When you're ready to fry, pour an inch of oil into a cast-iron skillet or pot. Heat the oil over medium-high heat, until it reaches 360°F, or until a pinch of flour sizzles but doesn't instantly darken. While the oil is heating, set a rack over a baking sheet, or line a plate with paper towels or brown paper bags to receive your fried pies.

When the oil is hot, carefully place in your pies one or two at a time depending on the size of your skillet. Cook until the first side is a nice golden color, then flip (gently—the crust is flaky and delicate, so a slotted spoon or spatula is best), and cook until they color on the second side. This should take about 5 minutes total—the lamb filling is so thin that it will easily be cooked when the dough is golden. When your chebureki are golden on both sides, gently remove them from the oil, and place on your prepared rack or paper towels to drain. Give them a sprinkle of salt, and serve hot. Repeat with remaining chebureki.

---

* To freeze chebureki, lay them out on a parchment-lined baking sheet until just frozen, then store them in a sealed container. Frozen chebureki can be fried directly from the freezer, sans thawing—just add a few additional minutes of cook time. They are a bit more delicate while frozen, so handle carefully to avoid breakage.

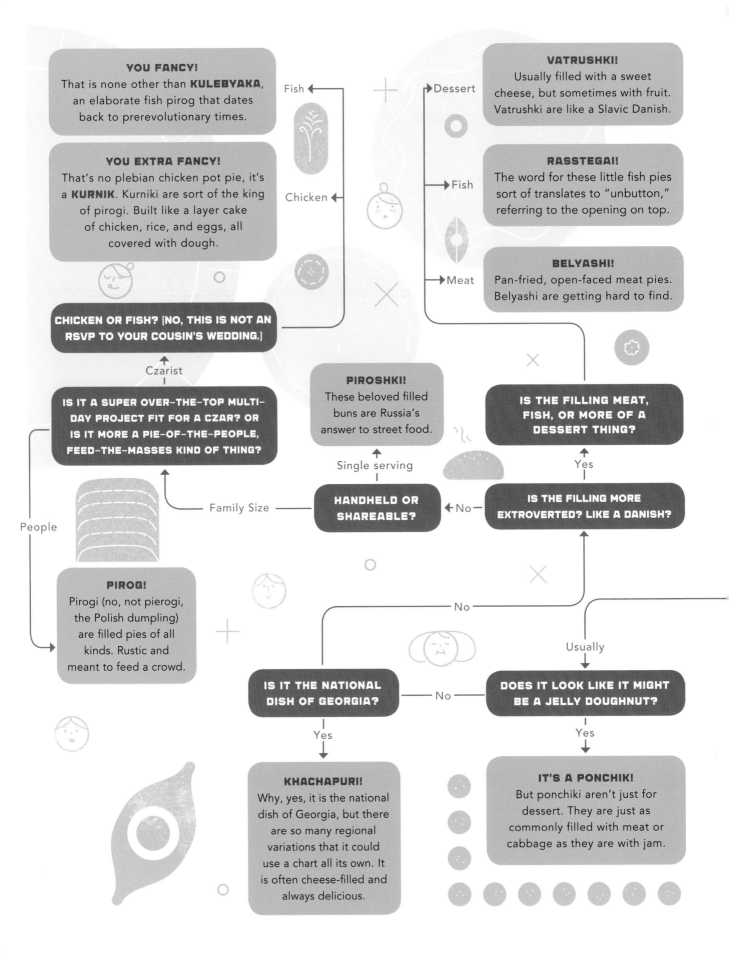

YOU FANCY!
That is none other than **KULEBYAKA**, an elaborate fish pirog that dates back to prerevolutionary times.

Fish

YOU EXTRA FANCY!
That's no plebian chicken pot pie, it's a **KURNIK**. Kurniki are sort of the king of pirogi. Built like a layer cake of chicken, rice, and eggs, all covered with dough.

Chicken

CHICKEN OR FISH? (NO, THIS IS NOT AN RSVP TO YOUR COUSIN'S WEDDING.)

Czarist

IS IT A SUPER OVER-THE-TOP MULTI-DAY PROJECT FIT FOR A CZAR? OR IS IT MORE A PIE-OF-THE-PEOPLE, FEED-THE-MASSES KIND OF THING?

Family Size

People

PIROG!
Pirogi (no, not pierogi, the Polish dumpling) are filled pies of all kinds. Rustic and meant to feed a crowd.

VATRUSHKI!
Usually filled with a sweet cheese, but sometimes with fruit. Vatrushki are like a Slavic Danish.

Dessert

Fish

RASSTEGAI!
The word for these little fish pies sort of translates to "unbutton," referring to the opening on top.

Meat

BELYASHI!
Pan-fried, open-faced meat pies. Belyashi are getting hard to find.

PIROSHKI!
These beloved filled buns are Russia's answer to street food.

Single serving

HANDHELD OR SHAREABLE?

No

IS THE FILLING MEAT, FISH, OR MORE OF A DESSERT THING?

Yes

IS THE FILLING MORE EXTROVERTED? LIKE A DANISH?

No

Usually

IS IT THE NATIONAL DISH OF GEORGIA?

No

DOES IT LOOK LIKE IT MIGHT BE A JELLY DOUGHNUT?

Yes

KHACHAPURI!
Why, yes, it is the national dish of Georgia, but there are so many regional variations that it could use a chart all its own. It is often cheese-filled and always delicious.

Yes

IT'S A PONCHIK!
But ponchiki aren't just for dessert. They are just as commonly filled with meat or cabbage as they are with jam.

DOES IT RESEMBLE A MINI BURRITO?

— No →

Yes ↓

IT'S A BLINCHIK!
Blinchiki are essentially crepes wrapped around a filling and pan fried. Known as a blintz in the New York City Jewish deli scene.

IS IT BURSTING WITH JUICY, MEATY GOODNESS?

— No →

Yes ↓

OH, BOY! A BOWL OF PELMENI!
Originally from Siberia, these meaty little dumplings are extremely popular all over Russia and many parts of the former Soviet Union. How you dress them can be very personal—everything from ketchup to soy sauce to butter and vinegar is game.

VARENIKI!
Ukraine's answer to pelmeni. Vareniki are typically slightly larger and half-moon shaped, and are filled with potatoes, veggies, fruit, or cheese.

THINGS WRAPPED IN DOUGH

From yeasted buns to slippery dumplings to grab-and-go fried pies, Russians *love* them some things wrapped in dough. But how do you know what's in front of you? Consult this chart for the full taxonomy of this delicious genre.

ALL RIGHT, IS IT USUALLY STEAMED OR BOILED?

Steamed ↓

MANTI!
Influenced by China, these Uzbek dumplings are prepared in a special steamer called a mantovarka.

Boiled ↓

IS THE DOUGH YEASTED?

No

Never ↓

LOOK UNDER THE HOOD. IS IT LAMB-FILLED?

No

Yes ↓

IS YOUR LAMB-Y BUNDLE OF JOY FRIED?

Yes ↓

BEHOLD! THE CHEBUREK!
Chebureki are the Crimean Tatars' gift to the world. Half-moon-shaped dough filled with lamb and then fried.

LOOK, KHINKALI!
A Georgian specialty, these dumplings are shaped into something of a beggar's purse before being boiled. Pro tip: Eat khinkali with your hands. Hold on to the knot on top. Bend over your plate when taking the first bite—they should be juicy! And last, but not least, DO NOT EAT THE KNOT OF DOUGH!

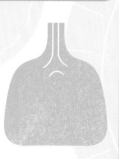

CHAPTER 5

DUMPLINGS

пельмени и вареники

+ + +

My husband, Israel, and I fell in love over bowls of pelmeni. Well, that's how I see it—he says that I seduced him with dumplings. In our early days working at Chicago restaurants, we'd stumble home in the predawn hours after service, and I'd pull out a bag of store-bought frozen dumplings and scour the kitchen for leftover broths or garnishes we could use to amp things up. Maybe a quick gremolata for brightness, or last weekend's rich oxtail braise. As soon as the pelmeni were done boiling away and dressed with that night's additions, we'd sink into the couch and forget the world.

Because pelmeni were new to Israel, he saw them as some secret weapon that I unleashed in the service of our courtship. But the truth is that these magical dumplings make us all weak in the knees. And while those store-bought ones require some doctoring to make memorable, making them yourself yields results that need nothing more than a little butter and a splash of vinegar. So go forth and seduce your special someone.

HOW TO MAKE PELMENI AND VARENIKI

What's the difference? In general, pelmeni are filled with meat, vareniki with vegetables, fruit, or cheese. Traditionally, vareniki are shaped a bit larger than pelmeni, but this is less critical. In order to make either, you will need one batch of dough (page 195), and one batch of a filling of your choosing (pages 198–204). After both are made, proceed to pages 206–211 for instructions on assembling, cooking, and serving. Each batch yields about 100 dumplings by hand, more if you've got a pelmenitsa (page 196).

DUMPLING DOUGH

тесто для пельменей и вареников

✢ ✢ ✢

There's a reason handmade dough is so much better than the dough in the freezer section. Industrial machines need to use a tougher, drier dough—all the better for standing up to mechanized production. But when you turn out pelmeni by hand, you can use a tender dough like this one, for slippery, delicate dumplings that pretty much melt in your mouth.

YIELDS DOUGH FOR ABOUT 100 DUMPLINGS MADE BY HAND, 148 WITH A PELMENITSA

3½ cups (450 grams) all-purpose flour

1 tablespoon kosher salt

1 large egg

¾ cup plus 2 tablespoons cold water

In the bowl of a stand mixer fitted with a dough hook, mix together the flour and salt. Add the egg, then slowly drizzle in the water. Mix until a dough forms, then knead for 10 minutes, until the dough comes together into a smooth, elastic ball. If you don't have a mixer, you can do this by hand, but knead for 20 minutes. (And be prepared to sweat!) Wrap the dough in plastic wrap or place in a covered container, and let rest at room temperature for at least 1 hour.

THE PELMENITSA

I absolutely love this thing. The pelmenitsa mold, with its thirty-seven hexagons, is a perfection of Soviet design, all angles and efficiency striving toward a utopian future of dumplings for all. There's a reason Russian émigrés would tuck the heavy metal mold inside their suitcases, with its unchanging price stamped in the side. It's form and function, nostalgia and dumplings, all together in a beautifully weird metal beehive.

SPEED!
Thirty-seven pelmeni all at once.

CONSISTENCY
Like tasty little soldiers.

The circular opening in the center of each mold creates the **IDEAL VOID** to pack in more filling.

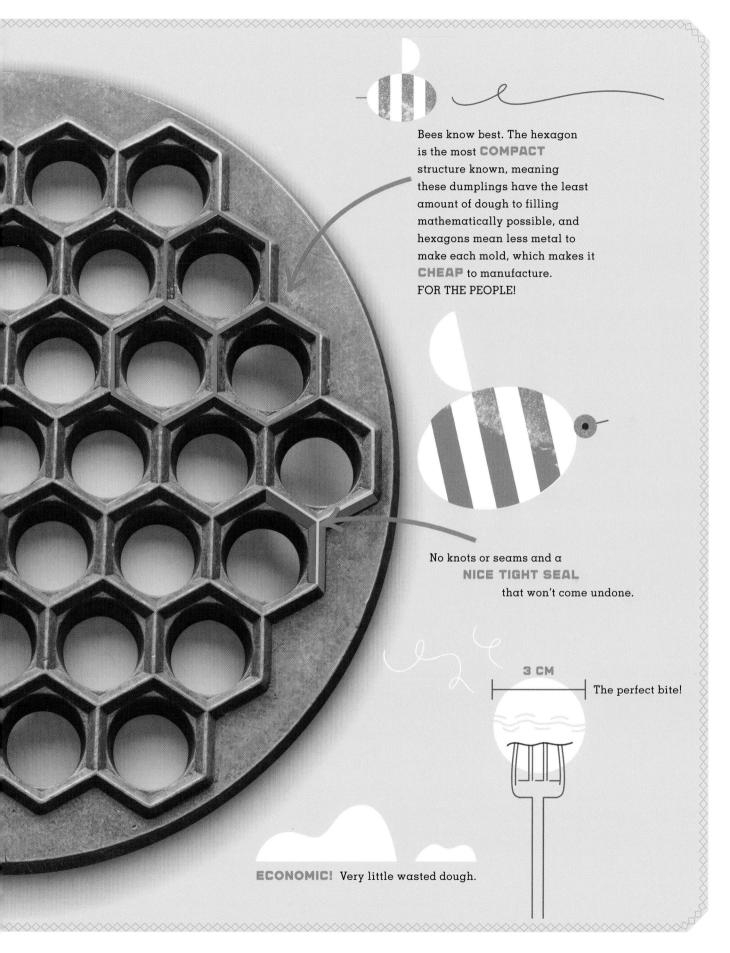

Bees know best. The hexagon is the most **COMPACT** structure known, meaning these dumplings have the least amount of dough to filling mathematically possible, and hexagons mean less metal to make each mold, which makes it **CHEAP** to manufacture. FOR THE PEOPLE!

No knots or seams and a **NICE TIGHT SEAL** that won't come undone.

3 CM

The perfect bite!

ECONOMIC! Very little wasted dough.

SIBERIAN PELMENI

сибирские пельмени

+ + +

The name here is arguably a bit redundant—pelmeni *are* Siberian. They're the original frozen food. Way before refrigeration, families in Siberia would gather together to make hundreds at a time and throw them out the window into the snow as they worked. Back then, the meat of choice was equine, but that has, understandably, fallen out of favor. I use a mix of pork, beef, and veal, which mirrors the dumplings of my childhood.

YIELDS FILLING FOR ABOUT 100 DUMPLINGS MADE BY HAND, 148 WITH A PELMENITSA

½ pound ground beef

½ pound ground pork

½ pound ground veal

½ onion, finely grated (include liquid)

⅔ cup ice water

1 tablespoon plus 1 teaspoon kosher salt

Place all the ingredients in the bowl of a stand mixer fitted with the paddle attachment and mix until the mixture comes together. You're looking for the fat to emulsify, which will incorporate all of the ice water and onion liquid, and coat everything with a nice fat-smeared sheen. If you stop the mixer and grab a pinch, it will stick to your fingers with a very tacky feel. Under- or overprocessing will lead to dry meat, so try to hit this nice sticky sweet spot—stop and check. The entire process should take 1 to 2 minutes tops, with the paddle attachment (longer by hand). Refrigerate until ready to assemble (page 206). This filling is best made the same day you are assembling, but can be made up to a day ahead if needed.

To cook and garnish, follow the instructions on pages 210–211.

LAMB PELMENI WITH ADJIKA BUTTER

пельмени с бараниной с аджиковым маслом

✤ ✤ ✤

I riffed this variation for a "dumpling week" event (one of Portland's best made-up holidays). With lamb, a bit of heat, and fresh herbs, these pelmeni bridge from Siberia to the sunny Caucasus. Instead of regular butter for finishing, toss these with an adjika butter—mix 1 part adjika (page 358) with 3 parts butter, and then finish the bowl with a bit of cilantro and mint instead of dill.

YIELDS FILLING FOR ABOUT 100 DUMPLINGS MADE BY HAND, 148 WITH A PELMENITSA

1½ pounds ground lamb

½ onion, finely grated (include liquid)

⅔ cup ice water

1 tablespoon plus 1 teaspoon kosher salt

Place all the ingredients in the bowl of a stand mixer fitted with the paddle attachment and mix until the mixture comes together. You're looking for the fat to emulsify, which will incorporate all of the ice water and onion liquid, and coat everything with a nice fat-smeared sheen. If you stop the mixer and grab a pinch, it will stick to your fingers with a very tacky feel. Under- or overprocessing will lead to dry meat, so try to hit this nice sticky sweet spot— stop every so often and check. The entire process should take 1 to 2 minutes tops with the paddle attachment (longer by hand). Refrigerate until ready to assemble (page 206). This filling is best made the same day, but can be made up to a day ahead if needed.

To cook and garnish, follow the instructions on pages 210–211.

TVOROG VARENIKI

вареники с творогом

✦ ✦ ✦

Every once in a while, a guest will ask for a side of jam with their tvorog vareniki. And if you were eating tvorog vareniki pretty much anywhere else, that would make sense—these farmer's cheese dumplings are almost always sweet. But since I get to make the rules around here, our tvorog vareniki are savory. The farmer's cheese is reinforced with some grated parmesan, tangy kefir, and chives, giving these vareniki a sour cream 'n' onion vibe. In order to get just the right oozy texture, this loose filling needs to be good and cold before piping— be sure to start things the night before.

YIELDS FILLING FOR ABOUT 100 DUMPLINGS MADE BY HAND, 148 WITH A PELMENITSA

1 pound tvorog (also labeled farmer's cheese—page 369)

1 large egg

½ cup kefir

¾ cup grated parmesan cheese

Scant ½ cup all-purpose flour

2 teaspoons kosher salt

¼ cup minced chives

Place the tvorog, egg, kefir, parmesan, flour, and salt in a food processor. Process for several minutes, scraping down the bowl a few times, until the mixture is very, very smooth. The cheese has some graininess, but if you keep processing, it will break down to a warm, smooth, liquidy mixture.

When you've reached this nice, smooth result, transfer the mixture to a covered container, and stir in the chives. The mixture will be thick but runny (don't worry!). Refrigerate overnight. By the next day, the filling will have thickened to the texture of a sticky whipped cream cheese or mascarpone. Keep refrigerated until ready to assemble (page 206).

To cook and garnish, follow the instructions on pages 210–211.

SOUR CHERRY VARENIKI

вареники с вишней

✢ ✢ ✢

These store-bought frozen dumplings were the easiest thing to "make" myself when I was a teenager. Fruit and pasta for dinner? Sign me up! But the reality was always disappointing. Each dumpling was filled with a single pitted sour cherry—add pasta and boiling water, and you end up with muted, watery flavors.

In order to help these dumplings realize all they can be, I concentrate the cherry flavor as much as possible—dried sour cherries (always in season!), reconstituted in sour cherry syrup for fruit-on-fruit intensity. The filling will be thick enough to mound into the dumplings after a few hours of chilling, but will melt back into a lusciously molten syrup after simmering. Equally suited to serving as a light meal or dessert.

YIELDS FILLING FOR ABOUT 100 DUMPLINGS MADE BY HAND, 148 WITH A PELMENITSA

1 cup sour cherry syrup*

½ cup water

1 pound (about 3 cups) dried sour cherries

1 tablespoon potato starch dissolved in 1 tablespoon water

Pour the cherry syrup and water into a medium-sized pot, and add the dried cherries. Bring the mixture to a boil, let bubble for 1 minute, and then stir in the potato starch slurry (mix vigorously to make sure everything is well combined). Boil, stirring, until the mixture thickens, 1 to 2 minutes. Remove from the heat and let chill until completely cold—a few hours, or overnight. Keep refrigerated until ready to assemble (page 206).

To cook and garnish, follow the instructions on pages 210–211.

---

* Available in Eastern European markets—and leftovers make for a delicious mixer.

THE ASSEMBLY

сборка

+ + +

YIELDS ABOUT 100 DUMPLINGS MADE BY HAND, 148 WITH A PELMENITSA

1 recipe dumpling dough
(page 195)

1 recipe filling of your choosing
(pages 198–204)

All-purpose flour for rolling

IF USING A PELMENITSA:

Divide the dough into 8 equal balls, and grab a spray bottle of water (or, if you don't have one, a dish of water and a pastry brush), a straight-sided rolling pin, and a rimmed baking sheet dusted with flour. Liberally dust the top of your pelmenitsa with flour. Take one ball (leaving the rest covered with a dish towel so they don't dry out), and roll it out on a lightly floured countertop until it's slightly larger than your mold. Drape the rolled-out dough over your pelmenitsa, so that it reaches over the ends of the mold. Press or pat the dough lightly so that an imprint of the mold below is made on the dough.

With two spoons, or a pastry bag fitted with a nice wide tip, scoop or pipe a little blob of filling into each of the 37 divots. You'll need just a heaping teaspoon or so in order to still be able to seal things (don't get carried away!). When you have piped filling into all the slots, roll out a second piece of dough until it's slightly larger than your mold. Lightly spray some water over the top of your filled pelmeni, or lightly brush the exposed dough with water if you don't have a spray bottle, and then gently place the second round of dough over the top. Firmly roll over the top with your rolling pin, several times as needed, to seal the pelmeni and cut the dough between them. Turn the pelmenitsa upside-down over the prepared baking sheet, and nudge the filled dumplings out, separating them with your fingers if needed. Repeat with remaining dough and filling. At this point, the dumplings can be cooked, or frozen for future use (freeze on the baking sheet, then transfer to a sealed plastic bag).

(continued page 208)

IF YOU DON'T HAVE A PELMENITSA:

Grab a spray bottle of water (or, if you don't have one, a dish of water and a pastry brush), and a rimmed baking sheet dusted with flour. Take one-quarter of the dough (leaving the rest lightly covered with a dish towel so it doesn't dry out), and roll it out on a lightly floured countertop until it's the thickness of fresh pasta sheets—just shy of being transparent.

FOR TORTELLINI-STYLE HAND-SHAPED DUMPLINGS:

Take a 2-inch round cutter (or a drinking glass), and cut out rounds of dough. Using two spoons, a small scoop, or a pastry bag, fill each round of dough with a generous blob of filling—about 2 teaspoons. Brush or mist the edges of the dough with water, then fold the round into a half-circle, pressing the edges to seal. Take the edges and pull them to each other, pinching to seal in a tortellini shape. As you shape a few dumplings, you'll get a sense of how much filling you can stuff into each dumpling and still seal it. Transfer the shaped dumplings to your prepared baking sheet, and gather the scraps together back into a ball. Repeat with the remaining dough and filling, rerolling the scraps at the end after they've rested. At this point, the dumplings can be cooked, or frozen for future use (freeze on the baking sheet, then transfer to a sealed plastic bag).

FOR A POTSTICKER MOLD:

Use the cutting edge of the dumpling mold to cut out rounds of dough. Brush or mist the edges of the dough with water, place the dough in your dumpling press, and, using two spoons, a small scoop, or a pastry bag, fill the round of dough with a generous blob of filling—about 2 teaspoons. Press the dumpling mold firmly closed to seal. Transfer the shaped dumplings to your prepared baking sheet, and gather the scraps together back into a ball. Repeat with the remaining dough and filling, rerolling the scraps at the end after they've rested. At this point, the dumplings can be cooked, or frozen for future use (freeze on the baking sheet, then transfer to a sealed plastic bag).

COOKING AND SERVING DUMPLINGS

варка и подача

✦ ✦ ✦

Depending on where in Russia (or America) your family is from, pelmeni can be served with anything from ketchup to sriracha to soy sauce. They can be served plain or floated in broth, or pan-fried in butter after their boil (especially good for leftovers). Below you'll find a template for all sorts of dumplings. But feel free to experiment to your taste—just don't try to use a broth and pan-fry (because why sog up those crisp edges?), and don't ever skip the secret sauce.

Dumplings

Butter

Vinegar

Salt

Broth (optional)

Smetana

Herbs

Bring a large pot of salted water to a boil. Add the dumplings, about 20 pelmenitsa-sized per person (12 to 15 per person if they're larger). Adjust the heat as needed to maintain a healthy-but-not-too-vigorous boil. While the dumplings cook, give a few good stirs, making sure to get your spoon all the way to the bottom of the pot to free any dumplings that may have stuck to the bottom. Cook until the dumplings rise to the surface, and then for 1 more minute (this will take 4 to 5 minutes for pelmenitsa-sized and slightly longer for the larger hand-shaped, depending upon the heat of your burner and whether your dumplings are fresh or frozen). If you're not certain whether they're done, remove a dumpling, and cut it in half. Meat fillings should be cooked through, and non-meat fillings should be hot in the center.

While the dumplings are cooking, prepare a mixing bowl to dress your dumplings. Consult the dumpling matrix (facing page)—for each serving of dumplings, place one measure of the secret sauce ingredients in your mixing bowl. When the dumplings are cooked, skim them out of the boiling water with a slotted spoon or drain in a colander, shaking off the residual water. Place them in the prepared bowl, and toss—the softened butter and vinegar will come together with the heat of the dumpling and the motion of stirring, emulsifying into a sauce. Keep whirling them around in the bowl until all of the butter is incorporated. Transfer the dressed dumplings into a dish, pour in hot broth if using, and top with a healthy amount of smetana (page 359), crème fraîche, or European-style sour cream, and then the fresh herbs.

THE DUMPLING MATRIX

DUMPLING	SECRET SAUCE (TOSSED WITH HOT DRAINED DUMPLINGS)	BROTH (OPTIONAL)	SMETANA (PAGE 359), CRÈME FRAÎCHE, OR EUROPEAN-STYLE SOUR CREAM	HERBS (GENEROUS PINCH OF FRESH MINCED)
SIBERIAN PELMENI	1 tablespoon butter, 1 teaspoon white vinegar, pinch of kosher salt	Fancy (page 351)	Y	Parsley, chervil, chive, celery leaf
LAMB PELMENI	1 tablespoon adjika butter (page 201), 1 teaspoon white vinegar, pinch of kosher salt	N	Y	Cilantro and mint
TVOROG VARENIKI	1 tablespoon butter, 1 teaspoon white vinegar, pinch of kosher salt	Garlic (page 353) Mushroom (page 352)	Y	Scallions
SOUR CHERRY VARENIKI	1 tablespoon butter, 1 teaspoon white vinegar, pinch of kosher salt	N	Y	Mint and basil

CHAPTER 6

SOUPS

супы

✣ ✣ ✣

When Campbell's soup was trying to break into the Russian market, their research team found that Russians eat soup *six times a week*. Yet they couldn't actually get Russians to buy their iconic red and white cans—because in Russia, to eat soup is to *make* soup. And make it we do.

Sure, soup is the backbone of any peasant culture (especially one that has had to live off of the root cellar for large portions of the year, and stretch meager ingredients into a variety of preparations). But Russians take it to extremes. Refreshingly cold and tangy dairy-based summer staples, stick-to-your-ribs meaty borsch, broths fortified with salami, and everything in between. It's actually one of the best ways to see the full range of Russian cuisine.

PORCINI BARLEY SOUP

суп перловый из белых грибов

✣ ✣ ✣

I am always forgetting just how much I love mushroom barley soup, how deeply satisfying it can be—especially when made with porcinis. Known as *belyi grib*—literally "white mushroom"—porcini are one of the favorites of Russian foragers. Unlike our white mushrooms, porcini are meaty and firm, holding their own against the toothsome barley. If you can't find fresh porcini (usually available from April to June), most Eastern European markets carry bags of frozen ones year-round.

SERVES 6 AS A MAIN COURSE, OR 10 AS A SOUP COURSE

1 tablespoon cooking oil (I use refined sunflower)

½ onion, cut into a ½-inch dice

3 to 4 stalks celery hearts (the small yellow center stalks), sliced ¼-inch thick (reserve leaves for garnish)

1 carrot, peeled and grated on the large holes of a box grater

½ pound porcini mushrooms (fresh or frozen), stems and caps cut into a ½-inch dice

2 quarts mushroom broth (page 352, or store-bought)

Kosher salt

⅔ cup pearl barley

½ cup smetana (page 359) or European-style sour cream

¼ cup thinly sliced scallions

Freshly ground black pepper

Heat a large stockpot over medium heat, and add the oil. Add the onion and cook, stirring occasionally, until well caramelized, adjusting the heat as needed so that it browns fully (about 15 minutes). Add the celery, carrot, and mushrooms, sauté for a few minutes until softened and starting to brown, then add the broth. Salt to taste, and bring to a boil. Reduce the heat until it's just high enough to maintain a simmer, and simmer for 30 minutes. Add the barley, give everything a stir, and simmer for another 45 minutes to 1 hour.

When the soup has simmered, taste and add more salt if needed. To serve, ladle into bowls and finish with a dollop of the smetana, the reserved celery leaves, scallions, and black pepper.

CHOLODNIK

ХОЛОДНИК

✢ ✢ ✢

If I had to pick one thing to eat all summer long, it might just be this soup. First off, it's Just. So. Refreshing. Served bracingly cold, it'll cool you down on the hottest of hot days in much the same way that a bowl of steamy stew will warm up the doldrums of winter. Add to that a balance of savory-sweet-rich-tangy-smooth-crunchy, and a stunning shade of magenta to boot.

To really take advantage of the ease of this soup, make the base ahead (it will keep for up to a week in this state). Do this, and you'll always be just five minutes away from a bowl of awesome. For my go-to meal, serve with pieces of salt-cured herring and freshly boiled new potatoes.

SERVES 6 TO 8

BASE:

2 quarts cold water

Kosher salt

1 bunch beets, with greens attached

Granulated sugar

TO FINISH:

1 cup smetana (page 359) or European-style sour cream

Fresh lemon juice

Kosher salt

4 pickling or Persian cucumbers, peeled and cut into a ¼-inch dice

½ cup thinly sliced scallions

½ cup coarsely chopped dill

Place the water in a large stockpot, and salt generously. Bring to a boil.

While the water is heating, remove the leafy stems from the beets, and wash and finely chop them. Set aside.

Wash and peel the beets themselves, then grate them on the large holes of a box grater.

When the water is boiling, throw in the grated beets and greens. Reduce the heat until it's just high enough to maintain a gentle simmer, and cook, uncovered, until the vegetables are tender, about 20 minutes. Season to taste, adding a touch of sugar if needed to bring out the beets' sweetness. Let cool, and then refrigerate until totally chilled (the base will keep for up to 1 week).

When you're ready to serve, season the base: Place some of the smetana in a bowl (about ¼ cup for every 2 cups base), and whisk in the base, bit by bit, until well combined (it should turn a gorgeous light pink). Add enough lemon juice to make it bright, and salt to taste. Pour into individual bowls, and top each with a handful of the cucumbers, scallions, and dill.

OKROSHKA

окрошка

✤ ✤ ✤

There are two schools of *okroshka*—those made with kefir, and those made with kvas (page 62). Every time I see the kvas version, I order it. Maybe this time I'll fall in love? But so far it's been a bust. Frankly, it's two tastes that don't seem to belong together—like a salad that somebody poured their soda into.

But kefir-based okroshka—*this* makes sense. Tangy, creamy, crunchy, with a hint of smoke from the meat. I love it as an alternative to the usual turkey sandwich sack lunch, or as a light summer dinner. I tend to make this soup in the heat of summer, when the garden is bursting with edible flowers. If you have some at your disposal, toss them in the bowl as well.

YIELDS ABOUT 2 QUARTS

1 large Yukon Gold potato, cut into a ⅓-inch dice

6 large hard-boiled eggs, divided

¼ cup dijon mustard

1 cup smetana (page 359) or European-style sour cream

1 quart plain kefir

1 cup water

Kosher salt

¼ pound hot-smoked salo (pork belly) or ham, cut into a ⅓-inch dice

1 bunch radishes, cut into a ⅓-inch dice

2 pickling cucumbers, peeled and cut into a ⅓-inch dice

½ cup sliced scallions (reserve some for garnish)

½ cup finely minced dill (reserve some for garnish)

Freshly ground black pepper

Place the potato in a small pot, and add water to cover by 1 to 2 inches. Bring to a boil over high heat, then reduce the heat until it's just high enough to maintain a simmer. Cook until the potato is tender when pierced with a knife. Drain and let the potato cool to room temperature.

While the potato is cooking, take 5 of the hard-boiled eggs (set aside the remaining egg for garnish), and separate the yolks from the whites. Dice the whites into ⅓-inch pieces, and set aside.

Place the yolks in a large bowl, and mash them with a fork. Add the mustard, and keep mashing to form a uniform, lump-free paste. Whisk in the smetana, then the kefir, then the water. Season to taste with salt, and refrigerate.

In a large bowl, mix together the reserved egg whites, potato, salo, radishes, cucumbers, scallions, and dill. Mix well, and season with salt and pepper. Place ¾ cup of the salad mixture into soup bowls. Add 1 cup of the kefir mixture to each bowl, then top with slices of the reserved hard-boiled egg, scallions, and dill. Serve very cold. If you're not eating all the okroshka at once, store the kefir base and the prepared vegetables separately, and combine them just before serving. The kefir mixture will keep for up to 1 week, but the vegetables are best mixed up the day they are to be used.

SCHAVEL

холодник из щавеля

✛ ✛ ✛

Okay, I know I just told you how cooling cholodnik (page 217) is. And it's all true. But *schavel* (sorrel) soup is the epitome of summertime. It's so clean, so green, so light on its feet.

Schavel is a soup my mother has been making for as long as I can remember. Except, as it turns out, I'd never had the real thing. Nowadays you can find sorrel in any farmers' market, but in 1980s suburban Chicago my mother had to make do with a combination of spinach and lemon juice to replicate sorrel's tangy bite. If you can't find sorrel either, spinach does make a fine alternative. But consider adding it to your backyard garden—it grows like a weed, and requires very little maintenance.

YIELDS ABOUT 10 CUPS

BASE:

2 quarts water

Kosher salt

1 small bunch sorrel (about the same size as the spinach), stems removed, washed and finely chopped

1 small bunch spinach, tough stem bottoms removed, washed and finely chopped

TO FINISH:

1 cup smetana (page 359) or European-style sour cream

Fresh lemon juice

Kosher salt

2 large hard-boiled eggs, diced

Scallions, thinly sliced

Dill, coarsely chopped

Bring the water to a boil, and salt generously. Add the sorrel and spinach, stir, and remove from the heat. Cool, and then refrigerate overnight—you want time for the greens to infuse into the liquid, and for the whole mixture to become bracingly cold. This base will keep for 1 week.

When you're ready to serve, season the base: Place some of the smetana in a bowl (about ¼ cup for every 2 cups base), and whisk in the base, bit by bit, until well combined. The result should look more like whole milk than skim, and taste rich yet light. Add lemon juice and salt to taste—you're looking for an end result that is lemony, but pleasantly so. Top each bowl of soup with a handful of hard-boiled egg, scallions, and dill.

SHORT RIB BORSCH*

борщ с говяжьими рёбрами

⁘ ⁘ ⁘

If you open a Russian restaurant, be prepared to have borsch on the menu—people assume it's part of the contract. And if you (like us) don't want to have it on your menu year-round, be prepared for a lot of furrowed brows (by the way, "There's more to Russia than borsch" is not always deemed an acceptable explanation). Also, be prepared for a lot of opinions about what makes for a good borsch. Then, be ready for those who are shocked that borsch has meat in it (aka Americans).

As everyone at Kachka can attest, borsch is a dish that people have quite a few strong feelings about. Like every good Russian, I learned to make borsch from my mom—and, with just a few tweaks, this recipe is pretty much hers. So, of course in my opinion, it's the best version out there.

SERVES 6 AS A MAIN COURSE, OR 10 AS A SOUP COURSE

¼ cup high-heat oil (I use canola or peanut)

2½ to 3 pounds bone-in beef short ribs

Kosher salt

1 medium yellow onion, halved and sliced into thin half-moons

2 large red beets, scrubbed thoroughly

2 quarts beef stock (homemade if possible)

2 large Yukon Gold potatoes, peeled and cut into a ¾-inch dice

1 carrot, peeled and grated on the large holes of a box grater

½ cup smetana (page 359) or European-style sour cream

1 handful thinly sliced scallions

1 handful coarsely chopped fresh dill

1 loaf dark Russian or Lithuanian-style bread, and Russian mustard (page 355, or store-bought) for serving

Heat a large stockpot over high heat, and add the oil. While the pot is heating up, season the short ribs with salt on all sides. When the pot is hot, carefully add the short ribs, and brown to a nice dark sear on all sides (a few minutes per side), using tongs to flip (you may need to do this in batches). The sear on the bottom of the pot will give your soup flavor, so make sure it doesn't burn—turn the heat down if needed. When the ribs are browned, remove them from the pot and set aside on a plate. Discard the excess grease from the pot.

Reduce the heat to medium, and add the onion. Sauté, stirring occasionally, until caramelized (about 30 minutes), adjusting the heat as needed so that it doesn't burn. When the onion has softened and browned, add the beets and stock.

Bring up to a boil, then reduce the heat until it's just high enough to maintain a simmer. Simmer until the beets are about half cooked—a knife will go in with some resistance—about 1 hour.

When the beets are half cooked, carefully remove them from the pot with a ladle and set them aside in a bowl to cool—this may seem fussy, but it allows you to get the beet flavor in the pot early on without overcooking the beets themselves. Add the

(continued page 223)

---

* Borsch does not have a "t" at the end—somehow the "t" got added on in German (as did a few other unnecessary consonants—borschtsch), so if you want to pass with the Brighton Beach babushkas, lose the "t."

browned short ribs back to the pot, and cook at the gentlest simmer, uncovered, for 3 to 4 hours, or until the short ribs are totally falling-apart fork-tender (and going longer won't hurt). Taste about halfway through cooking, and add salt as needed.

When the reserved beets are cool enough to handle, peel away the skin using a paring knife (if it doesn't just rub off on its own), and coarsely grate them on the large holes of a box grater or in a food processor.

When the short ribs have fully cooked, taste the soup, and add more salt as needed. Use a large slotted spoon to remove the short ribs. Add the potatoes, and continue to simmer until they are just cooked through, another 10 minutes or so. While the potatoes cook, pull the short rib meat off the bones, removing any bits of connective tissue. Discard the bones and connective tissue, and chop the meat into bite-sized chunks. When the potatoes are cooked, stir the meat back into the pot, along with the grated beets and carrots. Turn off the heat, and let cool— the pot will take a few hours to cool enough to go in the refrigerator, and the vegetables will cook in the residual heat. Refrigerate overnight.* The next day, discard the hardened fat from off the top. Reheat before serving.

Ladle the borsch into bowls, and garnish with a dollop of the smetana and sprinkling of the scallions and dill. Serve with slices of dark bread and spicy mustard. If you want the full Russian approach, try stirring some of the spicy mustard directly into your soup—to me, it's not borsch without this finishing touch.

---

* If you want to serve the soup the same day it's made, simply keep it simmering after adding in the beets and carrots. The borsch will be ready as soon as the beets are cooked through. Be careful not to let the soup cook any longer, or else you will drain the beets of all of their color and flavor.

SOLYANKA

МЯСНАЯ СОЛЯНКА

✦ ✦ ✦

My grandfather Naum was a fantastic cook. And one of his specialties was his *solyanka*—ask anyone in my mother's family, and their eyes close dreamily remembering it.

Solyanka has many variations, but as a general rule, it contains odds and ends of smoked meat (or, in some regions, smoked fish), paired with a piquant element (olives, capers, maybe tomatoes). Dedushka Naum's version involved loads of Russian salami and pickles. And my riff is basically just a bit of a reboot, with slightly more refined garnishes. No reason to mess too much with a good thing.

YIELDS 8–10 SERVINGS

BROTH:

¼ pound hot-smoked salo*

¼ pound Moskovskaya salami*

¼ pound basturma*

1 large onion

4 Israeli pickles

½ cup marinated peppers (page 75) or store-bought pickled peppers

2 dozen pitted Castelvetrano olives

1 ham hock

4 quarts water

TO FINISH:

1 stick (½ cup) unsalted butter

⅓ cup fresh lemon juice

1 lemon, halved and thinly sliced

½ cup smetana (page 359) or European-style sour cream

½ cup hot-smoked salo,* cut into a ¼-inch dice

½ cup Moskovskaya salami,* cut into a ¼-inch dice

½ cup Israeli pickles, cut into a ¼-inch dice

½ cup marinated peppers (page 75), cut into a ¼-inch dice

½ cup thinly sliced pitted olives

1 handful parsley, coarsely chopped

To make the broth, roughly chop the meats, onion, pickles, and peppers, and toss them into a large stockpot. Add the olives, ham hock, and water, and bring to a boil over high heat. Reduce the heat until it's just high enough to maintain a gentle simmer, and cook for 2 hours (too much evaporation and you will end up with a salt bomb, so keep the heat low). After 2 hours, strain the broth, discarding the solids. The solyanka broth will keep for up to 1 week in the refrigerator or can be frozen.

To serve, bring the broth to a simmer, and whisk in the butter one pat at a time. Add a splash of lemon juice, a slice of lemon, and a dollop of smetana to each soup bowl. Throw in a pinch each of the salo, salami, pickles, peppers, olives, and parsley. Pour about 1½ cups of the broth into each bowl, and stir well to mix everything together. Serve hot.

If you want to get fancy, arrange all the garnishes in a shallow bowl, and serve the hot broth in a tea pot at the table. Instruct your tablemates to pour the broth onto the composition and stir everything together themselves.

---

* This soup is all about using up odds and ends. If you don't have the cured meats listed, substitute with whatever is knocking around in your fridge.

KING SALMON UKHA

уха из чавычи

✦ ✦ ✦

When I was in culinary school, it was drilled into us to never use the bones of oily fish like salmon—they make for horrible fish stock. And for some of the more delicate sauces of the French canon, this is undoubtedly true. But for a rustic, brothy soup like ukha, it's just the thing you need. And there's something very satisfying (and delicious) about going against the grain of those stodgy ideologues. For an out-of-this-world ukha, ask your fishmonger for the trim of a very fresh whole fish (the classic fish head with spine and tail still attached).

SERVES 4 TO 6

BROTH:

2 pounds salmon bones, broken into 6-inch pieces—heads, trim, gills removed, etc.

½ onion, coarsely chopped (trim off any dirty roots, but don't peel)

3 fresh bay leaves, or 1 dried

TO FINISH:

2 large Yukon Gold potatoes, peeled and cut into a ½-inch dice

Kosher salt

½ red bell pepper, seeded and cored, cut into a ½-inch dice

½ pound king salmon fillet, skinned, pin bones removed

2 lemons, 1 cut into slices and the other juiced

Butter

Smetana (page 359) or European-style sour cream

Red pepper flakes

1 handful thinly sliced scallions

A few sorrel leaves, cut in a chiffonade

1 ounce salmon roe (optional—if you're feeling fancy)

To make the broth: Place the bones, onion, and bay leaves in a large stockpot, and add cold water just to cover (should be about 2 quarts). Bring to a boil, then reduce the heat until it's just high enough to maintain a gentle simmer. Cook, skimming occasionally, for 2 hours. Add more water if needed to keep things submerged, though if the simmer is gentle you should be okay.

When the broth has simmered for 2 hours, strain it, keeping the liquid and discarding the solids. Return the strained broth to the pot. Add the potatoes, and salt the broth to taste. Bring to a boil, then reduce the heat until it's just high enough to maintain a simmer. Cook until the potatoes are just tender, about 5 minutes. Add the pepper, let simmer 1 to 2 minutes, and then gently lay in the salmon fillet. Cook until the salmon is just beginning to think about flaking, about 5 minutes. Turn off the heat.

Ladle out the salmon fillet onto a cutting board, and dice it into bite-sized pieces (it'll cook further when the hot broth hits it, so don't worry if it's a touch undercooked in the center). Divide the cooked fish evenly among bowls, then ladle in the hot broth with the potatoes and pepper. Add a splash of lemon juice, a pat of butter, a dollop of smetana, and a small pinch of pepper flakes to each bowl, and stir together until butter melts and smetana is completely mixed in. Garnish with a lemon slice, scallions, sorrel chiffonade, and salmon roe (if using).

WINTER SCHI

щи из квашеной капусты

✦ ✦ ✦

As with borsch, *schi* is a soup with a ton of variations (page 232). This is a version of *kislyi schi*—(sour schi) made with sauerkraut instead of fresh cabbage, a scrape-the-pantry wintertime recipe with just a few ingredients. All you really need to do is cut the potatoes, and let the flavorful meat and sauerkraut do all the work. As with so many soups, this is best made a day in advance.

SERVES 8 AS A MAIN COURSE, OR 10 AS A SOUP COURSE

¼ cup high-heat oil (I use canola or peanut)

4 pounds pork ribs, cut into 4-rib sections (you don't want bony spare ribs, but the meatier style— usually sold as country ribs or Kansas City style)

Kosher salt

3 quarts water

¼ cup dried mushrooms, swished around in a bowl of water to remove any lingering sand

2 pounds Yukon Gold potatoes (3 to 4 very large potatoes), peeled and cut into a ½-inch dice

1½ quarts sauerkraut (page 84, or store-bought*), brine included

1 large carrot, peeled and grated on the large holes of a box grater

Smetana (page 359) or European-style sour cream and black bread for serving

---

* Store-bought sauerkraut varies widely in flavor and texture. If you wouldn't eat it on its own, don't use it in this soup.

Heat a large stockpot over high heat, and add the oil. While it's heating, salt the ribs on both sides. Working in several batches, sear the ribs on both sides. You want nice color, but no char, so adjust the heat as needed—it should take 1 to 2 minutes per side. Set aside the ribs as they sear, discarding any oil remaining in the pan when you're done.

Place the seared ribs back in the pot, and add the water and mushrooms. Bring to a boil over high heat, and then reduce the heat until it's just high enough to maintain a gentle simmer. Cook, uncovered, skimming as needed, until the ribs are fall-off-the-bone tender, 2 to 3 hours.

Remove the ribs from the pot (tongs are helpful), and set them aside to cool. Add the potatoes, and continue simmering until the potatoes are tender, about 10 minutes. While the potatoes are cooking, pick the meat off the bones. Discard the bones and any bits of gristle or fat, and roughly chop the meat. Add the meat back into the pot.

When potatoes are cooked, add the sauerkraut, its brine, and the grated carrot (if you add the kraut before the potatoes are cooked, the acidity can keep the potatoes from becoming tender, so patience, patience, patience), then turn off the burner and let them cook in the residual heat to meld the flavors. Taste and adjust the seasoning.

Let the mixture cool to room temperature, then refrigerate overnight. The next day, remove the hardened fat from the top, heat, and serve garnished with a dollop of smetana and sliced black bread on the side.

MONDAY SOUP

суп "понедельник"

✤ ✤ ✤

My mother's in-home day care was famous in Chicago's Russian Jewish immigrant community (complete with a waiting list). And part of her full-service operation included serving the kids an early dinner, at around 3:00 p.m. Over the years, she worked out a set menu: Fridays were chicken noodle soup; Wednesdays were mashed potatoes with hot dogs. Mondays always featured this vegetable soup made with cauliflower and broccoli, bolstered with butter and sour cream. And on Tuesdays, this soup made a second appearance—this time with meatballs and no dairy.

When our first son was born, we lived with my parents while Israel was managing a wine bar. And every Tuesday before service, he would pull up a chair and sit with the rest of the children for a bowl, which he lovingly coined "Tuesday" soup. But I personally feel that the meatballs are highly optional, and prefer the Monday version.

SERVES 6 AS A MAIN COURSE, OR 10 AS A SOUP COURSE

2 quarts water

2 quarts garlic broth (page 353, or vegetable or chicken broth)

1 head cauliflower

1 head broccoli (about the same size as the cauliflower)

Kosher salt

4 medium carrots, peeled and grated on the large holes of a box grater

2½ pounds Yukon Gold potatoes, cut into a ½-inch dice

1 cup rolled oats

½ cup finely chopped dill

½ cup finely chopped parsley

Butter and smetana (page 359) or European-style sour cream for serving

Pour the water and broth into a stockpot, and bring to a boil. While they're heating, core the cauliflower, and chop the florets into ½-inch pieces. Remove any tough ends and peel any thick stems from the broccoli, and chop the florets into ½-inch pieces.

When the broth is simmering, taste and add salt as needed—those vegetables will soak up a lot, so you want it well seasoned. Add the cauliflower and broccoli, along with the carrots and potatoes. Reduce the heat until it's just high enough to barely maintain a simmer, and gently cook, uncovered, for 30 minutes. Stir in the oats, and cook another 20 minutes, then add the dill and parsley, and remove from the heat. Taste and add salt as needed.

To serve, stir a pat of butter into each bowl, and top with a dollop of smetana.

TUESDAY VARIATION

For a heartier soup, take the filling for *golubtsi* (page 269), and roll it out into Ping-Pong-ball-sized meatballs. Gently plop them into the soup after you've stirred in the oats. Give a careful stir to make sure the meatballs haven't stuck to the bottom, then let them gently simmer with the oats for 20 minutes (they'll sink at first, but then float back up).

THE THING ABOUT SCHI

There's a popular saying in Russia: "*Schi da kasha—pishcha nasha*" ("Schi and kasha, that's our food"). The world of Russian soups is exciting and varied, yes—but nine times out of ten, it's schi that's for dinner.

Although I've spelled out a winter schi variation (page 229), at its heart, schi doesn't really have a recipe. It's the quintessential peasant stone soup, with no set ingredients (except cabbage—it must contain cabbage). To really cook schi like a Russian—to know its true soupy soul—you need less a recipe than a road map.

INGREDIENTS

BROTH

a braising cut of pork or beef

salt

water

AROMATICS

bay leaves

black pepper

BASE VEGETABLES

cabbage (or sauerkraut)

potatoes

OBZHARKA

onion

carrot

tomato

pepper

parsley

parsley root

celery

mushrooms

garlic

dill

TOPPINGS

smetana

scallions

dill

mustard

METHOD

1 **Make the broth.**

Brown the meat.

Add water and salt.

2 **Add the aromatics.**

Simmer until tender.

3 **Add the base vegetables and obzharka.**

Caramelize the onions.

Layer in all the other ingredients you're using.

Add the obzharka to the pot.

Turn off the flame and let the flavors marry for 15 to 20 minutes.

4 **Serve.**

Dish out.

Add the toppings.

Eat with black bread.

Proclaim "ochen' vkusno!" (very tasty!).

TO MAKE IT "LAZY"
omit the meat.

TO MAKE IT "SOUR"
use sauerkraut instead of cabbage.

TO MAKE IT "GREEN"
use sorrel or nettles instead of cabbage.

TO MAKE IT "BORSCH"
add beets! Yes, borsch is actually best described as a type of schi where beets are used in addition to or instead of cabbage.

OBZHARKA is basically Russian sofrito, a concentrated mixture of sautéed vegetables added to bolster things, like this soup. To make obzharka, start by caramelizing onions in a pan. Then layer in shredded or diced vegetables of your choosing. Classically, all obzharkas have onions, carrots, and tomatoes, but cooks add any of the other vegetables on the list (or vegetables that aren't on the list) for their own personal variations.

CHAPTER 7

THE MANGAL

мангал

✦ ✦ ✦

ecember 31, 1978, happened to be one of the coldest days on record in Borisov, Belarus (–22 degrees Fahrenheit!). But *shashlik* (kebab) was en vogue that year (and the meat already marinating) so my poor dad was dispatched to the outdoor grill. As guests stayed warm inside, he huddled over skewers that were sizzling on one side and freezing on the other.

Grilling on a *mangal*—a type of barbecue originating in the Caucasus—is still a cherished Russian pastime (albeit usually reserved for warmer times of the year). When my parents immigrated, they couldn't quite fit a mangal in their luggage, but their sword-like *shampuri* (skewers) were tucked into suitcases. All through my childhood, the smell of meat marinating in vinegar and onions (hallmarks of a good shashlik) was the smell of a party coming.

A GUIDE TO SHAMPURI

Called *shampuri*, skewers throughout the former Soviet Union are no joke. There are dozens of different styles, each with their merits, depending on what you're grilling and what kind of mangal you have. If you don't happen to live near a large Russian market (or mangal retailer), you can easily purchase these online.

❖ These are fantastic, all-purpose skewers—especially for smaller mangals. Easy to clean, lightweight, and super durable. This is the kind my parents immigrated with. Clearly, when you have to pack up your whole life and move to a new country, these skewers are on the "keep" list (because: priorities).

❖ This shampur is as big as they typically get, just under 2 feet long. You'll notice it's thick, too—about ½ inch wide. This is the skewer for lyulya kebab (page 242), giving a wide swath of metal to support all of that ground meat (anything skinnier, and you're likely to have a mess on your hands). The wide shampuri also ably handle the weight and size of whole fish (page 244).

❖ This is your typical standard grill model—and it'll work in a bind, but it's really not ideal. See how the metal is round, rather than flat? This is a nightmare for keeping your meat in place. Also, notice that the three other skewers have twisty metal near the handle. This ingenious design allows you to rotate the skewer by turns to ensure cooking (not so, smooth American skewer). If you really must use this kind of skewer, try running two of them parallel to each other through your grillables for better results.

❖ Notice the "V" shape of the metal here? This skewer is your best friend for smaller, cubed meats that might otherwise dance around as you try to turn them. The meat stays in place, and you get a much more even cook.

HOW TO MACGYVER A MANGAL

A mangal is Russia's take on a grill. In some ways, it's not too different from the Western variety—food + fire. But unlike our stateside versions, the narrow box of a mangal doesn't have grates, which lets you lay your skewers right over the coals (pages 240–241), avoiding major heat loss (and the whole food-sticks-to-the-grates-instead-of-the-skewers problem). Want to give it a go, but don't have your own? You can rig one up using any of the hacks below.

BUILD YOUR OWN

NEED: 20 to 24 paver bricks (4"x 8"x 2")

INSTRUCTIONS: Find a flat patch of dirt (or grass you don't mind scorching) outside. Stack the bricks according to the diagram. Build this box shorter if desired, using fewer bricks.

COST: $12

PROS: As close to a real mangal as you can get. Can be built and dismantled quickly. Carbon is good for your soil! It's modular, so you can really build any size you want.

CONS: You're gonna have to squat on the ground while grilling (maybe a pro if you're looking for a good quad workout).

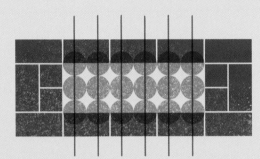

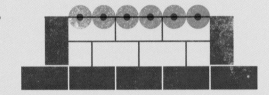

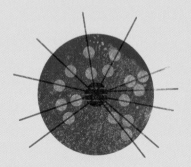

WEBER GRILLS

NEED: 1¼ quart stainless steel bain-marie (available online or in restaurant supply stores)

INSTRUCTIONS: Remove the top grilling rack. Place the bain-marie in the very center of the lower rack in the grill. Prepare coals on the bottom rack around the bain-marie. Skewers rest on the bain-marie, fanning out to the grill edge.

COST: $7 (or $106 if you are buying the grill, too)

PROS: Requires very little additional equipment. Finally, a use for that old grill rusting in the far corner of the shed!

CONS: Grilling around a circle might make you dizzy.

GAS GRILLS

NEED: Good oven mitts

INSTRUCTIONS: By removing the main grates on your gas grill, you can simply rest skewers across the frame. This can be a little tricky if your grill is really wide—if so, take the top warming rack in your grill and remove it. Place it along the back of the grill.

COST: Probably $0 (don't go and purchase a gas grill just for this purpose)

PROS: Fast and easy.

CONS: The skewers will be at a bit of an angle, so one end will cook a little faster than the other. You won't have any smoky flavors that come with grilling on live coals. The skewer handles may get very hot (use good mitts or tongs to handle).

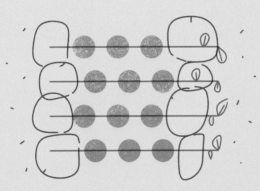

FOUND MATERIALS

NEED: A bunch of large rocks

INSTRUCTIONS: This is ideal if you're camping or such. Build a free-form mangal using rocks—kinda like a campfire. For extra authenticity (and flavor), use tree branches for skewers.

COST: $0

PROS: Good for when you're packing light.

CONS: Requires you to find the right materials. May be a bit uneven/rustic.

⚠ WARNING

YOU ARE PLAYING WITH FIRE HERE. BE SMART AND USE YOUR HEAD. KACHKA IS NOT RESPONSIBLE FOR ANY FLAMEY BAD DECISIONS (BUT TAKES FULL RESPONSIBILITY FOR A DELICIOUS GRILLED MEAL).

PORCINI
SHASHLIK
(PAGE 250)

MANGAL-ROASTED
WHOLE TROUT
(PAGE 244)

LAMB
SHASHLIK
(PAGE 248)

CHICKEN THIGH
SHASHLIK
(PAGE 246)

LYULYA
KEBAB
(PAGE 242)

GRILLED EGGPLANT
WITH KEFIR AND
HERBS (PAGE 256)

LYULYA KEBAB

люля кебаб

✦ ✦ ✦

Starting in the 1960s, my mother's father would travel to Azerbaijan for a month every year to treat his ailing back in the healing muds of Naftalan. And he would return to Belarus with suitcases stuffed with the then-rare culinary treasures of the Caucasus—persimmons, pomegranate molasses, adjika, tkemali—and notebooks filled with recipes for the dishes he had encountered. Like lyulya kebab.

Making a good lyulya kebab can be a tricky task. You want to hit the sweet spot of meat that's moist and tender, but with enough structure so that it actually stays on your skewer (instead of ending up on your coals). Your best friend in this endeavor is a nice, broad shampur (page 237). If you can't get ahold of these wide skewers, just form the mixture into patties, and grill like you would burgers (and for some real fusion, you can even serve on a bun swiped with mayo spiked with adjika, page 358).

SERVES 6 TO 8

1 teaspoon whole coriander seeds

1 teaspoon whole fenugreek seeds

1 teaspoon whole dill seeds

1 teaspoon whole cumin seeds

1 teaspoon ground turmeric

1 onion, chopped into a ¼-inch dice

½ bunch cilantro, finely chopped

2½ pounds ground lamb

1½ tablespoons kosher salt

½ cup ice water

---

* If you're making adjika (page 358) to go along with your grilled items, both start with the same spice mixture—simply triple the amount of spices, from 1 teaspoon to 3 teaspoons. Toast and grind as instructed, then use one-third of the resulting spice mixture for the lyulya kebabs, and the remaining two-thirds for the adjika.

Heat a small saucepan over medium heat. Add the coriander, fenugreek, dill, and cumin seeds and toast, stirring occasionally, until fragrant (about 2 minutes). Cool to room temperature and transfer to a spice grinder. Grind to a fine powder, then mix in the turmeric. *

Place the onion, cilantro, lamb, salt, ice water, and ground spices into a food processor (make sure the onions are on the bottom, otherwise the lamb will become overworked before the onions are incorporated). Process until the mixture comes together—you're basically looking for the fat to emulsify, which will incorporate the water, and coat everything with a nice fat-smeared sheen. If you stop the processor and grab a pinch of the mixture, it will stick to your fingers. Under- or over-processing will lead to dry meat, so try to hit this nice, sticky sweet spot—stop between pulses and check. The entire process should take 1 to 2 minutes tops. Transfer the lamb to a covered container, and refrigerate for a few hours (and up to overnight)—the meat will firm up somewhat as it chills.

When the meat is cold, set up the grill or mangal (see pages 238–239) and prepare the coals (coals are ready when they are white-hot, with no black showing). Grab a half-dozen broad shampuri and a bowl of cold water.

To shape, take a handful of the meat—about ⅓ pound—and mold it around the shampur. Squish the meat down the length of the shampur, evenly covering it with a coating that's less than ½ inch thick. Dip your hands in the water as you go, keeping them cold and wet, so that the meat sticks to the shampur instead of your hands. Repeat with remaining meat and shampuri.

When the coals are ready, place the shampuri over your mangal. Cook on all sides, until they've got a nice golden-brown color, with a bit of char. By the time you get that color, the meat should be cooked through, 5 to 6 minutes total. As fat starts to drip into the coals, you might get some flames licking the meat, which can lead to off flavors. Move the shampuri and coals around if you see this happening. When the shampuri are done, remove them from the heat, and use a fork to push the cooked meat off (in my experience, the used shampuri are very attractive swords for young kids, so you might want to hide them—or not, depending on your taste for danger). Serve with lepyoshki (page 252) and achichuk (page 254), and dipping sauces like adjika (page 358) or tkemali (page 361).

(see the photograph on page 241 for reference)

MANGAL-ROASTED WHOLE TROUT

форель на шампуре

+ + +

Trout—known as *forel* in Russian—are easily speared on large, broad shampuri (page 237). And, when you cook mangal-style (pages 238–239), there are no pesky grates for the delicate fish to stick to. Don't skip the brining, which does the double duty of making the trout both flavorful and also harder to overcook. The delicate-yet-smoky result is a classic summer meal, especially when paired with a simple dacha salad (page 99), and boiled new potatoes tossed with butter and fresh herbs.

SERVES 4 TO 6

2 quarts water, divided

½ cup kosher salt, plus more for salting fish

¼ cup granulated sugar

2 fresh bay leaves, or 1 dried

1 tablespoon whole black peppercorns

1 lemon

4 whole trout (8 to 10 ounces each), cleaned

Pour 2 cups of the water into a large stockpot. Add the salt, sugar, bay leaves, and peppercorns. Let the mixture come to a boil, stirring to dissolve the salt and sugar. Turn off the heat, then add the remaining water (if you want, you can use all of the water in the beginning, but this nifty trick cuts down your cooling time). Cut the lemon in half, squeeze the juice into the brine, and then toss the rinds in as well. Let the mixture cool to room temperature, about 30 minutes.

When the brine is cool, add your trout. Refrigerate for 4 to 8 hours.

When the fish have brined, grab 4 broad shampuri. Remove the fish from the liquid, and pat dry with a paper towel. Discard the brine. Skewering the fish isn't difficult, but takes a bit of care—it's all about winding the fish on the skewer evenly, so that it holds on to the shampur as it cooks. To assemble your shampur, start by holding the fish in one hand so that it's facing you, belly up. Take your shampur in your other hand so that its flat sides, like the fish's, are perpendicular to the ground. Go in through the mouth, and find the backbone with the tip of your skewer. Wind the shampur back and forth around the backbone—you should be able to make a couple passes on either side of it. As you wind through to the end, make sure your shampur leaves the fish through the midline, right through the tail.

After your fish are brined and skewered, set up your grill or mangal (see pages 238–239), and prepare your coals (coals are ready when they are white hot, with no black showing). When the coals are ready, salt inside the bellies of the fish, and place the shampuri over the mangal on an angle so that the whole fish are over the coals. Cook on all sides, until the fish have got a nice golden-brown color, with a bit of char. By the time you get that color, the fish should be cooked through, 8 to 10 minutes. Check the thickest part of the trout—the meat at the "shoulders"—and peek inside the belly to be sure. When the trout are done, remove from the skewers by using the tines of a fork to push them off. If they resist, scrape the tails off the skewers and try again.

(see the photograph on page 240 for reference)

CHICKEN THIGH SHASHLIK

шашлык из куриных бёдрышек

✛ ✛ ✛

My husband and I married in the courthouse of a tiny town in the foothills of the Smoky Mountains—just the two of us and our officiant. And while the intimacy and informality of our ceremony was perfect for us, my parents were decidedly nonplussed with these plans. *"Ti shto!* [What's wrong with you!] No chuppah?!?" So we agreed to a party—complete with a rabbi, four poles, and a sheet. But I had three conditions: (1) It had to be at their house; (2) They could only invite as many people as could fit around one table (so naturally, my dad built a table to *just* fit inside the walls of their living room); (3) They serve this shashlik.

SERVES 4

1 quart kefir

1 small yellow onion, coarsely chopped

1 large handful each cilantro and dill, coarsely chopped, plus more for garnish

2½ tablespoons kosher salt

2 pounds boneless, skinless chicken thighs, cut into 1½- to 2-inch chunks

1 yellow onion, cut into 2-inch chunks (optional)

In a large container, mix together the kefir, chopped onion, herbs, and salt. Add the chicken, and mix well to fully cover the chicken pieces. Let the mixture marinate for 24 hours in the refrigerator.

After marinating, remove the chicken pieces from the marinade, discarding the marinade. Thread the chicken onto shampuri (for more information about shampuri, see page 237—the V-shaped skewers work especially well here), leaving a small bit of space between cubes. Alternatively, if desired, thread pieces of the additional onion between chicken pieces. When the chicken is skewered, set up your grill or mangal (see pages 238–239) and prepare the coals (coals are ready when they are white hot, with no black showing).

When the coals are ready, place the shampuri over the mangal and cook, turning the shampuri so that all sides cook evenly. The meat should brown, with a bit of char in some spots, and should take about 10 minutes to cook. When you think the meat is done, take off one of the biggest chunks, and see if it's cooked to your liking. If so, pull the shampuri off the grill and onto a rack, and let them rest for 5 minutes. Garnish with chopped cilantro and dill. Serve with lepyoshki (page 252), achichuk (page 254), and adjika (page 358).

LAMB SHASHLIK

шашлык из баранины

＋ ＋ ＋

Chicago has a vibrant Soviet refugee community brimming with Russian-language publications—which means local Russian recipes. My mother clipped an article on shashlik from the *Reklama* newspaper back in the 1990s, and has been devoutly using the recommended pomegranate juice marinade for lamb ever since. Though there are as many recipes for lamb shashlik out there as there are sheep in Uzbekistan (read: a whole lot), using pomegranate juice is probably the most universal method. Be sure to give the meat enough time in the marinade—it makes a big difference.

SERVES 6 TO 8

2 cups unsweetened pomegranate juice

½ cup white vinegar

2 tablespoons kosher salt

3 pounds lamb meat, preferably top round or leg, cut into 1½-inch cubes (if there's any silverskin or chunks of hard fat, trim them off)

2 sweet onions, thinly sliced

1 yellow onion, cut into 2-inch chunks (optional)

½ bunch cilantro, coarsely chopped

Onion relish (page 249) for serving

In a large container, mix together the pomegranate juice, vinegar, and salt. Add the lamb and sliced onions. Mix to combine, making sure that all of the meat is completely submerged. Let the mixture marinate in the refrigerator for 24 hours.

The next day, take the marinated lamb from the refrigerator, and drain, discarding the liquid. Pick out the onions and reserve to make the onion relish.

Thread the cubes of marinated lamb on the shampuri (see page 237 for more information about shampuri—the V-shaped skewers work especially well here), making sure to leave a bit of clearance between the cubes of lamb so that they'll cook evenly. Alternatively, if desired, thread chunks of the yellow onion between the lamb pieces. When the lamb is skewered, set up the grill or mangal (see pages 238–239) and prepare the coals (coals are ready when they are white hot, with no black showing).

When the coals are ready, place the shampuri over the mangal and cook, turning the shampuri so that all sides cook evenly. The meat should brown, with a bit of char in some spots, and should take about 8 minutes to cook to medium. As fat starts to drip into the coals, you might get some flames licking the meat, which can lead to off flavors. Move the shampuri and coals around if you see this happening. When you think the meat is done, take off one of the biggest chunks, and see if it's cooked to your liking. If so, pull the shampuri off the grill and onto a rack, and let them rest for 5 minutes. Garnish with the cilantro. Serve with onion relish.

(see the photograph on page 240 for reference)

ONION RELISH

My dad is a bit obsessive when it comes to onions (he eats them like apples), and was always a bit sad when my mom would discard the onions flavoring the shashlik marinade. So she started sautéing them down and serving them on the side. I took it from there, amplifying the mixture with a few more Central Asian flavors to make a tangy yet balanced relish.

YIELDS A GENEROUS CUP

1 tablespoon cooking oil (I use refined sunflower)

Sliced onions left over from one batch of lamb shashlik marinade, drained

½ cup kefir

1 tablespoon adjika (page 358, or substitute a hot pepper paste such as harissa)

1 tablespoon pomegranate molasses

1 tablespoon chopped cilantro

½ teaspoon kosher salt

Heat a frying pan over medium-high heat, and add the oil. Add the onions from the marinade and cook, stirring often, until they are softened and starting to caramelize, about 15 minutes. Adjust the heat as needed—the onions will be a little wet from the marinade, but this will evaporate as they cook.

When the onions have cooked down and gotten some color, remove the pan from the heat, and let it cool slightly. Stir in the remaining ingredients, and adjust seasonings to taste. Cool to room temperature before serving, or refrigerate if not grilling immediately.

PORCINI SHASHLIK

шашлык из белых грибов

✛ ✛ ✛

I first came across a porcini shashlik at a restaurant in Brest, Belarus. Porcini are common there, and this dish was an inspired use of local ingredients in an unconventional way (most restaurants in Belarus tend to stay inside the lines).

The secret weapon here (if meaty porcinis and salo aren't enough) is mayonnaise. After a long marinade, the mayo is grilled away, leaving behind just a hard-to-place-but-delicious flavor, fat-supplied richness, and nice bit of tang. Serve with boiled new potatoes dressed with butter and herbs, and dacha salad (page 99).

YIELDS ABOUT 5 TO 6 SKEWERS

1 tablespoon kosher salt, plus more to season water

1 pound fresh porcini mushrooms, cut in half (or frozen, cut into 2-inch cubes)

½ cup mayonnaise (page 357, or store-bought)

2 tablespoons fresh lemon juice

½ cup coarsely chopped parsley

2 cloves garlic, peeled and coarsely chopped

½ medium sweet onion, peeled and cut into 1-inch cubes

½ pound salt-cured salo (pork fatback), rinsed and cut into 1-inch by ⅛-inch squares, or ¼ pound thick-cut bacon, cut into 1-inch squares (optional)

Grab a large skillet and pour about ½ inch of water into it. Season with salt, and bring to a boil over high heat. Place the porcini in the skillet in a single layer, and cover the pan with a lid. Reduce the heat until it's just high enough to maintain a gentle simmer, and steam for 5 to 10 minutes, or until the porcini become supple. Strain the porcini, and let them cool slightly.

While the porcini are cooling, place the mayo, lemon juice, parsley, salt, and garlic in the food processor, and pulse to combine (alternatively, you could just chop the parsley and garlic as finely as possible, and stir everything together).

Transfer the marinade to a container, and add the warm (not hot) mushrooms and the onion chunks. Mix well and cover. Marinate, refrigerated, for at least 2 hours (and up to 24 hours).

Pour the marinated mushroom and onion mixture into a colander, giving a few shakes to remove any excess marinade. Spear the chunks on the shampuri, along with the salo or bacon (if using), alternating (see page 237 for more information about shampuri—the V-shaped skewers work especially well here).

When you're ready to grill, set up the grill or mangal (pages 238–239), and prepare the coals (coals are ready when they are white hot, with no black showing).

When the coals are ready, place the shampuri over the mangal and slowly grill, turning to allow even cooking. The shampuri are ready when the mushrooms and onions are fully cooked, with some caramelized bits, and the salo is golden and rendered, about 10 minutes (adjust the coals or heat as needed if the shampuri are burning before this happens).

(see the photograph on page 240 for reference)

LEPYOSHKI

лепёшки

+ + +

If you've got the grill going, you really should throw some lepyoshki on as well. These round Uzbek flatbreads (sometimes called *non* or *lavash*) are usually fired in a type of tandoor oven. But luckily, that environment is easily simulated using a cast-iron skillet and a mangal or grill. Use this bread to wrap up your shashlik, or swipe through a dish of brindza pashtet (page 106).

YIELDS 8 LEPYOSHKI

1½ cups water, warmed to body temperature

1½ tablespoons honey

1 teaspoon active dry yeast

4¼ cups (550 grams) all-purpose flour

1 teaspoon kosher salt, plus additional for sprinkling

Olive oil

In the bowl of a stand mixer fitted with a dough hook, stir together the water with the honey and yeast. Let the mixture sit for a few minutes for the yeast to wake up.

Add the flour and salt, and mix for 5 minutes. The dough will clear the sides of the mixer, and by the end will be soft, supple, and only slightly sticky.

Lightly oil a large bowl, and turn the dough out into it. Swish it around, then flip it over, so that the top is oiled as well. Cover the bowl with plastic wrap, and place in the refrigerator to rise (slowly) overnight.

The next day, remove the dough from the refrigerator, and punch down to expel the air. Let it come to room temperature, and rise again until doubled in volume (this may take a few hours, depending on the temperature). Punch the dough down again, and divide into 8 even balls of dough, each about the size of a tennis ball.

If you're not ready to bake yet, you can wrap the dough balls and transfer them to the refrigerator for a few hours, and let them come to room temperature when you're ready. Otherwise, let the dough balls sit and relax on a lightly floured countertop, covered with plastic wrap or a sprinkling of flour and a clean dish towel, for about 30 minutes. While the dough is resting, set up the grill or mangal (see pages 238–239) and prepare the coals (coals are ready when they are white-hot, with no black showing).

When the dough has rested, stretch out each ball to a 7- to 8-inch circle, as you would a pizza crust. If it resists, let it rest a few more minutes, then try again. When your dough has been stretched, rub or brush the rounds of dough with olive oil, and season with a sprinkling of salt.

Once the mangal is rocking, place an upside-down cast-iron skillet in the coals (or grill directly on the grate if using a gas grill). When the pan is hot, place a round of dough on the surface. Cook until the dough puffs and starts to char, about 2 minutes. Flip the bread over, and bake the other side until that begins to char as well.

Repeat with all of the remaining dough. Serve immediately, or wrap in a dish towel to keep the lepyoshki soft and warm.

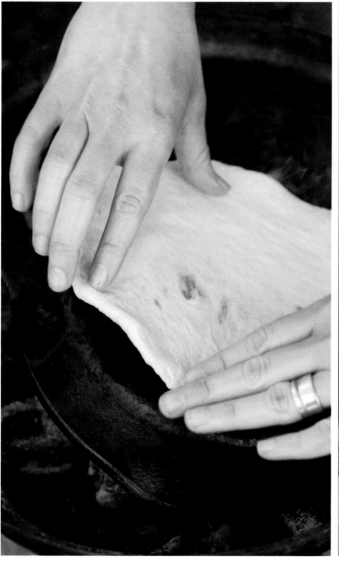

ACHICHUK SALAD

салат "ачичук"

✦ ✦ ✦

Tomatoes, onions, maybe a cucumber, mixed with herbs and vinegar and oil—for much of the former Soviet Union, this isn't so much a salad as it is *the* salad. Achichuk is Uzbekistan's version with the addition of cilantro and a few peppers, but the essential bones are the same. I find something comforting in the universality of this dish—whether you're in a dacha outside of Vilnius, a hole-in-the-wall cafeteria in Moscow, a kitchen in Tashkent, or at our Portland table, you're eating the same thing (with just a few regional variations). And though achichuk can (and should) be used for all manner of meals, it is considered compulsory alongside most anything from the mangal.

YIELDS 4 TO 6 SERVINGS

1 quart ripe tomatoes, cut in half and then quartered (I like Early Girls for their small size and intense flavor)

2 pickling or Persian cucumbers, peeled and sliced into ¼-inch half-moons

½ large sweet onion, thinly sliced

1 Cubanelle/Italian sweet pepper, seeded and thinly sliced

¼ cup chopped dill

2 tablespoons chopped cilantro

2 tablespoons thinly sliced basil leaves

¼ cup unrefined sunflower oil

2 tablespoons white vinegar

1 teaspoon Turkish hot pepper paste (you can substitute harissa, but you might want to start with a smaller amount, as heat levels can vary)

Kosher salt

Place the tomatoes, cucumbers, onion, pepper, and herbs in a large bowl, and gently mix.

In a small bowl, whisk together the oil, vinegar, pepper paste, and a pinch of salt to make vinaigrette. Dress the tomato mixture with vinaigrette, taste for seasoning, and serve.

GRILLED EGGPLANT WITH KEFIR AND HERBS

баклажаны на шампурах с кефиром и зеленью

✦ ✦ ✦

Eggplants are a sacred vegetable in the Caucasus, and this Azerbaijani-inspired treatment is pretty much the best thing that could happen to them. So many people think they don't like eggplant—most of the time, that's because it's not cooked right. Put an eggplant on the grill until it's charred outside and molten and creamy inside, and it's just intoxicating. And then top that hot, smoky dish with a cold, herb-spiked kefir sauce? Kind of a game changer.

While I think live coals are the best way to experience eggplant, this dish translates incredibly well to the oven, should you find yourself with an eggplant but without a grill.

SERVES 4 AS A MAIN DISH, 8 AS A SIDE DISH

2 large eggplants

2 tablespoons olive oil

Kosher salt

SAUCE:

½ cup kefir

1 teaspoon ground cinnamon

1 clove garlic, coarsely chopped

1 small handful cilantro sprigs

2 sprigs mint

2 sprigs basil

Kosher salt

1 tablespoon pomegranate molasses

* If you don't have a grill, wrap the split and seasoned eggplants well in heavy-duty foil, and bake at 500°F for about 45 minutes, or until molten on the inside and charred on the outside. Proceed with the recipe.

Remove the stems from the eggplants. Cut a slit along one side of each eggplant going halfway through. Gently pry them open a bit, and season the insides liberally with the olive oil and salt. Season the outsides as well.

Skewer the eggplants on two wide shampuri, running them perpendicular to the skewers (see photo on page 241). Set up the grill or mangal (see pages 238–239) and prepare the coals (coals are ready when they are white hot, with no black showing).

When the coals are ready, place the shampuri over the mangal and cook until the eggplants are tender and molten, offering no resistance—about 15 minutes on each side. The skin will be charred a bit, but not burned completely black.*

While the eggplants are cooking, make the sauce. In the bowl of a food processor, combine the kefir, cinnamon, garlic, cilantro, mint, basil, and salt to taste. Pulse a few times, until the mixture comes together and the herbs are well chopped.

When the eggplants are cooked, split them open on a large platter. Spoon the sauce over everything, and drizzle the pomegranate molasses over the top.

THE DACHA LIFESTYLE

Dachas are often described as Slavic summer homes—but there's so much that's lost in that translation. Traditionally, dachas were doled out by the czars as gifts to loyal subjects. In the Soviet era of state-owned land, they were given to city dwellers for summer farming. At their heart, dachas are rustic summer retreats, a place to live off the land and make the most of Russian summers. Yes, during the worst of Soviet shortages, getting the maximum yield out of dacha gardens was a practical matter. But even then, dachas were never just about filling your larder—they were always about refreshing your soul.

Dacha summers are (even to this day) about fishing, foraging for berries and mushrooms, and harvesting birch juice from the neighboring forest. About grilling on the backyard mangal, and getting a breath of fresh air far from your Moscow multiplex. About exploring, cooking, and just generally living outdoors.

Even today, though they be privatized, the dachas are still going strong. Yes, the cabins now feature indoor plumbing, and a not-permissable-in-the-Soviet-era second floor. But the essentials remain the same. Hands down the best meal I've had in Belarus was served at a cousin's dacha—birch juice harvested that morning, eggs from the chickens, milk from the neighbor's cow, and vegetables picked from the garden plot I was sitting beside. It was so picture-perfect, it could have been staged for a farm-to-table spread in a lifestyle magazine—but it was just another lazy afternoon on the dacha.

CHAPTER 8

HOMESTYLE DISHES

блюда домашнего
приготовления

✦ ✦ ✦

When my *Amerikanski* friends show up to family parties, I've learned it's crucial to warn them to pace their zakuski consumption. MORE FOOD IS COMING. But perhaps I never emphasize this enough (or perhaps the zakuski are too tempting). Because without fail, when the table is cleared and reset, the uninitiated are thunderstruck. There's *more* food?!? Well, yeah—we haven't even had the main course.

Although I find this somewhat amusing, it's also something of a shame—because these dishes are so deeply satisfying. Simmer them on a back burner when you're fussing over piles of zakuski—or, if you take a more *Amerikanski* approach, serve them on their own as a simple weeknight dinner or lazy Sunday braise.

BRAISED CHANTERELLES AND POTATOES

лисички тушеные в сметане с картошкой

✢ ✢ ✢

My brother is a 1990s hippie: he toured with Phish every summer, wore the same Mexican poncho for weeks on end. In 2000, he followed his hacky-sack-playing brethren to Portland. He was the first in my very tight-knit extended family to move from Chicago, and this was viewed with much skepticism—why would he choose this wild western outpost? It turned out he had good reason—in addition to fine beer, good food, and actual civilization (who knew?), the Pacific Northwest is absolutely overflowing with forest treasures like chanterelles.

Chanterelles, or *lisichki* in Russian, are highly coveted in the motherland. My brother would bring bucketloads of them back to Chicago whenever he visited, hitting the farmers' market on the way to the airport to arrive with a sort of peace offering. My mother would instantly snap them up and cook this dish.

Chanterelles have a delicate taste, and take well to a hearty-yet-gentle preparation. The cream works its way into the mushrooms, the mushroom flavor suffuses the potatoes, and everything just becomes deliciously rich and transformed. Don't think about adding any other ingredients to this dish—the beauty is in its simplicity, letting the fragile flavor of chanterelles come through undisputed.

**SERVES 4 TO 6 AS
A MAIN DISH**

2 pounds chanterelles

1 tablespoon unsalted butter

1½ cups heavy cream

1½ cups smetana (page 359) or European-style sour cream

1½ tablespoons kosher salt

2 pounds Yukon Gold potatoes, peeled and cut into 1½-inch chunks

Crusty bread for serving (optional)

Fill a large bowl or salad spinner with water, then thoroughly clean the chanterelles by dunking them in and vigorously swishing them around to shake loose any debris. Remove quickly, and repeat the process with fresh water until all the chanterelles are clean. Spread the chanterelles out on clean dish towels to dry.

Tear any very large chanterelles into halves or quarters. Heat a medium-sized Dutch oven or heavy-sided pot over medium heat, and melt the butter. Add the chanterelles and cook down, stirring occasionally, until the chanterelles give off their liquid and it mostly evaporates, about 10 minutes (you can cover the pot until the liquid comes out, so that the chanterelles don't scorch, but then remove the cover to help the liquid cook off).

While the chanterelles are cooking, whisk together the heavy cream, smetana, and salt. When the chanterelles have cooked down, pour in the cream

(continued page 262)

mixture, and stir everything together. Add the potatoes and stir again, coating everything with the braising liquid. Bring the mixture to a simmer and partially cover (leave a small crack to let steam escape), then reduce the heat until it's just high enough to maintain the gentlest possible simmer. Simmer for 2 to 3 hours, or until the potatoes and cream have both turned a light golden brown, and the liquid has cooked down a bit but is still saucy. Check it once an hour or so to see that things are moving along (no need to stir). Serve hot, with a bit of crusty bread to sop up the sauce if desired.

GAME HEN TABAKA WITH GREEN BEAN BORANI

табака из куропатки с борани

✦ ✦ ✦

Tabaka is a dish that, although Georgian, has infiltrated *every* Russian restaurant menu. And since poultry had generally been an expensive protein, it's taken on a highfalutin status. To make tabaka, meat is cooked under a heavy weight, allowing for more surface area to make contact with the pan. Which, in turn, allows for more crispy deliciousness—but it also means that the meat is easier to overcook. As a sort of insurance policy, I give tabaka a kefir marinade first, to guarantee that it stays nice and moist.

Tabaka is traditionally served with a garlic sauce and green bean *borani*. The garlic sauce and the borani sauce can be made the night before (while the hens marinate), so all you need to do day-of is weigh the birds down and cook 'em up.

SERVES 4

GAME HENS:

1 quart kefir

2 small heads garlic, peeled

3 tablespoons smoked paprika

2½ tablespoons kosher salt

½ bunch cilantro (both leaves and stems), coarsely chopped

2 Cornish game hens

GARLIC SAUCE (NIORTSKALI):

Cooking oil (I use refined sunflower)

Backs and wing tips from 2 Cornish game hens

2 teaspoons kosher salt, divided

1 small head garlic, peeled (set aside 2 cloves)

1 quart water

Pinch of red pepper flakes

½ teaspoon paprika

High-heat oil (I use canola or peanut) or clarified butter

Green bean borani (page 265) for serving

Cilantro for garnish (optional)

Make the marinade: Pour the kefir into a blender, add the garlic, and process until pureed. Add the paprika, salt, and cilantro, and pulse a few times to combine (you don't want to liquefy the cilantro, so don't overdo it).

Prepare the hens: Using kitchen shears, cut out the backs, setting aside. With a cleaver or heavy knife, hack through the middle of the breastbones, so that each game hen is cut in half. Cut off the last joint of the wings, and set the wing tips aside with the backs.

Place the hens, skin side up, on a cutting board, and cover with plastic wrap. Pound with a mallet to flatten—you're not looking to pound the meat thin, just to break the bones until it loses its will and lies flat (try not to splinter the leg bones).

Place the hens in a container, pour the kefir marinade over them, and cover. Marinate, refrigerated, for at least 24 hours (and no more than 36 hours).

While the hens are marinating, make the garlic sauce: Heat a medium pot over high heat, and pour in enough oil to coat the bottom. Add the backs and wing tips, sprinkle with ½ teaspoon of the salt, and sear for a few minutes on each side, until they are a nice golden-brown color. Reduce the heat

(continued page 264)

to medium, add the garlic cloves (all but 2), and sauté for a few minutes, until they just begin to turn golden and aromatic.

Add the water and 1 teaspoon of the salt, and bring the pot up to a boil. Reduce the heat until it's just high enough to maintain a simmer, and cook until the garlic is tender and sweet, and the broth tastes meaty and has reduced by half, about 1 hour. Strain out the garlic and game hen scraps—discard these, and set the reduced broth aside.

With a mortar and pestle, or with your knife and cutting board, take the remaining 2 garlic cloves, the remaining ½ teaspoon salt, pepper flakes, and paprika. Pound or press until you make a nice, well-combined paste.

Whisk the paste into your reduced meaty garlic broth. Pour into cups for serving, or refrigerate if making in advance.

To finish the dish: Find something heavy to weigh down your game hens—I use 8-pound garden bricks wrapped in foil, but you can use a pan with heavy stuff stacked in it.

Preheat your largest cast-iron pan (about 12 inches) over medium-high heat. Take the marinated game hens from the refrigerator and remove them from the marinade, wiping off any excess. Discard the marinade.

When the pan is hot, add a little bit of high-heat oil or clarified butter to cover the bottom. You don't want your pan to be smoking, but hot enough that a drop of flour or water flicked across it bubbles and reacts (though not violently). When it's nice and hot, add the game hens, breast side down, then place your brick (or weighted pan) on top so that it's pressing things down evenly. Reduce the heat to medium and cook for 6 to 8 minutes, until the skin is a dark golden (if the hens begin to spit violently or blacken sooner, lower the heat as needed).

Remove your weight, and flip the birds (a slotted spatula can be helpful in releasing any particularly stubborn bits). Replace the weights, and cook for another 8 minutes on the second side, until the meat is cooked through. Transfer to a rack, and let rest 5 to 10 minutes.

If you've made your garlic sauce in advance, warm it up while the birds are resting. Serve the game hens with the garlic sauce and green bean borani. Garnish with cilantro, if desired.

GREEN BEAN BORANI

1 cup kefir

1 sprig basil, minced

1 sprig mint, minced

A few sprigs cilantro, minced

1 clove garlic, minced

½ teaspoon freshly ground black pepper

¼ teaspoon ground cinnamon

Kosher salt

½ pound green beans, washed and trimmed

Bring a pot of salted water to a boil. While waiting for the water to boil, whisk together the kefir, herbs, garlic, pepper, and cinnamon in a small bowl, and add salt to taste. Set aside (this can be made up to 1 day in advance).

When you're ready to serve, blanch the green beans in boiling water for 1 to 2 minutes, until bright green and just tender. Drain and transfer to a serving dish, then drizzle with the kefir sauce. Serve immediately.

RABBIT IN A CLAY POT WITH DRANIKI

кролик в глиняном горшочке с драниками

✧ ✧ ✧

There are dozens of classic dishes that get cooked in smetana. To the uninitiated, braising in cultured dairy just sounds wrong. But it's magic. And while the smetana can work its voodoo on the rabbit all on its own, I like cramming in a heady amount of garlic and porcinis, and then balancing all that earthy intensity with the sharp-sweet punch of sour cherries. Serve with *draniki* (potato pancakes). Or, if you're looking for a quick shortcut, add some potatoes right to the braise for a one-pot meal.

Having trouble tracking down rabbit hindquarters? You can modify this recipe to work with chicken thighs. Simply cook the smetana braising sauce for about an hour on its own at 350°F before adding the chicken thighs, then reduce the heat to 250°F and braise for another hour.

SERVES 4

2 cups smetana (page 359) or crème fraîche

1 cup garlic broth (page 353) or water

8 cloves garlic, peeled

⅓ cup unsweetened dried sour cherries

⅓ cup fresh porcini mushrooms (available frozen year-round at Eastern European markets), cut into a ½-inch dice

¼ cup dried porcini mushrooms, swished in some water to rinse off any silt

1½ teaspoons kosher salt, plus more for seasoning the rabbit

High-heat oil (I use refined sunflower oil)

2 pounds rabbit hindquarters (or bone-in chicken thighs)

2 medium Yukon Gold potatoes, peeled and sliced ⅛-inch thick (optional)

Draniki (page 268) for serving

Preheat the oven to 350°F.

In a mixing bowl, whisk together the smetana and broth. Add the garlic, cherries, fresh and dried porcinis, and salt. Taste, and add more salt if needed. Set aside.

Heat a large, heavy oven-proof skillet or Dutch oven on high heat, and pour in enough oil to coat the bottom. Liberally salt the rabbit hindquarters, and add them to the skillet, searing on each side until brown, about 5 minutes per side. Remove from the pan, and discard the excess oil.

Place the rabbit back in the skillet.* Pour the smetana mixture over the meat, making sure to get some liquid on top of each hindquarter. Cover the pan, and place it in the oven to cook for 30 minutes. After 30 minutes, reduce the heat to 250°F. Braise until the meat is completely tender and easily separates from the bone, another 2 to 3 hours.

(continued page 268)

---

* If using potatoes, place them under the seared rabbit before braising, and proceed with the steps as written. If not using potatoes, serve with draniki (page 268).

DRANIKI

Draniki is the Belarusian word for potato pancakes. Although potato pancakes are popular throughout many former Soviet republics, they are practically a national pastime in Belarus—eaten all day, every day (basically like bread, but better). Use them to sop up sauces, like rabbit in a clay pot (page 267) or machanka (page 287), or serve them on their own with smetana (page 359) and scallions, or smetana and smoked salmon, or smetana and jam (you get the idea).

SERVES 4 TO 6 AS AN ACCOMPANIMENT

1½ pounds russet potatoes

½ small yellow onion

1 cup all-purpose flour

½ cup buttermilk

1 large egg

1 tablespoon kosher salt

Butter (clarified is best) or sunflower or vegetable oil for frying

Scallions, sliced, for garnish

Peel the potatoes, and finely grate both the potatoes and the onion on the small holes of a box grater or with the shredding disk of a food processor. Place the grated potatoes and onion in a large bowl, and mix in the flour, buttermilk, egg, and salt (the resulting mixture will be closer to a pancake batter than to hash browns).

Heat a large skillet over medium-high heat. Add a generous amount of clarified butter or oil (about ¼ inch deep). If you're using butter, wait until it foams. Ladle out 2-tablespoon measures of draniki batter, then spread them out to form 4-inch pancakes. Fry until brown and crisp on the outside (yet squishy and gooey in the center), 3 to 5 minutes for the first side, 2 to 3 minutes for the second.

Serve immediately, garnished with scallions.

GOLUBTSI

голубцы

✛ ✛ ✛

People have been known to cry over their bowls of golubtsi at Kachka, overcome by deep-seated memories of babushkas long passed and families separated by oceans. The smell alone is a time machine—earthy, tangy, and transporting. It's amazing that a humble cabbage roll could stir up so much emotion, and there isn't a restaurant critic or food writer on this planet who could motivate me more. It's these moments that keep me going on the toughest of days.

I couldn't help tinkering just a bit, but these are pretty much just exactly what my mama makes. It's not the most visually arresting dish, but I'm okay with that. These are never coming off the menu.

YIELDS 12 TO 14 ROLLS

1 large cabbage, or 2 medium

SAUCE:

High-heat oil (I use refined sunflower oil)

1 medium carrot, shredded on the large holes of a box grater

1 medium yellow onion, sliced in thin half-moons

2 cloves garlic, minced

2 28-ounce cans crushed tomatoes

1 cup lingonberry jam (available at Russian markets, well-stocked grocery stores, and, surprisingly, IKEA—if you can't find it, a tart cranberry sauce makes an okay substitute)

½ cup water

Kosher salt

Place the cabbage(s) in a stockpot, cover with water, and bring to a boil. Cook at a rolling boil for 10 to 15 minutes until the leaves soften (larger = longer), then remove and allow to cool. Peel and discard the outermost leaves (they get a bit blitzed in cooking), then separate the remaining leaves, leaf by leaf, until you're left with something about the size of a baseball. With a paring knife, shave down any thick ribs, so that the leaves are pliable. Take the trimmed ribs and any too-small-to-stuff inner leaves, and slice them to the same thickness as your onions. Set aside.

Make the sauce: Heat a large pot over a medium flame. Add enough oil to coat the bottom, then add the carrot, onion, garlic, and cabbage trim. Sauté, stirring occasionally, until the vegetables soften and the onions turn translucent, about 10 minutes. Add the crushed tomatoes and jam, along with the water. Increase the heat to bring the mixture to a boil, then reduce it until it's just high enough to maintain a healthy simmer. Simmer for 20 minutes to combine the flavors. Add salt to taste (you'll have to be somewhat aggressive to counteract the sweetness). While the sauce is simmering, prepare the filling of your choosing.

(continued page 271)

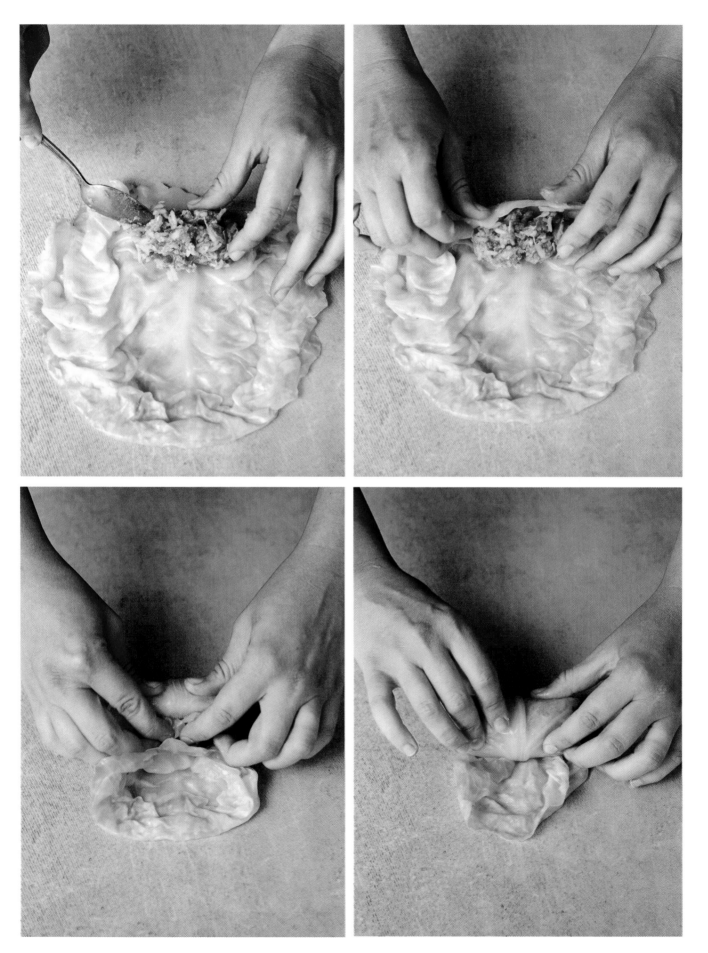

MEAT FILLING

½ pound ground pork

½ pound ground lamb

½ pound ground beef

2 cups cooked white rice

1 tablespoon kosher salt

Place the ground meats in the bowl of a stand mixer fitted with the paddle attachment, and mix until uniform, about 30 seconds. Add the rice and salt, and continue mixing until combined.

VEGAN FILLING VARIATION

(Because vegans should get a chance to remember their babushkas, too.)

High-heat oil (I use refined sunflower oil)

2 yellow onions, sliced into thin half-moons

6 to 8 king oyster mushrooms (also known as king trumpet), cut into a ½-inch dice (the stems are the most delicious part, so don't trim them away!)

4 cloves garlic, minced

2 cups cooked white rice

Handful coarsely chopped cilantro or parsley

Kosher salt

Heat oil in a large skillet over medium heat, and add the onions. Cook, stirring occasionally, until they fully soften and are just beginning to get golden, about 20 minutes, lowering the heat as needed so that they don't color before becoming entirely translucent. Add the mushrooms and garlic, and sauté until the mushrooms are cooked through and beginning to get a bit of color, and the onions are fully caramelized, about 20 minutes more. Cool the pan to room temperature, add the rice and herbs, and season to taste.

ASSEMBLY

High-heat oil (I use refined sunflower oil)

Smetana (page 359) or European-style sour cream

Handful fresh dill, coarsely chopped

Preheat the oven to 425°F. Grab the largest casserole dish/Dutch oven/roasting pan you have, and lay down about one-third of the sauce on the bottom. Set aside.

Take one of the precooked cabbage leaves on a clean work surface, and place about ⅓ cup of the filling in the center (the exact amount will depend upon the size of the leaf—you want to be able to form a neat little package). Roll up the cabbage leaf tightly around the filling, burrito style. See the photographs on the opposite page for reference. When you've made 3 or 4 in the same fashion, heat a large skillet over medium-high heat.

(continued page 272)

When the skillet is hot, pour in enough oil to coat the bottom, and place the stuffed cabbage parcels in it, seam side down. Let them cook for a few minutes per side, until golden brown—this helps seal the bundles, and also imparts a delicious caramelized flavor, so don't skimp! When browned, transfer them to your waiting sauce-lined dish. Repeat with the remaining cabbage and filling. If your dish isn't large enough to hold all the rolls, you can pile some of them on top in a second layer.

When you've finished filling and searing all of the cabbage rolls, pour the remaining sauce over the top. Cover the pan with a lid, then transfer to the oven. Bake for 1 hour, then reduce the heat to 350°F and bake another 1 to 2 hours for vegan golubtsi, or another 3 hours for meat-filled golubtsi.

Serve hot, garnished with a dollop of smetana and a sprinkling of fresh dill.

LAZY VARIATION

If you're not up for all of the filling and folding, golubtsi can also be made *lenivo*, the "lazy" way. There is a whole canon of classic dishes that have lazy versions (I love the self-awareness of owning your sloth). Simply make the sauce as above, but use half a head of fresh cabbage, shredded, instead of the trim. Make the meat filling as written, form it into 1½-inch-diameter meatballs, give them a quick sear on all sides in an oil-slicked pan over medium-high heat, then gently transfer them to the sauce, and continue simmering for another hour (longer doesn't hurt).

Lazy golubtsi are a natural fit for a meatball sub (a Super Bowl snack I've been known to make): Take a toasted hoagie bun and give it a swipe of adjika (page 358) and a few saucy meatballs. Top with melty cheese, and stick the sandwiches under the broiler to melt.

POTATO AND CARROT BABKA

картофельная бабка с морковью

✦ ✦ ✦

The popular translation of *babka*—from Seinfeld to pastry counters—has led us astray. Sure, I suppose that chocolatey bread *is* a babka—but it's not the *only* babka. To a Belarusian, babka is a type of casserole. Potato babka is the most common of the genre, and it's arguably far superior to any pastry.

I've given this version a bit of sweetness and color from grated carrot, but for the most part it's fairly traditional. In Belarus, having a potato babka sans pork is crazy talk, but I think it's equally enjoyable without. And instead of a sprinkling of streusel crumbs, Belarusian babka can be topped with souffléd mayonnaise. Optional, but there for you if you want to go big (you're welcome).

YIELDS ONE 13-X-9-INCH CASSEROLE

¼ pound slab bacon, cut into a ¼-inch dice

1 onion, cut into a ½-inch dice

6 medium (3 pounds) Yukon Gold potatoes, peeled and finely shredded

1 carrot, peeled and finely shredded

1 cup kefir

2 large eggs

1½ teaspoons kosher salt

OPTIONAL SOUFFLÉ TOPPING:

½ cup mayonnaise (page 357, or store-bought)

1 large egg

Heat a large skillet over medium heat, and cook the bacon, stirring occasionally, until the fat has rendered and the bacon is nice and crispy (about 15 minutes). Take the bacon out of the grease and set aside. Use some of the rendered fat to grease a 13-x-9-inch casserole dish, and set that aside.

Sauté the onion in the remaining fat until it's fully softened and starting to caramelize, about 20 minutes (adjust the heat as needed if it colors before it's softened).

While the onion is cooking, preheat the oven to 400°F.

When the onion is cooked, set it aside and let cool slightly while you prepare the rest of the babka. Combine the grated potatoes, carrots, kefir, eggs, salt, and caramelized onions in the food processor and pulse until the shredded potato and carrot are finely chopped and the ingredients are mixed together (just a few pulses). Stir in the rendered bacon.

Pour the mixture into the prepared casserole dish, and bake for 2 hours—covered for the first hour, uncovered for the second. Serve warm.

If you're going for the soufflé topping, when the babka is done, vigorously whisk together the mayonnaise and egg until well combined. Take the babka out of the oven, and evenly spread the mayonnaise mixture over the top. Place the casserole under the broiler, and broil 3 to 5 minutes, or until the mayo has puffed up and is golden brown and set. Remove from the oven, and let cool slightly before serving.

FOR A VEGETARIAN VERSION (SHHH, DON'T TELL THE RUSSIANS): Omit the bacon, and sauté the onions in refined sunflower or another cooking oil instead. Increase the salt to 1 tablespoon and toss in 3 tablespoons of butter (softened to room temperature) with the kefir, process it all together, and proceed as written.

CAULIFLOWER SCHNITZEL

шницель из цветной капусты

Pork schnitzel came to be as popular in Russia as it is throughout the rest of Europe (thanks, Habsburg Empire!). But while it holds an important place in the culinary landscape of Russian cookery, it has never really piqued my interest. Now, vegetable schnitzels—that's a brilliant adaptation that I can get behind. Somewhere along the way, Russians began to use the word *schnitzel* to refer to really any vegetable battered and pan-fried. In our home, cauliflower was most often given this treatment—though everything from beets to cabbage to celery root make for fantastic schnitzels.

My schnitzel gets a zippy flavor boost from some marinade time, and the result is not one of these poor-substitutes-for-meat numbers—it's head and shoulders above the standard meaty model. Serve with vinegret salad (page 105), parsley mayo (page 357), mashed potatoes, fries, or pretty much whatever you want.

SERVES 4 AS A MAIN DISH

2 medium heads cauliflower

MARINADE:

½ cup water

½ cup white wine vinegar

¼ cup coarsely chopped parsley

¼ cup Russian mustard (page 355, or store-bought)

2 tablespoons dijon mustard

1 clove garlic, minced

1 tablespoon granulated sugar

1 tablespoon kosher salt

TO FINISH:

All-purpose flour

2 large eggs

Kosher salt

Freshly ground black pepper

Plain breadcrumbs

Clarified butter or oil (I use peanut or canola) for frying

Set a large steamer basket above a pan of water, and heat the water to a simmer. If you don't have a steamer basket that'll fit the cauliflower steaks, then just heat a few inches of water in a large pan.

Slice the very bottoms off the cauliflower stems, then slice each head crosswise into ½-inch steaks. You should easily get at least two per head from the center, along with some smaller side bits. Don't remove the stalk (it gets a bad rap, but it'll be tender and tasty in the end). Reserve the steaks, and set aside the smaller florets and trim for another use (or you can en-schnitzel them as well—less dramatic but equally delicious).

Carefully place the cauliflower steaks in the steamer basket or poaching water, and cook until they're slightly softened but still firm, and can be pierced with just a little resistance, about 8 minutes.

While the cauliflower is steaming, mix together the water, vinegar, parsley, mustards, garlic, sugar, and salt in a small bowl. Set aside, and grab a casserole dish.

When the cauliflower is finished, pour a little of the marinade on the bottom of the casserole dish. Carefully place the hot cauliflower steaks on top of the marinade, and then pour the rest of the marinade over the top, for the cauliflower to drink up. Let sit for 1 hour to absorb (or refrigerate overnight).

When the cauliflower has marinated and you're ready to fry, get three shallow bowls. Fill one with some flour, one with the eggs (beaten with some water to loosen and a bit of salt and pepper), and one with the breadcrumbs. Pour enough clarified butter or oil into a large skillet (or two, if you'd like things to go more quickly) to go halfway up the cauliflower, and place over medium heat.

Remove the cauliflower from the marinade and shake off the excess. Dredge the steaks in the flour, then the egg, then the breadcrumbs—if you want a vegan version, use the leftover marinade instead of the egg for the middle layer. Make sure each layer covers all of the cauliflower, including the sides, to fully encase it. You can do this right before frying, or up to 2 hours ahead of time.

Shallow fry the cauliflower until golden brown, about 3 to 5 minutes per side (it's precooked, so you don't need to worry too much). Serve immediately.

PORK KOTLETI AND GRECHKA

котлеты из свинины с гречкой

✦ ✦ ✦

Ah, kotleti. These meat patties were, and continue to be, *everywhere* in Russia. From the beloved frozen six-kopek packages of "Mikoyan" brand, to a standard item on the Soviet cafeteria menu, to my mom's present-day kitchen.

Back in the 1930s, Stalin's favorite food commissar, Anastas Mikoyan, took a coast-to-coast American scouting mission—and was particularly enamored of fast-food hamburgers. He brought hamburger mass-production methods back with him, and used them to propel the humble *kotletka* to cult status.

The propaganda machine clearly worked its magic. Every. Single. Week. My mother still makes kotleti. In her refrigerator, I always find either ground meat waiting to be turned into kotleti, or leftovers from a dinner featuring the patties. It's a vicious circle of meatiness. And I'm passing it on to you. For a real Soviet dinner, grechka and malosol'nye cucumbers (page 86) are a must.

YIELDS 10 PATTIES

1 medium yellow onion, peeled and cut into large chunks

1 clove garlic

2 pounds ground pork

½ cup unseasoned bread crumbs

1 large egg

1 tablespoon kosher salt

1 tablespoon mayonnaise

A few grinds black pepper

Cooking oil (I use refined sunflower)

Grechka (page 280) and Malosol'nye cucumbers (page 86) for serving

Combine the onion and garlic in a food processor, and process until somewhat uniform.

Transfer the mixture to a large bowl or a stand mixer fitted with a paddle attachment, and add the remaining ingredients, except for the oil. Mix or use a wooden spoon (or your hands), until the fat emulsifies to coat everything with a fat-smeared sheen. If you stop the mixer and grab a pinch, it will stick to your fingers with a very tacky feel. Under- or overprocessing will lead to dry meat, so try to hit this nice, sticky sweet spot—stop every so often and check. The entire process should take 1 to 2 minutes, tops, with the paddle attachment (longer by hand).

Shape the kotleti into 10 flat, oblong patties—like a burger that tapers a bit at the ends. If the mixture is hard to work with, dip your hands in a dish of cold water to keep it from sticking.

Heat a large, heavy skillet over medium-high heat, and pour in a slick of oil to coat the bottom. Pan-fry the patties until they've developed a nice golden-brown crust, about 5 minutes per side. Serve hot, with grechka and half-salted malosol'nye) cucumbers.

(continued page 280)

GRECHKA

Buckwheat kasha—that fundamental earthy grain that feeds the masses—is a staple of Russian cuisine, from village breakfast to Soviet cafeteria side dish. And now, to endless Russian amusement, it's been "discovered" by glossy food magazines. But even the fanciest grocery-store kasha can be somewhat lacking—stale from poor packaging, or roasted unevenly (or barely at all), resulting in a dish that's disappointingly mushy. Hit the Russian market, and you'll find fresh groats, roasted to an even, burnished brown, that will cook up nice and fluffy. Look for grains from the Altai region of Siberia, where this finicky crop thrives.

The hazelnuts here aren't strictly traditional, but they mirror buckwheat's earthiness, which is rounded out with a generous knob of butter (don't skimp!).

YIELDS 1 QUART

3 tablespoons unsalted butter, divided

1 cup roasted buckwheat groats

1¾ cups mushroom broth (page 352) or water

1 teaspoon kosher salt, plus more to taste

½ cup toasted hazelnuts, coarsely chopped

Heat a medium-sized pot over medium heat, and melt 1 tablespoon of the butter. When the butter starts to foam, add the buckwheat groats, and stir to coat them evenly. Stir for another 1 to 2 minutes, until you can smell them, then pour in the broth (or water) and salt. Bring the mixture to a boil, then reduce the heat until it's just high enough to maintain a gentle simmer, and cover with a lid.

Simmer for 30 minutes, then check—the groats should be soft, with a slight chewiness (like barley or wheat berries). If they're still wet and undercooked, replace the lid and simmer another few minutes, until the water has been absorbed and the groats are fully cooked.

When the groats are cooked, add the remaining 2 tablespoons of butter and the chopped hazelnuts. Stir until the butter is melted, and the hazelnuts are mixed in. Add additional salt to taste. Serve hot.

SHORT RIB ZHARKOYE

жаркое с говяжьими ребрами

✦ ✦ ✦

This dish is ingrained in my mother's repertoire—it makes an appearance at least once a week on the dinner table, and is also her go-to for big gatherings. And for good reason: it is ridiculously easy to make, and the payoff is huge. The hardest part is peeling the potatoes—and waiting patiently for the thing to slowly braise away on the stove. The prunes melt into everything, adding a bit of earthy sweetness, and the potatoes turn tan, filled with long-cooked flavors, becoming an almost otherworldly thing. You can pluck out the bay leaves before serving, or leave them in—the Russian's say is that the person who finds a bay leaf will soon receive a letter.

SERVES 6

High-heat oil (I use refined sunflower or canola)

3 pounds short ribs (you want the bone-in English cut, nice and meaty)

1 tablespoon kosher salt, plus more for seasoning the ribs

3 pounds Yukon Gold potatoes (6 or 7 good-sized potatoes), peeled and cut into 2-inch chunks

12 pitted prunes

4 fresh bay leaves, or 2 dried

Heat a large, heavy pot over high heat, and pour in enough oil to coat the bottom. While you're waiting for it to heat up, generously season the short ribs with salt on all sides. Place the short ribs in the pot in a single layer (this will likely take two batches), and let them brown on all sides. This should take about 2 minutes per side. The sear on the bottom of the pan will help contribute to the flavor, so make sure they color richly but don't burn—adjust the heat as needed. Remove the short ribs from the pot after they're seared, and set aside on a plate. When they're all seared, pour out the remaining grease from the pot (but leave the nice browned bits).

Return the pot to the stovetop, and evenly layer in the potatoes and seared short ribs. Add the prunes and bay leaves. Pour in some water, enough to just cover things (this should be about 1½ to 2 quarts), and sprinkle in 1 tablespoon salt. Cover the pot, bring it to a boil, then lower the heat until it's just high enough to maintain the gentlest simmer. Cook, without stirring, for about 2½ hours. Then remove the lid, and cook at a gentle simmer for another 2½ hours, or until the short ribs are fall-apart tender, the potatoes have darkened to a deep tan, and there's just a few inches of liquid remaining.

Serve hot, with a slotted spoon. If there are leftovers, the excess liquid will absorb overnight as it sits.

NA KARTOSHKU (POTATO HARVESTS)

The Soviet Union impacted food production and consumption in a variety of ways—from establishing state-run cafeterias (the meat kotleti!) to forcing city-dwellers into apartments with communal kitchens (the smells!) to communal agriculture. That's how my parents, a physicist and a bookkeeper, ended up out in a Belarusian field for a month every fall digging for potatoes.

Kholkhozy, or collective farms, first started after the revolution, pulling the old feudal system into a more cooperative model. In familiar was-it-intentional-or-was-it-incompetence Soviet irony, the collectivization of agriculture under Stalin's first Five-Year Plan actually led to horrific food shortages throughout the region, which caused the state to bring more and more people into the fields. By the time my parents were growing up in the fifties and sixties, the worst of the famines were over—but stints at collective farms continued.

Every September, students (from teenage years through college) were sent out to neighboring villages for a month, living in local houses or barracks and helping with the agricultural work. They harvested apples and bundled flax, but mostly they dug potatoes. So people started calling it "*na kartoshku*" ("out to the potatoes"). Even after graduation, citizens would still be sent na kartoshku, as each regional party office had to make a particular quota of work detail, to "battle for the harvest."

But as backbreaking as this sounds, many people harbor surprisingly fond memories. Yes, there were outhouses, and not much in the way of showers. But where my dad was stationed (perhaps *because* that's where my dad was stationed) there were also culinary competitions organized, songs sung, and card games to be played when the workday was rained out. Anthems were written, and satirical operas composed (often poking fun at the farmers' plight).

And despite the physicality of the work, there was the general buzz of excitement that comes when groups of young people are thrown together with minimal supervision (and farmhouse moonshine). My aunt Asya still remembers realizing that her then-boyfriend-now-husband was truly in love—when he would give the supervisor her ID number instead of his own when dropping off a load of potatoes. Because nothing says love like filling your partner's potato harvest quota.

Photographs on opposite page: My dad's shenanigans during a potato harvest.

CHAPTER 9

SHOWSTOPPERS

привлекательные блюда

✦ ✦ ✦

Russians are really into presentation. It might be that people who grew up in the single-option Soviet-gray days try to show their best with the limited resources available. Whatever the reason, I remember my grandmother, freshly off the proverbial boat, refusing to walk me through the neighborhood to my friend's house until she combed her hair and put on some lipstick. And this spirit comes out at the table.

For big celebrations—you know, when you want to gather a hundred or so of your closest friends—cities with large Russian populations have a slew of banquet halls for the occasion. And you will see bells and whistles *everywhere*—from diners' wardrobes to sparkler-studded lamb chops (don't ask). Six-inch heels and pyrotechnics aside, there's a lot of fun in putting on a show for your loved ones. Unfortunately, sometimes the food is more style than substance (the bane of banquet halls everywhere). But at home, you can truly bring it for your celebrations, creating showstoppers as delicious as they are impressive.

MACHANKA

мачанка

✦ ✦ ✦

Machanka is perhaps *the* signature dish of Belarus, a rich, warming roast for those cold winter nights (or mornings—machanka is also popular for breakfast, similar to biscuits and gravy). The exact meat used can vary—a mix of pork belly, sausages, ham hocks—but it's always cooked in a rich sauce, into which you can dip (the literal translation of *machanka*) buttery blini or fresh-fried potato draniki.

I like narrowing the focus a bit, and make machanka with just pork belly. The belly is roasted on its own, and its drippings give a deliciously porky depth to the gravy. A sea buckthorn relish spooned on top brightens the whole thing up. Serve with a crisp, leafy green salad. If you're making it for a crowd, feel free to scale everything up for a full pork belly—but increase the marinade time to 24 to 36 hours.

SERVES 6

PORK BELLY:

¼ cup Russian mustard (page 355, or store-bought)

¼ cup granulated sugar

¼ cup kosher salt

2 pounds pork belly (ask for the meatiest cut), skin removed (have the butcher do this, or slice it as close to the skin as possible and just peel it off)

GRAVY:

1 cup fat, divided (use the fat rendered from roasting the pork belly, supplemented with butter if/as needed)

1 onion, sliced into thin half-moons

Kosher salt

1⅓ cups all-purpose flour

1 quart meat broth—you can use fancy broth (page 351)

⅓ cup white wine

1 cup smetana (page 359) or crème fraîche

Sea buckthorn relish (page 362)

Blini (page 139) or draniki (page 268) for serving

Mix the mustard, sugar, and salt together to form a paste, and rub it all over the pork belly. Place the meat in a covered dish or plastic bag, and refrigerate for 18 to 24 hours.

The next day, preheat the oven to 375°F, and place the pork belly in a roasting pan or casserole dish.

Roast the pork belly, uncovered, for 45 minutes, then reduce the temperature to 250°F for another 90 minutes, or until the meat is totally tender. When it's done, remove the pan from the oven and let it cool slightly, then transfer the pork belly to another container, and pour the fat that has rendered into a measuring cup. If you don't have 1 cup, add some melted butter to make up the difference.

Set the belly aside, and make the gravy: Pour ¼ cup of the fat into a large, heavy pot, and heat it over medium-high heat. Add the onion, season with a generous pinch of salt, and sauté until caramelized to a uniform golden brown, about 30 minutes, reducing the heat to low and stirring more frequently as it cooks, to ensure it colors evenly. When the onion has caramelized, transfer it to a small dish and set aside.

(continued page 289)

Add the remaining ¾ cup fat to the pot (still on medium-low), let it melt, and then whisk in the flour. Cook, stirring occasionally (and more frequently as it colors), until the roux darkens to a light golden-brown/caramel color, about 10 minutes. Increase the heat to medium-high, and whisk in the broth and wine, bit by bit, letting it boil and continually thicken as you go (remember, you're making gravy). When the liquid has all been whisked in, stir in the reserved caramelized onions. Taste and add salt, and then simmer for 30 to 60 minutes, to let the flavors develop. Gravy can be made up to 3 days in advance.

To serve: Preheat the oven to 400°F. Cut the belly across the grain (as with a brisket) into ¼-inch slabs. Lay the sliced machanka in a single layer on a foil-lined tray, and place it in the oven until heated through and starting to crisp on the outside, about 5 minutes per side.

Heat the gravy (if it was made ahead), and stir in the smetana. The gravy should be thick, but pourable. If it's too thick, thin it out with a little water. Season with salt as needed. Pour the gravy into a deep-sided serving dish. Lay out the slices of machanka on top, and garnish with sea buckthorn relish. Serve with large blini or draniki on the side.

KULEBYAKA WITH CRÈME FLEURETTE

кулебяка с кремом "флюрет

✛ ✛ ✛

In a chapter of showstoppers, this one takes the cake. Or, rather, pastry. Pastry wrapped around brined salmon, herb-and-egg-spiked rice, and crepes, that is. And served with a beet-bright buttery sauce.

Simple versions of kulebyaka do exist—more akin to riffs on the standard pirog—but this over-the-top version is more true to kulebyaka's roots as a prerevolutionary indulgence. Also, it's amazing. You can (and should) break down the elements, preparing the dough, the filling components, and the crepes in advance, and assembling everything the day of. It might be a bit of an undertaking, but it's transporting—earthy and buttery and light at the same time, a dish truly fit for a czar.

SERVES 6 TO 8 AS A MAIN DISH

DOUGH:

½ batch pirog dough (page 165), made at least 1 hour (and up to several days) in advance

All-purpose flour for rolling

FILLING:

1 pound center-cut salmon fillet, skin and pin bones removed, brined in the trout brine (page 244) for 4 to 12 hours

4 cups cooked white rice

1 bunch chard, leaves finely chopped and blanched, stems pickled (see headnote, page 88)

2 large hard-boiled eggs, cut into a ¼-inch dice

¼ cup finely chopped fresh dill

¼ cup mayonnaise (page 357, or store-bought)

1 tablespoon kosher salt

8 crepes (page 177)

Egg wash (1 large egg lightly beaten with a dollop of smetana [page 359] or crème fraîche)

Crème fleurette (page 292) for serving

Let the pirog dough soften at room temperature for a few minutes, just enough so that it can easily be rolled. Preheat the oven to 400°F. Take the brined salmon out of the refrigerator, and let it warm up slightly.

In a large bowl, gently stir together the rice, blanched chard, pickled chard stems (along with a splash of their brine), eggs, dill, mayo, and salt, until just combined. Remove the salmon from its brine (you can discard the brine).

Cut the dough into two slightly unequal halves. On a clean, floured surface, roll the smaller piece out to be about 2 inches longer than your salmon fillet on each side, and the larger piece to be 3 inches longer. Lay the smaller piece out on a rimmed baking sheet.

Lay down 3 crepes on top of the pastry, overlapping them to fit. With a knife or scissors, trim any overhang, so that there's 1 inch of dough exposed on all sides. These are your moisture barrier! Then lay down half of the rice filling, spread out to an even layer (still leaving the exposed border of dough). Pat the salmon fillet dry, and lay it gently on top. Then top it with the remaining rice filling (you'll need to sort of pat it over the salmon fillet), and the remaining 3 crepes (overlapped and trimmed).

(continued page 292)

With a pastry brush (or your finger), brush the egg wash over the exposed dough, then top with the larger pastry piece, crimping the layers together with a fork. Trim away any crooked parts of the crust of the pie with a knife. Brush the top of the entire pie generously with egg wash, and cut a few vents through the top layer of dough to let steam escape. Feel free to get fancy with your vent cuts, or dress it up with decorative dough scraps.

Transfer the kulebyaka to the oven, and bake until the crust is golden brown and the fish is cooked through (stick a knife through to the fish, let it stay in for 15 seconds, then pull it out and touch it to the inside of your wrist to see if it's hot—or until a thermometer reads 130°F). This should take about 40 minutes. Pull it from the oven, and let it cool a bit. Cut the kulebyaka into individual portions, and serve with crème fleurette.

CRÈME FLEURETTE

This French sauce isn't well known, but it's just a derivative of hollandaise—with some dairy whisked in at the end. I give it a Kachka spin by using smetana instead of the standard crème fraîche, and using liquid from pickled beets instead of the classic vinegar and shallot reduction (which has the added bonus of turning everything a shocking pink). Once you have a go at it, you may not want to go back to that plain-Jane hollandaise ever again—try it on your next eggs Benedict, or with roasted asparagus.

YIELDS ABOUT 1½ CUPS

1 pint liquid left over from pickled beets (page 88)—if you're making kulebyaka, you can use this liquid to pickle the chard stems, before reducing it for the sauce

1 large egg yolk

1 tablespoon water

2 sticks (1 cup) unsalted butter

2 tablespoons smetana (page 359) or crème fraîche

Kosher salt

Pour the beet-pickling liquid into a saucepan, and cook it at a healthy simmer until it's reduced to just a few syrupy tablespoons, about 30 minutes (run a fan, vinegar is intense when cooking!). Transfer the liquid to a double boiler, along with the egg yolk and water.

Add the butter to your beet saucepan, and heat it gently over a low flame until the butter melts.

Heat the double boiler under the beet liquid, and whisk together until the mixture starts to thicken (this should just take a few minutes). Gently drizzle in the butter, continuing to whisk, to create a thick, fluffy sauce, incorporating all of the butter. Whisk in the smetana and season with salt as needed (the reduced pickling liquid packs a lot of punch, so it might not need much).

Serve right away. This sauce will break when it gets cold, so plan to make it immediatly before serving, or find a preheated thermos to store it in if making up to 30 minutes ahead.

CRAYFISH BOIL

раки вареные

✦ ✦ ✦

Crayfish are everywhere in Russia, and they're a natural summer meal for a crowd—many dachas aren't too far from a lake or river, where summering Russians catch them for free.

Cooking these little guys is as easy as boiling water. Set up a large burner outdoors, grab a boil pot, and chill the kvas and beer. Cover a big picnic table with newspapers, and bury it in cooked crayfish. Sure, there are a lot of shells to pick through. But those tasty little tails are worth the trouble—if gossiping around the table while drinking beer on a summer evening isn't reward enough.

SERVES 6 TO 8

6 cups kosher salt

¼ cup ground coriander (freshly ground is best, if you can swing it)

¼ cup smoked paprika

¼ cup onion powder

¼ cup mustard powder

¼ cup dried dill

2 tablespoons freshly ground black pepper

8 fresh bay leaves, or 4 dried

8 pounds small, young potatoes (fingerlings, butterballs, etc.), scrubbed but not peeled

4 heads garlic, scrubbed and halved through the equator

8 dill flower stalks, flowers picked off and reserved for garnish

6 gallons water

20 pounds live crayfish*

8 lemons, quartered, divided

2 12-ounce bottles of beer (Baltika 7 or another pilsner-style beer preferred), plus more for serving

---

* Remember: Crayfish, like crabs and lobsters, have claws. Always pick up crayfish from behind.

Place the salt, coriander, paprika, onion powder, mustard powder, dried dill, pepper, and bay leaves into a seafood boil pot, and give a stir to combine. Add the strainer insert, then add the potatoes, garlic, and dill stalks. Cover with the water, and bring to a boil (yes, this will take some time).

While you're waiting for the pot to come to a boil, clean the crayfish: Place the crayfish in a large vessel, and fill it with cold water. Use tongs or a wooden spoon to move the crayfish around, removing any dirt and debris. Strain off the water, and examine the crayfish—if they still appear dirty, or the water was very cloudy, repeat the soaking and straining process until clean. Discard any crayfish that appear dead.

When the pot has come to a boil, reduce the heat until it's just high enough to maintain a steady simmer. Let simmer for about 15 minutes, or until the potatoes are almost cooked through. Add the crayfish, bring the pot back up to a boil (3 to 5 minutes), and immediately turn off the heat. Add 4 of the quartered lemons, and all of the beer. Cover the pot with a lid and let it sit in the residual heat for 20 minutes.

To serve, pull out the strainer basket and pour the contents onto an oilcloth tablecloth or newspapers. Squeeze the 4 remaining lemons over the crayfish and potatoes, and garnish with the dill flowers. Serve with lots of beer and Wet Naps.

CHICKEN KIEV

КОТЛЕТЫ ПО-КИЕВСКИ

✦ ✦ ✦

Claimed by both Russians and Ukrainians as their own, Chicken Kiev is often the entry point into Russian cuisine. When I worried in the early Kachka days that nobody would order the herring, I figured at least they would order the Chicken Kiev—a dish both Russians and Americans get nostalgic for.

Yes, it does have some restaurants-of-yesteryear associations. And setting it up takes some fussing. But in the end, everyone gets their own little present of a dish—and who doesn't get excited when warm butter pours out?

SERVES 4

MARINADE:

1 quart kefir

½ sweet onion, coarsely chopped

1 bunch dill (both leaves and stems), coarsely chopped

2½ tablespoons kosher salt

TO FINISH:

4 small boneless, skinless chicken breasts (tenderloins removed)

1 stick (½ cup) salted butter

¼ cup minced dill

1 cup all-purpose flour

2 large eggs, whisked with a pinch of kosher salt

1 cup fine, unseasoned breadcrumbs

High-heat oil (I use canola or peanut)

Kosher salt

The day before you're making the dish, mix together all the marinade ingredients in a covered container (the cutlets will be delicate, so you don't want to use a bag). Pound out the chicken breasts to flatten them—basically you're looking for as thin as you can get them without tearing, about ¼ inch, nicely uniform (thinner cutlets make for an evenly cooked and properly sealed Kiev). Carefully place the flattened cutlets in with the marinade, coat them well, and refrigerate overnight.

At least 1½ (and up to 7) hours before you're ready to cook your cutlets, take the stick of butter and cut it in half widthwise, and then cut each half in half lengthwise, to create 4 planks (if you don't have salted butter, just add a generous sprinkling of salt). Roll each plank in the minced dill, to fully cover all sides. Set up your Kiev assembly station: Pour the flour, eggs, and breadcrumbs each into their own shallow bowl, and set aside.

Take the chicken from the refrigerator, and carefully remove the cutlets from the marinade, shaking off any excess. On a plate or cutting board, lay out a piece of chicken. Place the dill-coated plank of butter in the middle, and then fold the cutlet around it like a burrito—fold the bottom closest to you around the butter, then fold the sides in, then roll everything up. Make this nice and snug, so the butter is totally encased in the chicken.

(continued page 299)

Then comes standard breading: Place your chicken-butter burrito in the dish of flour, to coat it on all sides, then dip it in the egg to do the same, then finally in the breadcrumbs, patting them down so that they adhere. If any bald patches are revealed, you can troubleshoot with some dabbed-on spot repairs. Use both hands, and press in on your bundle on all sides to reinforce the breading a bit. Repeat with the remaining cutlets, and then place all of the filled packages on a rack and refrigerate, uncovered, for at least 1 hour (and up to 6 hours), allowing the egg to dry out and seal the parcel. If you're rushed, you can skip this step, but it improves your chances of success.

When you're ready to cook, pour 2 inches of oil into a pan, and heat over medium heat. When the oil is hot (a pinch of breadcrumbs dances in the oil, but does not burn), cook the cutlets 5 to 6 minutes per side, until golden brown. To test for doneness, carefully poke a metal skewer into the cutlet, leave it inside for 30 seconds, then remove and touch to your wrist to see that it's hot (make sure the butter doesn't pour out of the hole you just made!).

When the cutlets are done, remove them from the hot oil, and place on a rack for 1 minute to rest. Give them a sprinkling of salt, and serve while hot and buttery. For a real throwback, serve with french fries and buttered peas.

KASHA-STUFFED SUCKLING PIG

поросенок молочный фаршированный кашей

✦ ✦ ✦

If you're going for showstopper, it's hard to beat a whole stuffed pig. And this fact is not lost on Russian cooks. It's a prerequisite of any wedding or major celebration, as my parents can attest. They had several roast pigs at their wedding—and then again for their fortieth anniversary.

Of course, Russians are not the only ones aware of how delicious suckling pig can be. Nearly every part of the world makes some version of this. What sets the Russian take apart from the rest are two things: the filling and the rub. This suckling pig is stuffed with buckwheat, which gives the sweet meat an earthy perfume. And the entire outside of the pig is rubbed down—generously—with smetana. As the pig cooks, the buckwheat soaks up the juices, and the milk sugars in the smetana caramelize to a burnished glaze.

Although it looks intimidating, this is actually fairly easy to make—the hardest part is sourcing the pig (check out Latino markets, well-stocked meat counters, or local farms), and finding space in your fridge to hold it while brining.

SERVES A PARTY

BRINE:

¾ cup juniper berries

¾ cup whole black peppercorns

6 gallons water, divided

3 cups kosher salt

3 cups granulated sugar

1½ cups Russian mustard (page 355, or store-bought)

PIG:

1 15-pound whole suckling pig (anything larger is tricky in a home oven—you've been warned)*

FILLING AND FINISHING:

A double batch of buckwheat kasha (page 280), made up to 3 days in advance

Trussing pins, or a heavy-gauge needle, thread, and pliers

3 to 4 cups smetana (page 359) or crème fraîche

Heat a large stockpot over medium heat. Add the juniper berries and peppercorns and toast, stirring, until the spices are fragrant (this should just take a few minutes). When you start to smell the spices, pour in 3 gallons of the water, and stir in the salt, sugar, and mustard. Increase the heat to high, and cook, stirring, until the mixture comes to a boil and the sugar and salt dissolve. Take the pot off the heat, pour in the remaining 3 gallons of water, and let cool fully.

When the brine has cooled, figure out a good vessel that can fit both the pig and the brine, and pour the cooled brine over the pig. Refrigerate the pig in the brine for 48 to 72 hours.

About 4 or 5 hours before you'd like to serve the pig, get your filling, trussing supplies, and smetana ready. Find your largest roasting pan, or make one out of a rimmed sheet tray lined with a whole lot of heavy-duty foil. Preheat the oven to 350°F.

---

* Bonus if your pig came with innards—you can soak the liver in milk, then dice it up and add it to the buckwheat stuffing.

Pull the pig out of the brine, discard the brine, and dry the pig off with clean dish towels. Make sure the cavity has been fully cleaned out. Upend the pig on your work surface, and pack the cavity with the buckwheat filling. Take your needle and thread, or trussing pins, and close the cavity around the filling.

Carefully flip the filled pig over into your roasting pan, tucking the legs underneath. Rub the smetana generously over the entire pig, using your hands to work it in everywhere. Don't be shy. The brine will have seasoned everything, so there's no need for additional salt.

When the pig has been filled, trussed, and smetanaed, roast it for 1 hour. After the first hour wrap the ears (and tail, if you care) with little caps of foil to keep them from burning. Put it back in the oven for 1 hour more. If the skin is starting to get too dark, tent the whole pig with foil. If the skin is browning more heavily on one side than the other, turn it (all ovens have different hot spots). Starting at hour three, begin checking for doneness—you want a meat thermometer to read 155°F at the thickest part.

When the pig has cooked to temperature, remove it from the oven, and remove any foil. Let it rest for 30 minutes. Remove the twine or trussing pins and carve, making sure everyone gets a portion of both the meat and the buckwheat filling (and don't forget about the flavorful meat around the jowls). This doesn't need a sauce—it'll be plenty flavorful and juicy on its own.

ARMENIAN PUMPKIN DOLMAS

долма из тыквы по-армянски

✛ ✛ ✛

This might come as a surprise, but dolmas are not just stuffed grape leaves. A dolma refers to any stuffed vegetable, from the Middle East to the Balkans to the Caucasus. Here, pumpkins (or winter squash) are stuffed with *plov*, a Central Asian take on rice pilaf. The warming cinnamon and cooling fresh mint, rich lamb and tart sour cherries, all bathing the rice and baked squash—needless to say, your kitchen will smell amazing. You can easily omit the lamb to make a spectacular side for a holiday table, or a vegetarian-friendly main course.

YIELDS 4 GENEROUS SERVINGS

4 small, round squashes (1½ to 2 pounds each) with flat bottoms, such as Heart of Gold, Sweet Dumpling, Carnival, or Sugar Pumpkins

1 pound lamb shoulder, fat cap and silver skin/connective tissue removed, cut into ½-inch chunks

1⅓ cups long-grain white rice

1 large apple (whichever kind is eating best at the moment), peeled, cored, and cut into a ¼-inch dice

¼ cup dried unsweetened sour cherries

¼ cups golden raisins

1½ tablespoons kosher salt

1 teaspoon ground cinnamon

1 teaspoon paprika

½ teaspoon ground allspice

½ teaspoon freshly ground black pepper

1 handful fresh mint leaves, cut into thin ribbons, with some reserved for garnish

1⅓ to 2 cups garlic broth (page 353) or stock/broth of your choosing

½ stick (¼ cup) unsalted butter, divided into 4 tablespoon-sized pieces

Preheat the oven to 325°F.

Wash and dry the squash. Carve out the tops, like you're carving a pumpkin, and set them aside. Scoop out and discard the seeds and any stringy pulp. If the squash are wobbly, you can shave a bit off the bottom of each to help them stay upright.

In a large bowl, mix together the lamb, rice, apple, dried fruit, salt, spices, pepper, and mint. Place your squashes into a casserole dish and stuff each squash with ¼ of the filling mixture. Pour ⅓ cup broth in each squash to moisten the mixture, then top each with 1 tablespoon of butter.

Cover each squash with its reserved top and bake for 3 hours, uncovered, or until the rice in the center is done, and the squash has darkened and softened. Check halfway through, and add more broth to moisten if needed.

To serve, remove the squash caps and sprinkle on the reserved mint. If serving whole, replace the caps. If serving smaller portions, discard the caps and cut each squash in half to reveal the filling.

ROASTED VEAL CHOP WITH CAVIAR BEURRE BLANC

телятина с соусом из икры

+ + +

There is a classic prerevolutionary dish in which a whole veal leg would be larded with lamprey and pork fat and roasted—before getting the royal treatment of caviar sauce. In updating this dish, and paring it down for civilians, I've stripped it to the essential-yet-still-luxurious elements: caviar and veal, sort of the ultimate surf and turf. This is an especially indulgent meal meant for intimate events (I love it paired with scalloped potatoes and asparagus).

The caviar should be of high quality, but it doesn't need to break the bank. I like using Tsar Nicoulai's Estate grade of white sturgeon caviar, an exceptional product for the price. At a lower price point, try paddlefish or hackleback roes, both of which emulate caviar's flavors surprisingly well.

SERVES 2

2 2-inch-thick veal chops (if using thinner chops, reduce the cooking time)

Kosher salt

2 tablespoons high-heat oil (I use canola or peanut)

¼ stick (2 tablespoons) unsalted butter, melted, for basting

CAVIAR SAUCE:

¼ cup dry white wine

¾ stick (6 tablespoons) unsalted butter, cut into 4 pieces

Kosher salt

½ ounce black caviar

Remove the chops from their packaging and pat dry. Very generously season with salt, and rub it in. Let them sit out at room temperature for 30 minutes to 1 hour. Preheat the oven to 325°F.

When the chops are ready, heat a large cast-iron pan over high heat and add the oil. When the pan is very hot (the oil just shy of smoking), place the chops in the pan. Drop the heat to medium-high, and let the chops cook for 3 minutes on each side. When the chops have finished cooking on the second side, transfer the pan to the preheated oven, and roast, basting with the butter—about 10 minutes for medium-rare, longer if you prefer a more well-done chop. Transfer the chops to a cooling rack to rest.

While the chops rest, make the sauce: Pour the wine into a small sauté pan and simmer over high heat until it's reduced to just 1 tablespoon. Drop the heat to low, and begin whisking in the butter, one piece at a time, adding the next piece only when the one before it is incorporated. Make sure that the mixture does not boil, which may cause it to break. Continue until all of the butter is incorporated into the sauce. Whisk in just a pinch of salt. Remove from the heat and add the caviar, gently folding the eggs into the sauce. Plate the chops, and spoon half the sauce over the top of each veal chop. Serve immediately.

NOVY GODT (NEW YEAR'S EVE)

If you're going to throw one showstopping Russian party, it should be for New Year's Eve. No, not because the holiday is a natural fit for caviar and frosty booze (although, to be fair, it is). But because in the former Soviet Union, New Year's Eve is not just another holiday. It is *the* holiday.

I'm talking family gathered around the tree (*yolka*), complete with ornaments, presents, and a Kremlin-red star atop the highest bough. Special state-dispensed gift boxes, full of chocolates and mandarins. Who is that jolly white-bearded man in a red suit delivering presents? It's Ded Moroz, Father Frost! Delivering presents with Snegurochka, his granddaughter the Snow Maiden!

Sound eerily like Christmas? That's because it pretty much is. After a postrevolutionary crackdown where religion was banned and Christmas trees outed as class enemies, the USSR relented a small bit, allowing its brave new society to reclaim their trees and tinsel. But, in keeping with the party line, all of these newly state-sanctioned traditions were secularized and moved down the calendar from Christmas to New Year's.

And when I say this oh-so-clearly Yuletide-inspired celebration was secularized, I mean *totally* secularized—entire generations grew up gathered around the yolka having never heard of Christmas (the Soviet propaganda machine was shockingly good at its job). Which led to some confusion with the Jewish immigrant aid organizations, when their nice Soviet Jewish families proudly displayed trees. And could you believe those foolish Americans were throwing them out right before the holiday?

MAKE NOVY GODT
SUPER PREMIUM

᛭

Take a nap and start dinner between 9 and 10 p.m. (because it's not New Year's unless you're celebrating into the wee hours of the morning).

✤

Max out on zakuski: plentiful, varied, and luxe—bring out the seafood, caviar, and definitely Salat Olivier (page 152).

᛭

Have someone dress up like Ded Moroz and pass out fun little gifts for your guests.

✤

Be sure to put out a bowl of mandarins at dessert.

✤

Make it a family affair—in America, New Year's is for parties with friends, but in Russia, it's all about family.

CHAPTER 10

DESSERTS

сладости

✦ ✦ ✦

Dessert is when a good party becomes a great party (and I'm not just saying that because of my epic sweet tooth). My mom has finally stopped fluttering around the table making sure everyone has what they need. My dad and aunt Asya start singing, and if my uncle Mitya is there, the guitar comes out. If my dad's cousin's wife, Rita, is there, then it's the piano that gets involved. A few guests have headed home, and the party becomes smaller, more intimate. And as idle hands play with candy wrappers and orange peels, the stories come out.

When I was really little, this was the time when my cousins and I would run upstairs for some bonus late-night playtime. But as I got older, I started sticking around the table to hear the stories. My dad's coworker wrapping a goose around his leg to steal it from the factory, my gunslinging heroic grandmother and the cow that recognized her when she returned to her shtetl after the war. The Soviet Union was really hard on my family—but there were still roommate hijinks and underground matzo-baking and satirical songs. All of which spilled out around the dessert table. So make something worth lingering over, and savor the long-forgotten memories that resurface along the way.

BIRD'S MILK CAKE WITH GLAZED APRICOTS

торт "птичье молоко" с глазированными абрикосами

✦ ✦ ✦

"Bird's milk" is Russian shorthand for an unobtainable indulgence, the ne plus ultra delicacy for the person who has everything. In this case, the milk is actually evaporated, not avian—disappointing, I know—but enriched with butter, lightened with egg white, and gelled into a milky, featherlight soufflé. Bird's milk cake was first conceived at a popular restaurant in Moscow in the 1970s, inspired by a popular candy by the same name. We set ours atop a chiffon sponge, then top everything with chocolate ganache. The amaretto-poached apricots and almonds are just gilding the lily—but if you've gone as far as obtaining bird's milk, what's a little garnish?

CAKE:

Unsalted butter for greasing

½ cup (65 grams) pastry flour

¼ cup plus 2 tablespoons (75 grams) granulated sugar

½ teaspoon baking powder

¼ teaspoon kosher salt

2 tablespoons neutral oil (refined sunflower or canola)

2 large eggs, separated

3 tablespoons water

Zest of ½ an orange

¼ teaspoon almond extract

⅛ teaspoon cream of tartar

APRICOTS IN AMARETTO SYRUP:

½ cup water

½ cup granulated sugar

½ cup Amaretto liqueur

2 cups dried apricots, sliced into thin strips

Make the cake: Preheat the oven to 325°F. Line a 9-inch springform pan with parchment. Butter and flour the sides (if the pan is nonstick, you can skip this step), and set aside.

In a large bowl, whisk together the flour, sugar, baking powder, and salt. In a separate bowl, whisk together the oil, egg yolks (reserve the whites—you'll need them soon), water, orange zest, and almond extract until well combined. Fold this wet mixture into the flour mixture until *just* combined.

Place the reserved egg whites in the bowl of a stand mixer fitted with a whisk attachment (or use a large bowl and a hand mixer), and beat for a few minutes, until foamy. Add the cream of tartar, and continue to beat until stiff peaks form. Gently fold the egg whites into the batter, taking care not to deflate the whites, and pour the mixture into your prepared pan, smoothing out the top. Bake until the cake is set and a tester comes out clean, about 20 minutes.

While the cake is baking, prepare the syrup: In a small saucepan, stir together the water, sugar, and liqueur. Bring to a simmer to dissolve the sugar, then turn off the heat.

(continued page 313)

BIRD'S MILK SOUFFLÉ:

¾ cup (150 grams) granulated sugar

⅓ cup water

2 teaspoons (4 grams) agar powder*

1 stick (½ cup) unsalted butter, softened to room temperature (the butter needs to be very soft to mix easily, so give it ample time in a nice warm space)

¼ cup evaporated milk, at room temperature

1 vanilla bean

2 large egg whites

GANACHE GLAZE:

½ cup heavy cream

½ cup chopped dark chocolate (go for a fairly dark chocolate, at least 70%)

½ cup toasted almond slices (optional)

* Available at health food stores or Asian markets. I measured using Eden Foods, a reliable and widely available brand. Agar also comes in flakes—if using this form, make sure to measure by weight instead of volume, and give it an extra half hour to soften and bloom.

When the cake is done, remove it from the oven, and let it cool. Release the cake, peel off the parchment, and then return the cake to the pan, former parchment side up. Brush the top of the cake generously with the syrup, and set aside.

Add the apricots to the remaining syrup, and bring the mixture to a boil. Reduce the heat until it's just high enough to maintain a simmer, and simmer for 20 minutes to plump up the apricots. Turn off the heat and let the mixture cool, then set aside.

When the cake and apricots are done, make the soufflé: Place the sugar, water, and agar in a medium-sized saucepan, and let sit for 15 minutes for the agar to soften and bloom.

While it's resting, beat together the butter and evaporated milk in the bowl of a stand mixer fitted with a paddle attachment (or a large bowl with a hand mixer). Scrape the seeds from the vanilla bean and add them to the bowl (discard the pod). Beat until combined. If the butter hasn't been fully warmed, it may look somewhat curdled. Give it time to warm up, or mix the best you can—it should still turn out fine. Set aside.

When the agar has softened, give it a stir, turn the heat to high, and bring to a boil. Reduce the heat until it's just high enough to maintain a simmer, and cook for 15 minutes.

When there are about 3 minutes left on the agar, place the egg whites in the clean bowl of a stand mixer fitted with a whisk attachment, and beat until stiff peaks start to form. With the mixer running on high, slowly pour the hot agar syrup into the bowl (aim to hit the side of the bowl just above the egg, to avoid too much spattering). Continue beating until the agar is fully mixed in.

Gently fold the egg white mixture into the waiting butter/milk/vanilla mixture, until *just* fully mixed (no streaks), taking care not to deflate the mixture. Working quickly, gently pour the soufflé mixture on top of the sponge, smoothing the top. Refrigerate until the mixture is set, at least 30 minutes (it should feel like touching the center of a marshmallow).

(continued page 314)

CONTINUED

*bird's milk cake with
glazed apricots*

When the bird's milk soufflé has set, prepare the ganache: Place the heavy cream in a small saucepan, and bring it to a boil. As soon as it boils, remove the pan from the heat, and add the chocolate. Let sit for a few minutes for the chocolate to melt in the hot cream, and then whisk until smooth and combined. Take the cake from the refrigerator, and pour the ganache over the top— you can use an offset spatula, but you will likely be able to just tip the pan slightly, and let gravity help pull the ganache to the edges. Place the cake back in your refrigerator for 5 to 10 minutes to allow the ganache to set. When it's hardened somewhat, release the sides of the springform pan, and transfer the cake to a plate. Serve with the apricots and toasted sliced almonds (if using).

This cake is best served the day it's made (if doing so, you can leave it out at room temperature), but you can keep it, covered, in the refrigerator for up to 1 week. Be sure to bring it to room temperature before serving.

PLOMBIR WITH BLACK CURRANT TEA MILK CARAMEL

пломбир с соусом из карамельной сгущенки и черносмородинового чая

✦ ✦ ✦

GOST, the Soviet state standards for food manufacturing that were developed under Stalin, outlined guidelines for several types of frozen confections. There was the cheapest, *molochnoye*, a disappointingly thin ice milk, and the slightly better milk-plus-cream *slivochnoye* (my parents, who are eight years apart in age, both remember the same unchanging Soviet price of each treat). But the richest, creamiest, and most coveted was *plombir*. While many foodstuffs suffered in the Soviet era, plombir was a delicious exception. Food minister Anastas Mikoyan brought industrial ice cream production to the USSR after a trip to America, and ensured that the quality held steady (causing Stalin to remark that Mikoyan cared more about ice cream than Communism).

With both heavy cream and egg yolks, plombir is luxuriously rich. The higher fat content also means it melts more slowly, with a creamier mouthfeel. Although it's similar to ice cream, plombir was derived from a slightly different culinary route—folded and molded instead of churned, which means you can make this sweetly simple version without an ice cream maker.

YIELDS ABOUT 6 CUPS

1 large egg

3 large egg yolks

½ cup granulated sugar, divided

1 vanilla bean

2 cups heavy cream

Black currant tea milk caramel (page 316) and chopped toasted hazelnuts for serving (optional)

Prepare a mold for your plombir: Line a standard loaf pan or small casserole dish with parchment or smoothed-down plastic wrap, spread over the bottom and overhanging the sides. You can also use silicone baking molds or silicone ice cube trays, which allow the plombir to be easily popped out after freezing. Set the mold(s) aside.

Place a metal or glass mixing bowl atop a saucepan with a few inches of water to create a double boiler (there should be a few inches between the surface of the water and the bottom of the bowl). Whisk together the egg, yolks, and ¼ cup of the sugar. Scrape the seeds from the vanilla bean and add them, along with the pod.

Bring the water underneath your bowl to a simmer, and, using a hand mixer (or a whisk and a very strong arm), whisk the mixture as it heats. When the mixture has become thickened and pale (about 5 minutes), remove the bowl from the pan, and continue to whisk the mixture as it cools to room temperature.

(continued page 316)

CONTINUED
*plombir with black currant
tea milk caramel*

In a separate bowl, beat the cream, gradually adding the remaining ¼ cup sugar, until it forms medium-stiff peaks.

Gently fold the cream mixture into the egg mixture so that the two elements are well incorporated, without any streaks, but taking care not to deflate. Pour the plombir mixture into your prepared mold(s), cover, and freeze at least 4 hours or overnight.

To serve, unmold and slice into individual portions. Serve the plombir as is, or with black currant tea milk caramel and chopped toasted hazelnuts.

BLACK CURRANT TEA MILK CARAMEL

Back in the Soviet Union, milk caramel (known as *dulce de leche* in Spanish-speaking countries) is used prolifically. Beyond filling cookies (or grandchildren's mouths), it's also common to simply have a few spoonfuls alongside your tea. This sauce is inspired by that common pairing. Because it's addictively good and so damn easy to make, it might replace chocolate sauce as your go-to ice cream topping.

YIELDS ABOUT 1½ CUPS

3 black currant black tea bags (if black currant tea isn't available, try another fruity black tea or Earl Grey)

¾ cup boiling water

¾ cup milk caramel (available in Russian grocery stores) or dulce de leche (available in Latin markets), or make your own (page 363)

Place the tea bags in a cup, pour the boiling water over them, and steep. Remove the tea bags, and stir the tea into the milk caramel, blending until smooth. Let cool (it will thicken slightly as it cools), and serve.

CHOCOLATE KOLBASA

шоколадная колбаса

✦ ✦ ✦

The original versions of this no-bake confection appear to have been the result of ingenuity in the face of food shortages, using cocoa powder and butter to create a complex, fudgy treat seemingly out of nothing. I, of course, couldn't leave it be, and added some velvety dark chocolate to amplify the cocoa—because why not?

At Kachka, we use broken oreshki (page 320) as the cookie portion, but you can use any type of shortbread or tea cookies (and if they're stale, just give them a quick toast in the oven to revive them).

YIELDS 2 "LOGS" OF KOLBASA

2 generous cups broken cookies

⅔ cup toasted hazelnuts, chopped until they're fairly fine but still have some texture

1 stick (½ cup) unsalted butter

6 ounces sweetened condensed milk (leftover milk keeps for a while in the refrigerator, and is delicious stirred into your morning tea or coffee)

½ cup bittersweet chocolate chips or chopped chocolate (you're looking for something around 72%, as semisweet would be a bit too sweet)

1 tablespoon cocoa powder

1 teaspoon kosher salt

¼ cup powdered sugar

Crush the cookies so that the bits are no larger than ½ inch. Place in a large bowl, and add the hazelnuts.

In a saucepan, gently melt the butter over low heat, then whisk in the sweetened condensed milk. Add the chocolate, cocoa powder, and salt, and whisk until the chocolate has melted and the mixture is smooth.

Scrape the chocolate into the bowl with the chocolate cookie pieces. Mix everything together and let sit for 15 minutes—it will firm up enough to hold its shape as the chocolate cools.

Lay two sheets of foil on the countertop, and top each with a sheet of waxed paper. Scrape half of the mixture onto one of the sheets of waxed paper, and then roll the mixture up in the waxed paper, twisting the ends, to make a sausage-like log. Roll in the foil to secure. Repeat with the remaining mixture. The logs will be fairly soft.

Place the logs in the refrigerator. After 1 hour, check if the logs have flattened at all. Roll them around to restore them to an even cylinder. Return to the fridge another 1 to 2 hours to fully set.

To serve, remove the logs from the refrigerator, peel off the paper, and sprinkle them with the powdered sugar. Cut into ¼-inch slices, and serve like cookies. Wrapped logs will keep in the fridge for up to 1 week, though they're best the first few days.

ORESHKI
(PAGE 320)

ZEPHYR
(PAGE 331)

CHOCOLATE
KOLBASA
(PAGE 318)

ORESHKI

орешки

＋ ＋ ＋

My cousin Marina was an incredibly finicky eater as a child—so finicky that even downing some cookies was considered a victory. So when she fell in love with oreshki—caramel-filled butter cookies—my aunt Asya desperately searched for an *oreshnitsa*, the walnut-shaped mold used to make the oreshki shells. And, as always happened in the shortage-ridden Soviet Union, she couldn't find them anywhere. But she didn't let that stop her.

Because shortages existed for nearly every product, industrious citizens took matters into their own hands in whichever way they could. My grandfather was a screen printer, making everything from banners to dish towels—and so he smuggled out linens for trade. What could my father's physics lab possibly have of value? The pure alcohol used in cleaning slides and laboratory reactions, which was constantly disappearing. And my engineer uncle directed a crew making hydraulics for trucks—but, wanting to make his little oreshki-loving niece Marina happy, he directed the line to do a custom production of an oreshnitsa mold.

I have since inherited the resulting one-off oreshnitsa, and it is one of my most prized kitchen possessions—one I still use to make oreshki at home. Luckily, if you don't have an uncle running a machine shop, these days you can easily purchase an oreshnitsa—either the old molds like my uncle Boris made, or a modern electric version. As my cousin Marina will attest, it's totally worth the investment.

YIELDS ABOUT 5 DOZEN FILLED COOKIES

COOKIES:

1 stick (½ cup) unsalted butter (high-fat European butter yields the best texture), softened to room temperature

½ cup granulated sugar

2 large eggs

1 tablespoon white vinegar

1 teaspoon vanilla extract

¼ teaspoon baking soda

3 cups (380 grams) all-purpose flour

If you have an electric oreshnitsa, plug it in and let it come to temperature. If you're using a simple metal mold, heat it over medium heat. The dough is plenty buttery, so no need to grease the molds.

In a stand mixer fitted with a paddle attachment (or using a large bowl and an egg beater), cream together the butter and sugar until light and fluffy. Add the eggs, mixing until well incorporated, then stir in the vinegar, vanilla, and baking soda. Stir in the flour until just combined.

Scoop off about a ½-inch lump of dough, using a small cookie scoop or a spoon, and use your hands to roll it into a rough ball. The exact size will vary depending upon the size of the molds—put a sample ball of dough into the mold and press it to see. You want the dough to fully cover the entire mold when pressed, without too much dough being forced out the sides (the dough will expand a bit upon cooking as well). When you've figured out the right dough ball size, roll out enough balls to fill your mold, put them in the wells, and press the mold shut. Cook

FILLING:

1 13.4-ounce can milk caramel (available in grocery stores, substitute dulce de leche) or make your own (page 363)

¼ cup shelled walnuts, toasted and finely chopped

½ teaspoon kosher salt

½ teaspoon chicory concentrate syrup, or 1 teaspoon brewed espresso (optional, but gives a nicely complex, bitter note)

until golden brown and crisp, about 7 minutes. No need to flip the mold during cooking (and, in fact, don't, unless you fancy molten butter running out all over your kitchen).

When the cookies are golden brown, flip them out of the molds, and trim off any overhang. Repeat with the remaining dough. Any trim or incomplete/broken shells can be used for chocolate kolbasa (page 318). Cookie shells can be made 1 or 2 days in advance and stored in a covered container.

Make the filling: In a medium bowl, mix together all of the filling ingredients to form a smooth, nut-studded sweet caramel. The filling can also be made a few days in advance, but don't fill the cookies until the day you intend to serve them.

To finish the cookies: Scoop or pipe a bit of filling into a cookie shell, so that it mounds up slightly. Top with another cookie. Repeat with the remaining shells and filling, and serve. And if you're a bit overgenerous and run out of filling before you run out of shells, a chocolate-hazelnut spread like Nutella makes for an inauthentic-yet-delicious filling alternative.

(See photograph on page 319)

THREE–LAYER CONDENSED MILK CAKE

торт "три коржа"

✦ ✦ ✦

For much of my childhood, this was my mom's go-to cake. Each sponge cake layer is mixed with a different ingredient (poppy seed, prunes, walnuts), and then basted with sweetened condensed milk and left to soak. She just called it "three-layer cake"—so I pressed her for its actual name:

"It can't really just be called that. Where did you get it from?"

"From Lilya Gofman."

"So call Lilya."

"Well, maybe it wasn't Lilya . . ."

"But maybe it was, just ask her."

"No . . . Wait, this is not her handwriting."

"Okay, but it must have a name. Can't dad just Yandex it?"

My dad (the obstinate pessimist) chimes in: "Bonnie, you don't understand—we didn't have names for these things. I will not find it."

I roll my eyes. "Just try Yandex."

Yes. Yandex. It is Russia's answer to Google—but much more awkward and clunky. And it yielded dozens of names for this cake that don't translate particularly well. Including the name, of course, "Three-Layer Cake."

YIELDS 1 THREE-LAYER LOAF

SOAKING LIQUID:

2 14-ounce cans sweetened condensed milk

2 sticks (1 cup) unsalted butter, softened to room temperature

Preheat the oven to 350°F.

Butter and flour a 9-x-5-inch loaf pan (a straight-sided pan is easiest for creating a stackable cake, but if you have a sloped pan you can just trim the cake's sides). Line the pan with parchment—this serves as a sort of gurney to lift out the layers, so leave some overhang.

In the bowl of a stand mixer fitted with a paddle attachment, or large bowl with a hand mixer, stir together the sweetened condensed milk and butter until combined. Set aside.

(continued page 324)

CONTINUED
three-layer condensed milk cake

FOR EACH OF THE
THREE LAYERS:

Heaping ¾ cup (100 grams) all-purpose flour

2 teaspoons potato starch

1 teaspoon baking powder

¼ teaspoon baking soda

½ cup (100 grams) granulated sugar

1 large egg

½ cup (100 grams) sour cream

ADD-INS:

First layer: 1 cup (100 grams) walnuts, chopped into ¼-inch pieces

Second layer: ⅓ cup poppy seeds (I like to blanch these in a few changes of boiling water to soften them and leach out any bitterness or off flavors)

Third layer: 1 cup (150 grams) prunes, cut into ¼-inch pieces

In a small bowl, whisk together the flour, potato starch, baking powder, and baking soda. Set aside.

In the bowl of a stand mixer fitted with a paddle attachment or bowl, cream together the sugar and egg for a few minutes, until the mixture is light and fluffy. Add the sour cream, mix until combined, and then fold in the flour mixture until it's just combined. Gently mix in your add-in (the walnuts, poppy seeds, or prunes). Pour into the pan, place in the oven, and bake until a tester comes out clean, about 20 minutes.

While the cake bakes, line a rimmed baking sheet with waxed paper or parchment that's at least 6 inches longer than your loaf.

When the cake layer has baked, remove it from the oven, and run a knife around the edge to loosen it if needed. Using the parchment, flip the cake out onto your waiting tray (return the parchment to the loaf pan). Pour one-third of the soaking liquid over the top of the warm cake, spreading it around with a spoon so that it can soak in everywhere.

While the first layer sits in its milky bath, prepare the second layer—repeat the above process, but with a different add-in.

While the second layer is baking, sit down next to your first layer with a good book, and spoon up any soaking liquid that seeps out, ladling it back over the top and sides. By the time the second layer has finished baking, most of the liquid will have been absorbed. When the second layer has baked, run a knife around the edge to loosen it, and carefully place the second layer on top of the first. Pour half of the remaining condensed milk mixture over the top, and spread it around. Make the final layer, and while it bakes repeat the spooning and soaking with the second layer. Repeat with the final layer.

When you've finished all of the baking and soaking, let the cake sit overnight, so all that milky goodness has time to soak in (you can tent it with foil if needed). If any liquid seeps out overnight, you can gather it into a little dish to serve alongside. If your loaf pan has sloped sides, take a sharp serrated knife and trim off the edges to neaten everything up (this isn't necessary, but looks nice and has the added benefit of giving you some delicious end bits to eat while nobody's looking). Cut into slices and serve.

SIRNIKI WITH RASPBERRY KISSEL

сырники

✤ ✤ ✤

Back in the Soviet era, *sirniki* were a standard-issue kindergarten snack—alongside a glass of *kissel*. Russian adults raised on this regimen are downright giddy at seeing them on the Kachka menu.

This is compounded by the fact that babushkas are hardwired to administer sirniki to grandchildren. They can't help themselves. In fact, my mother sincerely thinks that my son's dislike of all things dairy is because he hasn't been fed enough of these farmer's cheese pancakes (she outwardly blames herself, but I know this game of Soviet Jewish motherly guilt—she is actually indirectly blaming me—and, as with most things that I won't openly admit to her, she's most likely right).

YIELDS 18 SIRNIKI, 4 TO 6 SERVINGS

SIRNIKI BATTER:

½ cup plain kefir

½ pound tvorog (also labeled farmer's cheese—page 369)

1 large egg

Heaping ⅓ cup all-purpose flour

2 tablespoons granulated sugar

1 vanilla bean

TO FINISH:

Unsalted butter

Smetana (page 359) or crème fraîche

Raspberry kissel (page 326)—you can also use jam or berry compote for a simpler option)

Turbinado sugar (optional—adds a nice little textural element)

Put the kefir, tvorog, egg, flour, and sugar in a blender. Scrape the seeds from the vanilla bean and add them (discard the pod). Blend for 2 to 3 minutes, until the mixture is as smooth as you can get it. Let the batter rest for at least 1 hour, and up to 3 days (if it'll be much longer than 1 hour, refrigerate, otherwise you can leave it at room temperature). The result will be similar to a thick pancake batter.

When you're ready to cook, let the batter come to room temperature if you've refrigerated it, and heat a skillet over medium heat. Melt a generous pat of butter in your skillet, and pour out 3-inch pancakes (about 2 tablespoons of batter each). Cook until the bottom is golden brown, and the top begins to dry out, then flip and cook until golden on the other side, about 2 minutes per side. Repeat with remaining batter, adjusting the heat and adding more butter as needed.

Serve hot from the skillet, with a dollop of smetana, a puddle of kissel, and a sprinkling of turbinado sugar if desired.

(continued page 326)

RASPBERRY KISSEL

Kissel is a loosely set fruit dessert, a standard Soviet-era sweet found everywhere from state cafeterias to army rations. Set with potato starch, kissel has a consistency ranging from gelatin-like firm to pourable-sauce soft. At Kachka we split the difference, honoring the classic sirniki and kissel combo by making a lightly gelled sauce.

YIELDS ¾ CUP

1 cup fresh raspberries

1 cup water

2 teaspoons potato starch dissolved in 2 teaspoons warm water

Combine the raspberries and the water in a small saucepan. Bring the mixture to a boil over high heat, then reduce the heat until it's just high enough to maintain a simmer. Cook the berries for 10 minutes, and then mash them with a fork or potato masher to release more flavor. Simmer for another 10 minutes after mashing, then remove from the heat.

Strain the raspberry liquid through a fine-mesh strainer (lined with a coffee filter, if you want a nice clear kissel) into a heatproof bowl. Let the mixture drip through (for 2 hours if using a coffee filter, less time for a strainer), giving it a gentle stir halfway through to release more juice.

When the raspberry mixture has drained, discard the solids, and measure out ¾ cup of the liquid into a small saucepan. Bring the liquid to a boil over a high heat. Stream the potato starch–water slurry into the saucepan, whisking continuously until the mixture comes to a boil and thickens. Remove from the heat, and chill completely. Serve cold.

ZEPHYR

зефир

✛ ✛ ✛

These pink-and-white swirled confections can be found in every Russian grocery store. They look like meringues, but *zephyr* are actually more akin to an apple marshmallow (likely adapted from *pastila*, Russia's version of pâte de fruit). I remember methodically going through the display, giving each one a squeeze in hopes of finding the rare freshly imported batch that still had a little give in the center. This was a bit of a unicorn—most of the time, the zephyr were hopelessly dry from their travels.

These days, manufacturers have overcorrected for their stale wares—you flat-out can't purchase zephyr without all forms of creepy additives. If you want the real experience, you're just gonna have to roll up your sleeves and make 'em.

YIELDS ABOUT 60 SANDWICHED ZEPHYR

SYRUP:

⅔ cup water

2 tablespoons (14 grams) agar powder*

2¼ cups (450 grams) granulated sugar

BASE:

1 cup thick apple puree (I toss whole apples in a 325°F oven for 45 minutes and then remove the skin and scrape out the puree after they've cooked down, but you can use any thick commercial sauce)

2 large egg whites

1¼ cups (250 grams) granulated sugar

1 teaspoon vanilla extract

2 tablespoons beet juice (optional— include it if you're nostalgic for pink zephyr)

TO FINISH:

Powdered sugar

Grab a pastry bag with a rosette tip (or a plastic bag with one corner snipped off, if you don't have one), and line a few rimmed baking sheets with parchment or Silpat liners. Set aside.

Pour the water in a small saucepan, sprinkle in the agar, and then let the mixture sit at room temperature for 15 minutes to soften and bloom. Add the sugar, and bring to a boil over high heat until the mixture reaches 225° to 235°F (if you dribble some of it off a spoon, it'll form a thin thread).

While the syrup is heating, prepare the base: In the bowl of a stand mixer fitted with a whisk attachment, whisk the apple puree and egg whites on high for 4 to 5 minutes (the mixture will become fluffy). With the mixer running, slowly add the sugar and the vanilla, and whisk on high for 5 more minutes.

(continued page 332)

* Available at health food stores or Asian markets. I measured using Eden Foods, a reliable and widely available brand. Agar also comes in flakes—if using this form, make sure to measure by weight instead of volume, and give it an extra half hour to soften and bloom.

When the base is ready and the syrup is hot, with the mixer running on high, slowly pour the hot syrup into the bowl (aim to hit the side of the bowl just above the egg, to avoid too much spattering). Continue beating until the bowl cools to room temperature, another few minutes. If using, stream in the beet juice at this point.

When the mixture has cooled, transfer it into your pastry bag. Pipe out small rosettes, about 1½ inches in diameter (or make them bigger if you like). If you're not sure if the mixture is cool enough, pipe out one rosette, and wait a few minutes—if it slumps at all, wait a bit longer for your mixture to cool more. When you've piped out all of the zephyr, dust with powdered sugar, and allow to dry, uncovered, overnight.

The next day, take 2 zephyr off of the parchment, and stick them together, base-to-base (they should stick easily). Repeat with remaining zephyr. Store in an airtight container for up to 1 week.

STRAWBERRIES AND SMETANA

клубника со сметаной

✦ ✦ ✦

When my parents immigrated in 1980, my mother didn't know any English. So she figured, why not have another child, since she wouldn't be able to find a job anyway? This is the very practical way in which I came to be. And once I was born the following year, she started watching other immigrants' kids, too—again, very efficient use of resources. One of her very first charges was Rosa Gordon, who became my close childhood friend. I loved playing at Rosa's house, and I especially loved the snack her mother would feed us: strawberries sprinkled with sugar and mixed with sour cream. Back in Belarus, this would have been made with *zemlyanika*—tiny, fragrant wild strawberries that cover the forest floor in early summer.

This recipe is heavily inspired by that midday snack at Rosa's—with a bit of influence from the classic American strawberry shortcake. Tangy cultured smetana, and strawberries that get a boozy kick from a little bubbly (I use Sovetskoye Shampanskoye, but anything you'd use in a mimosa would work). The cake here is a welcome addition, but highly optional if you're looking for a quick no-bake variation. What's not optional is the use of locally picked, super-ripe fruit. As a good Oregonian, I am required to preach the gospel of in-season berries!

SERVES 8

STRAWBERRIES:

2 pints strawberries (if it's past strawberry season, feel free to substitute raspberries, blackberries, or whatever berry is at its peak)

2 to 4 tablespoons granulated sugar

½ cup off-dry sparkling wine

CAKE:

Unsalted butter for greasing

½ cup (65 grams) pastry flour

¼ cup plus 2 tablespoons (75 grams) granulated sugar

½ teaspoon baking powder

¼ teaspoon coarse kosher salt

2 tablespoons neutral oil (refined sunflower or canola)

2 large eggs, separated

3 tablespoons water

Zest of ½ lemon

½ teaspoon vanilla extract

⅛ teaspoon cream of tartar

Wash and hull the strawberries, and halve or quarter them (depending on how large they are). Sprinkle over the berries enough sugar to sweeten them and make the juices come out—it'll vary depending on how sweet your berries are. Let them sit and get nice and juicy while you prepare the cake.

To make the cake: Preheat the oven to 325°F. Line an 8-inch-square pan with parchment. Butter and flour the sides (if the pan is nonstick, you can skip this step), and set aside.

In a large bowl, whisk together the flour, sugar, baking powder, and salt. In a separate bowl, whisk together the oil, egg yolks (reserve the whites— you'll need them soon), water, lemon zest, and vanilla until well combined. Fold this wet mixture into the flour mixture until *just* combined.

In the bowl of a stand mixer fitted with a whisk attachment (or a large bowl with a hand mixer), beat the reserved egg whites until foamy. Add the cream of tartar, and continue to beat until stiff peaks form. Gently fold the egg whites into the batter, taking care not to deflate them, and pour the mixture into the prepared pan, smoothing out the

(continued page 335)

TO FINISH:

2 cups smetana (page 359) or
crème fraîche

2 tablespoons sugar

Turbinado sugar

top. Bake until the cake is set and a tester comes out clean, about 20 minutes.

While the cake is baking, pour the sparkling wine into the strawberries, give it a good stir, and set aside.

When the cake is done, place it on a rack to cool. Place the smetana in a large bowl (or the bowl of a stand mixer fitted with a whisk attachment), and with an electric beater or a whisk, beat it until it balloons up a bit, like whipped cream. Sweeten with sugar to taste (there's a lot of sweetness in the strawberries and cake, so you just need a little bit). Strain the strawberries, reserving the syrup.

To serve, cut the cake into 8 pieces. Take a square of cake, and dunk it halfway down into the strained syrup (it'll soak up the sweet red boozy syrup, which is exactly what you want). Top each serving with ½ cup of the strawberries and a generous ¼ cup dollop of the whipped smetana, and sprinkle with the turbinado sugar.

POPPY SEED CHOCOLATE ROLL

маковый рулет с шоколадом

✦ ✦ ✦

It doesn't matter the time of day or the occasion—if someone calls to say they are stopping by, my mom mans the battle station for a full-on campaign. The towels in the bathroom need to be changed to the fancy ones with embroidery and shiny tassels. She swaps out the industrial black plastic kitchen trash can she actually uses for a shiny chrome one that gets put out when company comes by. The coat closet door must be closed, lest anyone SEE THAT WE WEAR COATS!

And if it's a quick impromptu visit—that in most homes would not warrant food at all—she puts on the kettle to treat the unsuspecting guest to "tea." Tea is code for a small feast of sweets and savories that could easily pass as dinner in most households. "Mom, the electrician is just coming by to discuss his quote—you do not need to feed him." She scoffs at this, and pushes my dad out the door to go pick up provisions—cured meats, smoked fish, nuts, fruits.

For these sorts of situations, my dad will undoubtedly return with a poppy-seed roll. It's the food equivalent of "I'm keeping my options open—let's keep it casual." It's equal parts dessert, breakfast, and late-night snack. Just the thing for next-door neighbors, book club—and, yes, electricians.

YIELDS 2 ROLLS

DOUGH:

½ cup milk, warmed to body temperature

½ cup granulated sugar

2½ teaspoons (1 package) active dry yeast

3 large eggs

4¼ cups (550 grams) all-purpose flour, plus more for rolling

1 teaspoon kosher salt

1½ sticks (¾ cup) butter, softened to room temperature

Pour the milk into the bowl of a stand mixer, then sprinkle in the sugar and yeast. Let the mixture sit for 10 minutes to allow the yeast to wake up.

Fit the mixer with a dough hook, and add the eggs, flour, and salt. Knead on a low speed, gradually increasing to medium, for a few minutes, until the dough is uniform (it'll be fairly stiff).

Add the butter, a few spoonfuls at a time, waiting until each addition is fully incorporated before adding more. After all of the butter has been worked into the dough, knead for an additional 10 minutes, scraping down the bowl as needed. The dough will become smooth and elastic.

Cover the bowl with plastic wrap, and place it in the refrigerator to rise overnight (if you need it the same day, you can let it rise at room temperature for 4 hours, but you'll get better flavor development if you give it a cold rise overnight).

POPPY-SEED FILLING:

¾ cup (100 grams) poppy seeds (poppy seeds are deliciously oily but can go rancid, so give a sniff to make sure they smell good)

¾ cup milk

½ cup granulated sugar

¼ stick (2 tablespoons) unsalted butter

1 teaspoon kosher salt

1 large egg

½ cup semisweet chocolate chips

3 tablespoons cocoa powder

TO FINISH:

1 large egg beaten with a splash of cream or milk to form a wash

¼ stick (2 tablespoons) unsalted butter, melted

Grind the poppy seeds in a coffee or spice grinder for 1 to 2 minutes, until the seeds are cracked and starting to form a paste. Set aside (if you don't have a spice grinder, you can skip this step, but grinding makes for a more cohesive filling).

Combine the milk, sugar, butter, and salt in a small saucepan, and heat it over medium heat until the mixture begins to steam. Crack the egg into a bowl, and then whisk in about ½ cup of the steaming liquid, pouring it in a thin stream and whisking constantly to keep the egg from setting. Pour this tempered mixture back into the pan, reduce the flame to medium-low, and whisk until the mixture thickens slightly and turns light yellow, 3 to 5 minutes. Remove from the heat, and add the chocolate chips. Let them sit for a few minutes to warm and soften in the residual heat, then whisk the mixture until it's smooth. Whisk in the cocoa powder, and then the ground poppy seeds. Let the mixture cool slightly, and then refrigerate until cooled fully (at least a few hours, and up to 1 week).

(continued page 338)

Remove the dough from the refrigerator about 2½ hours before you want to bake. Take the filling out of the refrigerator at the same time. Line two rimmed baking sheets with parchment.

After 2 hours, lightly flour a countertop. Roll half the dough into a 12-by-8-inch rectangle, landscape-style. Leave the other half of the dough covered in the bowl. If the dough springs back and fights you, roll it as best you can, spread a dish towel over it to keep it moist, then let it sit for about 5 minutes to relax and try again. Once the dough is rolled out, brush the long edge farthest from you with egg wash—just the last inch or so. Take half of the filling, and spread it in an even layer over the dough (except for the far edge with the egg wash).

Starting at the side closest to you, snugly roll up the dough into a thin log. Pinch both ends, torpedo style, and then tuck them under the roll. Transfer the roll to a prepared baking sheet. Repeat with the remaining dough and filling. Set aside the remaining egg wash. Preheat the oven to 375°F, and let the rolls sit out for 20 minutes to proof while the oven comes to temperature.*

When the oven has heated and the rolls have softened a bit, take a sharp knife. Cut diagonal slits about halfway through each roll, every 2 to 3 inches (these will let the rolls rise in the oven without bursting, plus it looks lovely). Brush the rolls with the reserved egg wash.

Bake the rolls for 30 minutes, until golden brown. When done, brush the just-baked cakes with melted butter, and transfer them to a wire rack. Let cool for about 1 hour before serving, to allow the cake to finish setting. Like any enriched bread, these are best the day they're made. Although stale leftovers make for an *amazing* French toast or bread pudding.

---

* If you want to be really prepared for impromptu guests, stash one of these rolls, tightly wrapped, in the freezer before the final rise. Thaw fully, and bake as instructed.

APPLE PONCHIKI
WITH THYME SUGAR

яблочные пончики с чебрецовым сахаром

✛ ✛ ✛

My dad often laments that as a kid, he never got to eat apples unless they were on the verge of spoiling. His father would fill up the root cellar with fruit in the fall, and then release only the ones that were going bad for consumption. This was his strategy to have apples all winter long. When my dad would complain, my grandfather would remind him that it was better to have mediocre apples all winter than an empty cellar in January.

These days, we go apple picking every fall (our Portland-adopted very American ritual). And what does my dad do? He picks hundreds of pounds: the Soviet ingrained habit of getting while the getting's good. My chef de cuisine, Olga, came up with this recipe a few autumns ago, after my dad dropped off one of these epic apple hauls at Kachka.

YIELDS ABOUT 4 DOZEN FRITTERS

THYME SUGAR:

2 tablespoons fresh thyme leaves

1¼ cups granulated sugar

APPLE PONCHIKI:

4 cups (515 grams) all-purpose flour

1 tablespoon plus 1 teaspoon baking powder

¾ cup kefir

2 large eggs

1 cup granulated sugar

1 tablespoon vanilla extract

2 teaspoons kosher salt

1 teaspoon ground cinnamon

1 cup apple puree (page 331), or thick applesauce

1 cup tvorog (also labeled farmer's cheese—page 369)

3 small apples, peeled and cut into a ⅓-inch dice

High-heat oil for frying (I use canola or peanut)

Lingonberry jam (optional) for serving

MAKE THE THYME SUGAR:

In a large bowl, mix the thyme and sugar, pressing them together to bruise the thyme leaves and scent the sugar (you can use a muddler, a mortar and pestle, or a wooden spoon). Set aside.

MAKE THE PONCHIKI:

Whisk together the flour and baking powder, and set aside.

In a stand mixer fitted with a paddle attachment, or in a large bowl with a wooden spoon, beat together the kefir, eggs, sugar, vanilla, salt, cinnamon, and apple puree until smooth and combined. Add the flour mixture and the tvorog and mix for just a few seconds—you want the flour to be fully incorporated, but you should still see small lumps of tvorog. The batter will be fairly stiff. Fold in the diced apple.

Pour 3 inches of oil into a large, heavy pot (like a Dutch oven), and heat the oil to 360°F (a pinch of flour should sizzle, but not darken immediately). While the oil is heating, line a rimmed baking sheet sheet with paper towels.

(continued page 341)

When the oil is hot, using a small scoop or two spoons, scoop out 2-tablespoon lumps of dough to form fritters, and slide into the hot oil. Repeat until the pot is mostly full, leaving some room for them to expand. Fry, turning as needed, until the fritters are a light golden brown, about 4 to 5 minutes total. When the ponchiki are cooked, skim them out of the hot oil with a spider or slotted spoon, let them drain on the paper towels for about 30 seconds, and then tip them into the bowl with the sugar. Shake the ponchiki around to coat them evenly with the sugar. Repeat with the remaining batter. Serve hot, with lingonberry jam if desired.

FARINA PARFAIT

мусс фруктовый из манки

✦ ✦ ✦

Farina mousse, known as *debesmanna*, is a classic Latvian dessert I was told I must try while traveling through the Baltics a few years ago. I had very low expectations—it is, after all, a mix of wheat porridge, sugar, and fruit, which sounds more like "gruel" than "mousse." But through some sort of kitchen alchemy, the grains and fruit transform into a light and fluffy confection.

This particular recipe is inspired by a version I had a few years ago at Lido, a hugely popular chain of Latvian cafeterias. My dad charmed someone in the kitchen into sharing their recipe, and, after quite a lot of unfluffy flops in the kitchen, I finally figured out how to make it work with local ingredients. At Kachka, we layer the mousse into a parfait with rosewater whipped cream, candied pumpernickel croutons, and sweet-yet-earthy rye tuiles. All of these components can be made far in advance, making it very easy to tackle—or do as the Latvians do, and try the mousse on its own, or with a simple splash of milk for breakfast.

FARINA MOUSSE:

1 pound fresh or frozen berries (black currants are my go-to, but you could also swap in lingonberries or gooseberries or any small, tart berry)

½ cup (100 grams) granulated sugar

¼ cup (45 grams) farina (finely ground Cream of Wheat style breakfast cereal)

Rosewater whipped cream (page 344)

Candied pumpernickel croutons (page 344)

Rye tuiles (page 345)

Place the berries in a saucepan, and splash in a few spoonfuls of water. Bring the mixture to a boil, and then reduce the heat until it's just high enough to maintain a healthy simmer. Cook until the fruit bursts and releases its juice, with few (if any) whole berries left, about 15 minutes. Pour the mixture through a fine-mesh strainer, keeping both the juice and the fruit.

Take the strained juice, and add enough water to measure 2 cups of liquid. Return this mixture to the saucepan. With a spatula, smush the remaining fruit through the strainer, leaving behind the seeds and skins, and passing the strained pulp through (you can also use a food mill if you prefer). Add the strained fruit puree to the saucepan as well, along with the sugar.

Bring the mixture to a boil, then reduce the heat until it's just high enough to maintain a healthy simmer. Cook for 5 to 7 minutes, until the mixture thickens slightly to a somewhat syrupy consistency. Slowly pour in the farina in a thin stream, whisking constantly for 3 minutes to keep it from clumping. Let the mixture simmer another 5 minutes, stirring occasionally. Remove from the heat and let cool slightly, then refrigerate until fully chilled (a few hours, or overnight—the mixture won't whip unless it's completely chilled, so make sure it's cold).

(continued page 344)

When the fruity farina mixture is cold, transfer it to the bowl of a stand mixer fitted with a whisk attachment. Whisk on the highest setting for 20 minutes. Over this time, the mixture will fluff up to nearly double its volume. After whipping, the mixture can be refrigerated for several days (and, surprisingly, will hold its volume quite well—it actually gets fluffier with time and is at its best the second day).

To serve: Grab eight glass ice cream dishes (if you don't have these, old-fashioned glasses also work well) or one large glass trifle dish. Lay down a scoop of mousse, about half as much rosewater whipped cream, and a handful of pumpernickel croutons in each glass. Repeat, then top with a couple of rye tuiles, and serve immediately.

ROSEWATER WHIPPED CREAM

YIELDS 2 CUPS

1 cup heavy cream

2 teaspoons granulated sugar

1 teaspoon rosewater

With a mixer or a whisk, whip the cream until it forms soft peaks, then whisk in the sugar and rosewater.

CANDIED PUMPERNICKEL CROUTONS

YIELDS 3 CUPS CROUTONS

½ stick (4 tablespoons) unsalted butter

3 cups ¼-inch cubes of pumpernickel bread (half a sleeve of canapé-sized slices, or a half-dozen pieces of thin-sliced bread)

3 tablespoons sugar

Heat a large skillet over medium-low heat, and melt the butter. When the butter starts to foam, add the bread cubes, tossing to make sure they're evenly coated. Cook, stirring regularly, until the bread cubes crisp—pumpernickel is a dark bread, so it's a bit hard to tell, but it should take a few minutes (adjust the heat as needed if they darken before becoming crisp). As the mixture is cooking, grab a rimmed baking sheet and line it with paper towels.

When the bread cubes have crisped, sprinkle on the sugar, and remove from the heat. Toss the mixture, letting the residual heat melt the sugar. When the sugar has melted and coated the bread cubes, tip them out onto the paper-towel-lined tray, spread them out, and let them cool completely. When the cubes are cool, transfer them into an airtight container.

RYE TUILES

YIELDS 16 TO 18 COOKIES

3 tablespoons granulated sugar

2 tablespoons rye flour

1 tablespoon unsalted butter, melted

In a small bowl, whisk together the sugar and rye flour, then whisk in the water, and then the melted butter. Cover the batter, and refrigerate until cold (about 1 hour).

Preheat the oven to 350°F, and line a couple of rimmed baking sheets with Silpat or parchment. Transfer the batter into a piping bag with a ½-inch tip, or a plastic bag with one corner snipped off. Pipe out quarter-sized rounds of batter (about 1 teaspoon or so per cookie—don't mound it high), leaving at least 3 inches between them. The cookies will spread significantly, so don't crowd them.

Transfer the cookies to your preheated oven, and bake for 10 to 12 minutes, until fully golden brown and lacy-thin. Let the cookies cool on the tray completely, then transfer to a sealed container (tuiles are delicate, so handle gently).

WHAT'S INSIDE THAT SHINY WRAPPER?

Walk into any Russian grocery store, and you'll see the same thing—an entire child-entrapping Technicolor wall of brightly wrapped candies. Sold in bulk and weighed at the counter, these are incredibly popular—every home has a candy dish filled with an assortment of household favorites. And, unsurprisingly, these sweets have a Soviet past.

After the revolution, the major candy factories were nationalized, given politicized names like Red October, and set to printing out candy labels emblazoned with heroes of the CCCP. The revolutionary rhetoric eventually toned down, but the state-run production had a clear impact—although recipes were codified and circulated, some factories did a better job than others, with variation in quality, wrapper details, and formulation among them (in addition to the subpar ingredients of the leaner Soviet times). It's as though each city had its own Snickers factory, putting its own slight tweak on an open-source recipe (and, of course, everyone is partial to their hometown's version). They have now all been privatized, but the iconic wrappers remain the same. Here's a guide to some of the most common sweets.

KOZINAKI/GOZINAKI *chopped walnuts (in Georgian)*
Chocolate-covered sesame candy
Georgian/Persian in origin. Can be any nut, seed, or a combination of both.

ROMASHKA *daisy*
Brandy-and-rum-flavored filling coated in chocolate
Candies inspired by the bucolic Soviet countryside.

KAROVKA *little cow*
Milk fudge candy with a gooey center (sometimes)
Fresher = softer—center might still be gooey.
Older = hard the whole way through.

RAKOVAYA SHEYKA *crayfish tail*
Hard candy with peanut-chocolate filling
Look for Roshen brand "Rachki"—usually fresher tasting.

BATONCHIK *little loaf*
Cocoa, peanut, and soy paste formed into batons
Candies like these stretched the ingredients—but are surprisingly tasty.

MISHKA KASOLAPY *clumsy bear*
Layers of alternating praline and wafers coated in chocolate. Soviet Kit-Kat!
Dates back to pre-Soviet times. Image on wrapper is based on a famous painting by Ivan Shishkin.

MISHKA NA SEVERYE _little bear in the north_

Almond praline and wafers coated in chocolate

First produced in Leningrad in the thirties. Production even continued through the siege!

HALVA _chocolate-covered sunflower paste_

Halva, in the Soviet Union, meant "sunflower seeds"

Makes an unusual savory-sweet flavor. This modern version, coated in chocolate, is a go-to.

KARA KUM _black sand_

Praline filling with wafer crumbs covered in chocolate

Created after the 1954 "kara kum canal" water pipeline project as a commemoration.

GRILYAZH _comes from the French word for "roasted" grillées_

Roasted nut brittle coated in chocolate

Different factories used different varieties of nuts. This is a family favorite—the one we always have in our house.

PTICHYE MOLOKO _bird's milk_

Vanilla soufflé covered in chocolate

Based on a Polish candy. Zotov, a Soviet-era food minister, tasted this in Czechoslovakia in 1976 and demanded candy makers in the USSR figure out how to make at once.

YUZHNAYA NOCH _southern night_

Chocolate-covered fruit jelly (pâte de fruit)

Look! A chocolate with something other than praline filling!

VASILKI _cornflowers_

"Crème brûlée"–flavored filling with roasted cashews and brandy, coated in chocolate

Cornflowers cover the Russian countryside.

ZOLOTOY KLUCHIK _golden key_

Caramel hard taffy

Caution: Notorious for ripping the crowns off people's teeth (as my dad can attest).

KRASNI MAK _red poppy_

Praline mixed with ground hazelnut and wafercrumbs coated with chocolate

Poppy flowers also cover the Russian countryside. You'd think there'd be poppy seeds in here. Nope!

ALONKA _it's a girl's name, loosely "Helen"_

Chocolate-coated wafers and praline

The original Alonka is a chocolate bar, but she comes in all shapes and sizes these days. The brand is so loved that the little girl is as well known as the Mona Lisa.

TEA CULTURE

If someone comes to the house for dinner but leaves before tea, they'd better have a damned good excuse. In Russia, tea isn't just a beverage—it's a ritual, the closing digestif of hospitality. Even though my mother now serves coffee, she hasn't shaken the shorthand, and still asks if we're ready for some tea. And a hot drink comes out after every meal, brought to the table with a little candy or a cookie or jam (for a three-times-a-day sugar hit that's the likely source of my sweet tooth). Even Russia's overnight trains, which these days serve microwaved meals on styrofoam plates with plastic utensils, still pour a proper cup of tea in a real glass, slipped into a fancy metal holder called a *podstakanik*.

But traditionally, when you're talking about Russian tea, you're talking about a ritual centered around a samovar. Samovars are essentially self-contained stoves, where a coal fire heats an enormous pot of water topped with a container of tea concentrate, called *zavarka*. The mass production underlines tea's role as a social beverage—this is no single-serving appliance. The samovar-heated water is served with the zavarka, allowing people to dilute a cup to taste. Over time, samovars eventually switched from actual fire to electricity. Even so, they're barely used anymore. But their legacy remains: although my parents never used a samovar after they came to America, all of their tea sets (of which they seem to have several) come with two teapots—one large and one small—to hold the water and zavarka to drink samovar-style. Even in households (like ours) that have since converted to the ease of tea bags, the samovar is still a prized possession on prominent display.

CHAPTER 11

PANTRY

бульоны и приправы

‡ ‡ ‡

You've probably heard that football is a game of inches. Well, so is cooking. Meaning that the difference between mediocre and life-changing food is in these tiny, seemingly insignificant steps. Seasoning with *just* the right amount of salt, using produce that is at its peak, and preparing ingredients with care. I know it's asking a lot to make your own broths, mayo—sometimes even butter! But these things are worlds apart from their store-bought counterparts, transforming dishes from good to phenomenal. Wondering why food from a simple kitchen in the old country can taste so amazing? This is why.

Now that I've preached a bit, I'll concede it's not always easy to carve out enough time to, let's say, make your own cultured dairy when you can just buy it in the store. So go ahead and do what you need to do—but do yourself a favor, and try making these little details from scratch at least once.

FANCY BROTH

бульон "фэнси"

✢ ✢ ✢

I am a hoarder of leftover braising liquids. My home chest freezer is always full of little bags of the red wine broth that bathed last week's beef cheeks, or the stock that spent four hours simmering with veal tongue (page 147). These are flavor powerhouses, imbued with meaty richness—capable of elevating all sorts of dishes. So when I witnessed my mother dumping out a WHOLE STOCKPOT full of braising liquid after making saltison (page 143), my head almost exploded. This is the woman who saves every single plastic bag from the grocery store, but she was pouring liquid gold down the drain. I stopped her midway, and rescued a few quarts.

A few weeks later, my husband and I were hosting a dinner party (testing future Kachka dishes on friends), and I needed a broth for serving pelmeni. So I defrosted the rescued saltison broth, along with other brothy remainders of beef tongue (page 183) and kholodetz (page 154), and mixed them all together. It was undeniably ahh-mazing. And because it would take making three different dishes and then mixing the broths from them and simmering them again with more stuff, we decided it was pretty darn fancy.

But for those who aren't making three types of long-cooked Russian meats in a single week, I've figured out a home cook version. Note that this recipe yields a lot—it's hard to do heads and shanks in half-measures—but it freezes beautifully, leaving quarts of this secret weapon to add some instant flavor boost to your home cooking any time you need.

YIELDS 12 TO 16 QUARTS

5 pounds veal feet (if unavailable, substitute veal bones)

8 pounds beef bones

1 yellow onion, sliced in half, but not peeled (remove any dirty roots)

Strained liquid from 1 recipe of saltison (page 143)

1 cup dried mushrooms, swished around in water to remove any lingering sand

3 cloves garlic, peeled

4 sprigs parsley

2 sprigs thyme

1 tablespoon whole black peppercorns

1 tablespoon yellow mustard seeds

Preheat the oven to 425°F. Place the veal feet and beef bones on two rimmed baking sheets, and roast until the bones turn golden, and your kitchen smells amazing, 30 to 40 minutes. Turn halfway through.

While the bones are roasting, heat a large stockpot over high heat. Add the onion, cut side down, and cook until it chars, about 5 minutes. Pour the saltison liquid into the stockpot and bring to a boil, then reduce the heat until it's just high enough to maintain a gentle simmer. Add the roasted veal feet and beef bones, along with all of the remaining ingredients.

Gently simmer, uncovered, for about 6 hours.

After simmering, strain the broth, reserving the liquid but discarding the solids. Chill the broth overnight, then remove and discard the fat from the top. Use anywhere you'd use meat stock—soups, pelmeni, etc.—or freeze for future use. Salt to taste before using.

MUSHROOM BROTH

грибной бульон

✤ ✤ ✤

It takes upwards of six or more hours to really get a flavorful meat broth or stock made. And there is a place for that. But when I don't have time (or when I'm cooking for vegetarians), I make mushroom broth. It's the base for a good porcini barley soup (page 215), or giving a bit of mushroom-on-mushroom oomph to your julienne (page 161), or making a killer vegetarian gravy. Most of the flavor comes from the dried mushrooms, but if you can save any mushroom scraps from other projects (tossed in the freezer until you're ready to use them), they'll make the results even richer.

YIELDS 2 QUARTS

½ yellow onion, sliced in half but not peeled (remove any dirty roots)

2 quarts water

½ cup dried mixed mushrooms, washed clean of any silt

4 dried porcini, washed clean of any silt

Mushroom stems and trim, if you've got them

1 sprig thyme

1 sprig parsley, leaves removed

2 teaspoons whole black peppercorns

Heat a medium-sized soup pot over high heat. Add the onion, cut side down, and cook until it chars, about 5 minutes. Pour in the water, then add the rest of the ingredients. Bring to a boil, then reduce the heat until it's just high enough to maintain a simmer. Simmer for about 1 hour (though an extra hour won't hurt). Add enough water to bring it back to the original level in the pot, then strain. Salt as needed, and season to taste.

GARLIC BROTH

чесночный бульон

✛ ✛ ✛

There is absolutely nothing Russian about this recipe—it's inspired by the delicious Provençal soup *aïgo bouido*. I use it all the time as a huge flavor boost anywhere you would use meat or vegetable stock. The long, gentle simmer melts away any harshness, leaving a roasted garlic sweetness. It's especially good paired with cheese vareniki (page 202), or for sipping alongside piroshki (page 173).

YIELDS 2 QUARTS

2 heads garlic, very well scrubbed and dried (roots intact, as long as they're very clean)

Olive oil

2 quarts water

Cut the garlic in half (around the equator). Heat a large pot over medium-low heat, and add a slick of oil. Add the halved garlic, cut sides down, and cook, stirring occasionally, until aromatic, about 3 minutes. Be careful to not burn the garlic.

When the garlic is aromatic, add the water. Bring the pot to a boil, then lower the heat until it's just high enough to maintain a gentle simmer. Simmer until the garlic is fully tender and sweet and the broth is infused with its flavor, about 1 hour. Strain and discard the garlic, add water if needed to replace any that's evaporated, and season to taste.

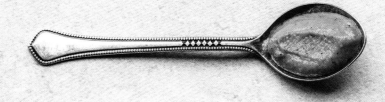

RUSSIAN MUSTARD
(PAGE 355)

TKEMALI
(PAGE 361)

SMETANA
(PAGE 359)

ADJIKA
(PAGE 358)

SMETANA
BUTTER
(PAGE 359)

PICKLED
MUSTARD
SEEDS
(PAGE 356)

RUSSIAN MUSTARD

русская горчица

✤ ✤ ✤

Russian mustard is always on my table, whether for stirring into your borsch (I can't eat a bowl without it) or cutting through the fat of a nice salami. It's closer to those Chinese mustard packets than a standard dijon or ballpark version, and with good reason—instead of yellow mustard seed, Russian mustard powder comes from the same hotter brown mustard seeds. It's an entirely different plant, with seeds that have a sharper, horseradishy bite.

I can slather on a good swipe, but my husband will just barely let it kiss the bread (he's gradually building up his tolerance, but servers always give new diners a fair warning). Behind the sting, there's a nice round flavor from the allspice, garlic, and bay leaves. This will keep in the refrigerator for a while, and temper slightly as it sits—the fresher, the spicier.

YIELDS ABOUT 2 CUPS

1¼ cups water

3 tablespoons granulated sugar

2 teaspoons kosher salt. plus more as needed

½ cup white vinegar

1½ teaspoons allspice berries

4 fresh bay leaves, or 2 dried

4 cloves garlic, peeled and roughly chopped

1½ cups brown mustard powder (page 367)

Pour the water, sugar, and salt into a pot. Bring to a boil, stirring to dissolve, then remove from the heat and let the mixture cool to room temperature.

While the liquid is cooling, pour the vinegar into a nonreactive container, then add the allspice berries, bay leaves, and garlic. Set the mixture aside overnight, covered, to steep.

When your water-sugar-salt mixture has cooled, whisk in the mustard (gradually, so there are no lumps), forming a thick mixture. Set out at room temperature overnight, covered, to rehydrate.

The next day, uncover the mustard and vinegar containers (the built-up mustard fumes are no joke, so let the container breathe for a minute or two before you take a whiff, unless you want to be reduced to tears). Take a strainer, and pour the vinegar through it into the mustard mixture. Discard the allspice berries, bay leaves, and garlic caught in the strainer, and whisk the vinegar into the mustard. Add additional water, if needed, to create a smooth, spreadable mustard consistency (different mustard powders will vary in how much water they absorb). Season to taste with additional salt if needed. Store in the refrigerator.

PICKLED MUSTARD SEEDS

маринованные семена горчицы

✣ ✣ ✣

This recipe is my adaptation of something I learned working at Craft, a restaurant in New York City. For a young cook it was a huge *aha* moment to realize that I could actually eat these seeds whole once they cooked a bit. I love having a jar of them in my fridge to throw into all sorts of dishes—from smoked trout salad (page 141) to a cabbage pirog (page 165)—adding more texture than just the average swipe of mustard (and, as they are pickled, they'll keep for quite a while). Mix them with a bit of jam for a sort of cheater mostarda, add a few tablespoons into potato salad, or throw them into a vinaigrette.

YIELDS ABOUT 1½ CUPS

¾ cup water

¾ cup apple cider vinegar

½ cup yellow mustard seeds

¼ cup granulated sugar

2 teaspoons kosher salt

Place all ingredients in a saucepan, and bring to a boil. Be sure to run the fan—hot vinegar is, um, *aromatic*. Reduce the heat until it's just high enough to maintain a gentle simmer, and cook until the liquid is absorbed and the mustard seeds have swelled and softened, about 1 hour.

To make pickled raisins for the cabbage pirog (page 165): Follow the instructions above. When the mustard seeds are done, add ½ cup golden raisins to the saucepan, along with an additional ¼ cup water. Bring to a boil, then turn off the heat, letting the raisins cool and swell in the residual heat, absorbing the pickled flavors. Store in the refrigerator.

MAYONNAISE

майонез

It is impossible to overstate the Russian obsession with *mayonnaise*. The Soviet state really pushed mayo, and was beyond successful—you find it *everywhere*. It's even used à la frosting, piped into florets and flourishes on unassuming salads and whole fish presentations (in a fashion you may have thought disappeared in the 1970s).

As a proper American kid, I hated the stuff myself. It didn't really matter whether it was the beloved Provansal style of the Soviet era or Hellmann's—it was all the same gloppy white stuff to me. It wasn't until I went to culinary school that I had a revelation—mayo doesn't have to be this terrifying, jiggly refrigerator staple. It's just a sauce. Yolks, oil, water, and a bit of lemon. Make mayo yourself (spoiler alert: it's surprisingly easy), and it's like meeting a whole new condiment—one you might be inspired to consume in near-Russian amounts.

YIELDS ABOUT 2 CUPS

2 large egg yolks (if you're worried about consuming raw eggs, you can use pasteurized)

1 tablespoon dijon mustard

Juice of ½ lemon

Kosher salt

2 cups refined sunflower oil (or any fresh, high-quality neutral oil)

Up to ½ cup water

Grab a large bowl (glass or stainless steel), and place it on a damp towel to keep it still as you whisk, whisk, whisk. Whisk together the yolks, mustard, lemon juice, and a good pinch of salt. Slowly whisk in the oil—a few drops at first (I find a squeeze bottle particularly handy for this), and then a bit more of a stream once things come together. If the mixture tightens up too much before you've added all the oil, add some water (a spoonful or two at a time) to loosen it, up to ½ cup (you likely won't need that much). Keep adding oil (and water, if needed) until it's all incorporated. Taste and add salt as needed.

Mayonnaise is best used the same day it is made, but can be kept for 2 days in the refrigerator (longer if using pasteurized eggs).

PARSLEY MAYONNAISE

майонез с петрушкой

YIELDS ABOUT ¾ CUP

½ cup mayonnaise

¼ cup parsley, finely minced

1 small clove garlic, finely minced

1 tablespoon fresh lemon juice

In a bowl or food processor, mix together all of the ingredients until combined.

ADJIKA

аджика

✦ ✦ ✦

Every spice seller in the Moscow market has their own adjika. This pepper paste is rich, layered, and addictive—earthy and bright and almost unplaceable, with spices that evoke both Eastern Europe and the Middle East, all bound with a gentle burn of chiles. This version, with the uncommon addition of walnuts, comes from a cousin's wife from Abkhazia, the disputed territory on the eastern coast of the Black Sea rumored to be adjika's birthplace.

The recipe here will yield a thick, intense paste for maximum versatility. Feel free to dilute with water for more of a sauce when needed. Use adjika anywhere you would use a hot sauce—on Russian and Georgian dishes, sure (especially anything hot off the mangal, see chapter 7), but you can also spread a swipe across your sandwich bread, mix it with mayo and dollop on a burger, jazz up your hummus with it—you get the idea.

YIELDS ¾ CUP

2 teaspoons whole coriander seeds

2 teaspoons whole fenugreek seeds (if you are just back from Georgia and have a stash of blue fenugreek, you can throw it in as well, added later with the turmeric)

2 teaspoons whole dill seeds

2 teaspoons whole cumin seeds

¼ cup coarsely chopped walnuts

2 tablespoons coarsely chopped parsley leaves

2 tablespoons coarsely chopped cilantro leaves

6 tablespoons tomato paste

3 tablespoons Turkish hot pepper paste (you can substitute harissa, but you might want to start with a smaller amount, as heat levels can vary)

2 tablespoons fresh lemon juice

2 tablespoons olive oil

2 teaspoons ground turmeric

2 teaspoons kosher salt

1 clove garlic

Heat a small saucepan over medium heat. Add the coriander, fenugreek, dill, and cumin seeds, and toast, stirring occasionally, until fragrant, about 2 minutes. Transfer to a spice grinder and grind to a fine powder.

Place the ground spices and remaining ingredients in a food processor and blend, scraping down occasionally if needed, until the mixture is smooth. Store in the refrigerator.

SMETANA

смета́на

✦ ✦ ✦

Obligatory Dairy Nerd Rant: *Smetana* means "sour cream." But all too often, commercially produced so-called sour cream in the United States is actually not sour cream! It's made with a fraction of the butterfat that it needs, and is not cultured (the "sour" in sour cream). Instead, thickeners and acids are added to give an approximation of the body and tartness that would come naturally if it were truly cultured full cream.

Where I come from, smetana is kind of a big deal. It's the mother sauce of Mother Russia. Used as a braising liquid, a salad dressing, rubbed on roasts, mixed into soups—you name it. At Kachka, we go through gallons of the stuff every week. Luckily, making it yourself takes nothing more than two ingredients and a couple of days of waiting.

YIELDS 1 QUART

1 quart heavy cream

⅛ teaspoon 901 Buttermilk & Sour Cream Culture,* or ¼ cup buttermilk

Bring the heavy cream to room temperature, and mix it with the culture. Let the mixture sit out at room temperature, loosely covered, for 12 hours. Transfer the container to the refrigerator for 12 hours, then return to room temperature to finish, 10 to 18 hours, depending upon the temperature—it's done when it has thickened. Store in the refrigerator.

SMETANA BUTTER

ма́сло на смета́не

If you've ever overwhipped cream before, then you've basically made butter—it's just that easy. Using smetana instead of cream adds a tangy complexity to butter's richness that's totally addictive. Spread it thickly on your preferred bread (brown or otherwise) for a life's-simple-pleasures kind of moment.

YIELDS ABOUT 2 CUPS

Smetana (above)

Kosher salt

To churn this into deliciously rich cultured butter, use smetana that has been properly chilled in the refrigerator overnight. Transfer the smetana to the bowl of a stand mixer fitted with a whisk attachment, and use a splash guard if you've got one (or else be prepared for a bit of spatter). Whisk on high speed, past the point of whipped cream, until the mixture clumps around the whisk, and a pool of liquid separates out at the bottom. You can't overmix, so don't hold back.

* Available online at www.getculture.com

(continued page 360)

CONTINUED
smetana butter

Strain off the liquid (which is actual buttermilk) through a fine-mesh strainer. Transfer the curds to a bowl, add cold water to cover, and knead the mixture until it comes together and the additional buttermilk comes out—this creates a more refrigerator-stable no-spatter product, but if you're just using it as is/right away you can skip this step. Transfer the butter mass to a paper towel and blot any excess liquid. Sprinkle salt all over and knead (or mix in a bowl with a spoon) to incorporate.

TKEMALI

ткемали

Tkemali is the ketchup of the Georgian cookout. Traditionally, it's made with a Georgian variety of fresh sour plums, but since they're nearly impossible to find, I started using dried (and have come to even prefer their concentrated flavor). Commercial tkemali can be a bit heavy-handed with the seasonings, so I scale it back a bit—if you're making a plum sauce, let the plums shine through. Pair with any of the rich and smoky meats that come off the mangal (chapter 7).

YIELDS ABOUT 2½ CUPS

1 pound (about 3 cups) dried sour plums (these dark yellow plums can be found at Middle Eastern grocery stores—you can substitute ¾ pound halved dried apricots, but make sure they're the deep orange, very sour variety)

2½ cups water, plus more to cover plums

½ teaspoon whole coriander seeds

¼ teaspoon whole fenugreek seeds

1 tablespoon Turkish hot pepper paste (you can substitute harissa, but you might want to start with a smaller amount, as heat levels can vary)

3 cloves garlic, peeled and coarsely chopped

¼ cup coarsely chopped fresh cilantro

¼ cup coarsely chopped fresh dill

1 teaspoon kosher salt

Place the plums in a saucepan, and cover with water. Bring the water to a boil, then immediately strain and discard the liquid. Place the plums back in the saucepan, and add 2½ cups water. Bring to a boil, then reduce the heat until it's just high enough to maintain a simmer. Simmer for 10 minutes, skimming off any foam that rises to the top. By the end, the plums will have plumped somewhat, and the water will have dropped below the level of the fruit.

While the plums are simmering, toast the whole spices: Heat a small skillet over a medium-low flame, and add the coriander seeds, shaking the pan periodically, until they smell fragrant and just begin to darken, about 2 minutes. Transfer to a spice grinder or mortar and pestle. Repeat with the fenugreek seeds. Grind to a fine powder.

When the plums have cooked, strain them, reserving the liquid. Let the plums cool until you can handle them easily, then remove and discard the pits and any lingering bits of stem. Place the pitted plums in a food processor, along with the reserved cooking liquid, toasted spices, pepper paste, garlic, cilantro, dill, and salt. Process, scraping down the bowl as needed, to form a thick, spreadable sauce, adding additional water if needed. Taste and adjust the seasonings—if the plums are too sour, you may need to add a pinch of sugar. Serve with any of the grilled meats from the mangal (chapter 7), khachapuri (page 167), or spread it onto grilled cheese, shake it into a salad dressing, etc., etc., etc.

SEA BUCKTHORN RELISH

приправа из облепихи

✦ ✦ ✦

Sea buckthorn berries have a surprisingly tropical flavor, and with their winter-hardy thick skins are a prime source of vitamin C in the colder months. Traditionally, these were more medicine than food—my mother makes a tonic every year, which everyone in my family has a spoonful of every winter morning, and my grandmother is always suggesting a poultice made with the fruit for all sorts of skin ailments. But the berries are being explored more and more as a culinary ingredient, especially in the Baltics.

Sea buckthorn's acidity makes the berries a bit tricky to figure out—often recipes just dump a lot of sugar on them, but I think they work beautifully with savory stuff as well. I use the brilliant orange berries to create a sort of Russian chutney. Use this relish to perk up meats (especially rich dishes like machanka, page 287), cheese plates, or some ricotta-topped toast.

YIELDS ABOUT 3 CUPS

1 cup granulated sugar

1¾ cups water, divided

3 sprigs rosemary

1 pound sea buckthorn berries,* rinsed, hard woody stems removed (soft stems are fine)—if unavailable, substitute cranberries

¼ cup brown mustard seeds

¾ cup apple cider vinegar

1 tablespoon kosher salt

In a medium-sized saucepan, bring the sugar, 1 cup of the water, and the rosemary to a boil, and add the berries. If you're using cranberries, let sit for 5 minutes, but if you're using sea buckthorn, let them sit 1 hour (they have tougher skins, which need to soften). Strain, reserving both the liquid and the berries but discarding the rosemary.

Pour the liquid back in the saucepan, and add the mustard seeds, remaining ¾ cup water, vinegar, and salt. Give the mixture a stir, and bring it to a boil over high heat, then reduce the heat until it's just high enough to maintain a gentle simmer. Simmer gently until the liquid is mostly absorbed and the mustard seeds are softened, about 2 hours. Stir in the reserved berries, and cool.

* Available in Russian markets, usually in the freezer section

MILK CARAMEL

вареная сгущенка

❖ ❖ ❖

I didn't meet my grandparents until I was six, when my mom's parents emigrated. Forget about Skype—you could hardly get a paper letter from Borisov to Chicago in the early eighties. So when they finally arrived, they had to make up for all that lost time—with food, of course. My grandfather would fry up potato pancakes on a dime, while my grandmother would boil cans of sweetened condensed milk on the stove for hours.* And she would spoon the resulting milk caramel to me, still warm from the can.

Use this recipe for black currant tea milk caramel (page 316), oreshki (page 320), or filling grandchildren's mouths.

YIELDS ¾ CUP

1 14-ounce can sweetened condensed milk

Warm water

Preheat oven to 400°F. Pour the sweetened condensed milk into a pie pan or 8-inch square pan, and cover it with foil. Set the pan inside a large casserole dish, transfer it to the oven, and pour warm water into the casserole dish so that it comes at least halfway up the sides of the inner pan (being careful not to flood water into the condensed milk).

Bake until the mixture thickens and darkens to a peanut-butter–like color and consistency, about 1½ to 2 hours, stirring every 30 minutes (more frequently as it nears the end of its cooking time), and adding more water as needed to keep the dish halfway submerged. When the milk has caramelized, carefully remove it from the oven, and let cool.

* Disclaimer: Don't go and try this yourself—one wrong move and you'll have a milk caramel bomb on your hands.

STOCKING THE RUSSIAN PANTRY

In the phone-free Belarusian days when my parents grew up, you sometimes didn't know you were entertaining company until you heard a knock on the door. And so being a good host (one of the holy grails of Russian culture) meant having a well-stocked pantry. Whether you're preparing for impromptu guests, or just stocking up for your own weeknight dinners or snacks, here's a guide to the classics of the Russian market (as well as a few of my own personal picks).

BAIKAL SODA байкал
Soviet Russia's answer to Coca-Cola (but much more delicious). Named after a large freshwater lake in Siberia, it's full of roots and herbs—there's a lot going on in here.

BIRCH WATER березовый сок
The sap from birch trees is collected in the spring for a refreshing, healthy drink. Birch water has a very delicate, lightly sweet flavor, but is also highly perishable—most bottled versions will have sugar or citric acid added to preserve it.

BRINDZA брынза
Brined sheep's milk cheese, very similar to feta (and often sold interchangeably with it at Eastern European markets). As with feta, there are many cow's milk versions these days—try to find sheep's milk, which is much more flavorful and creamy than its bovine alternative.

BUCKWHEAT GROATS гречневая крупа
You can find buckwheat groats in many grocery stores these days, often labeled "kasha." Skip these, and head for your nearest Eastern European market—the stock will be fresher, and more deeply and evenly roasted (more roast = more flavor). Look for groats from the Altai region of Siberia.

BUCKWHEAT HONEY гречишный мёд
A delicious, strongly flavored honey that has a pleasantly medicinal note. Use sparingly—a little goes a long way.

COD LIVER печень трески
Inside these iconic yellow cans with red Cyrillic writing you'll find several lobes of rich, delicious cod liver packed in its own oil. Cod liver pashtet (page 125) is the most known

use, but it is also commonly served with roughly chopped hard-boiled eggs and onions for a quick salad. There are many inferior brands, so be sure you're buying the top-of-the-line stuff from Norway.

KOMPOT MIX компотные смеси
A mix of dried fruits, for an easy winter version of kompot (page 58).

DRIED MUSHROOMS грибы сушеные
Dried mushrooms will keep forever in your pantry, and are just so jam-packed with flavor. Throw them in soups and braises, or make mushroom broth (page 352). Remember that dried mushrooms are usually not very well cleaned before drying, and will harbor silt and sand—wash well before using. Pretty much any international market will give you dried mushrooms with far more variety (and a cheaper price) than a conventional grocery store.

EGGPLANT SALAD салат из баклажанов
There are tons of different eggplant caviars, spreads, and roasted salads at Eastern European markets—I love keeping one or two jars on hand the way some people keep pasta sauce in the pantry. I've used them to braise chickpeas and chicken thighs, or just eat straight from the jar with a little bread. The Todorka brand "Eggplants with Prunes" is of particularly high quality and is minimally processed.

FRUIT PRESERVES варенья
Rosehips, Cornelian cherry, sea buckthorn berry, barberry, cloudberry. Mix up your PB&J game with a new-to-you fruit each time you visit the store.

FRUIT SYRUPS сиропы фруктовые

Best bang for your buck when it comes to packing intense fruit flavors into dishes. Russian markets feature a whole host of amazing options, but the sour cherry syrup is what I use for sour cherry vareniki (page 204). Try adding a few of these syrups to your bar for mixers—ZerGut brand is my go-to.

FRUIT TEAS AND TISANES фруктовые чаи

Sure, you can find rows and rows of black tea at Eastern European markets. But what's exceptional are the wide range of tisanes, bursting with a host of dried fruits, berries, and herbs. And be sure to grab a box of black tea mixed with dried black currants as well. Not only does it make a tasty cup, but you need it to make black currant tea milk caramel (page 316).

HERRING селедка

Look for salt-cured herring packed in oil with salt—meaning fish, salt, and oil should be the only three ingredients listed.

HOT PEPPER PASTE паста из острого перца

This is a Turkish product that most closely resembles Georgian pepper pastes. Your best bet is to look in Middle Eastern or Mediterranean markets. Look for Sera brand Hot Pepper Paste (there is also a mild version, which is a fine substitute if you don't love heat).

ISRAELI PICKLES огурцы бочковые

If you can find "barrel-style" Russian pickles, grab them, but I find Israeli pickles are the best substitute—made of thin-skinned Persian or Armenian cucumbers, and packed in a particularly salty, tangy brine. So good!

KEFIR кефир

With its healthy probiotics, kefir is becoming more popular—you can now find it in pretty much any grocery store. Look for plain, whole-fat kefir when using it for recipes in this book. As any Russian will tell you, it is pronounced "keh-FEAR"—not "KEE-fur" (this is yogurt, people, not a Hollywood star).

KHMELI SUNELI хмели-сунели

In Georgian, *khmeli suneli* just means "dried spices"—and this dried seasoning mix can vary greatly from brand to brand. But in general it will be packed with savory, almost unplaceable flavor, full of everything from blue fenugreek to coriander to marigold petals. Add to bean salads, sprinkle on rice, or use as a dry rub or marinade for meats and poultry.

KVAS квас

Kvas (page 62) is essentially a fermented drink made from bread (and sometimes from beets or even lettuce—though purists will tell you that that's technically a *rassol*). The

kvas you can buy in grocery stores is usually not fermented at all, more like a sweet malt soda. Which can still be delicious—try Ochakovsky Kvas in the yellow cans. Fermented kvas can be harder to find, but here and there I've found large plastic jugs of a good version called Nash Kvas Perviy Klass (Our Kvas Is First Class).

LECHO лечо

Lecho (sometimes spelled *lecso*) is a Hungarian jarred pepper condiment, but well-known and widely used in Russia. It makes a good base for stew, or a quick side dish on its own. Just like with eggplant salad (page 365), I like keeping a couple of jars on hand when I'm too lazy to prep a sauce or a bunch of veggies.

LITKOVSKY (LITHUANIAN) CHEESE
сыр литовский

Lithuania is known throughout the former Soviet Union for its excellent dairy products and breads (and after being at the markets in Vilnius, I can see why). This simple, unfussy cheese melts well, and makes for a nice tweak on the standard deli sandwich when paired with a few slices of Moskovskaya salami (page 13) and some nice Borodinsky bread (page 13). Add some Russian mustard (page 355) for the ultimate sandwich.

MARINATED MUSHROOMS грибы
маринованные

Russian markets feature *dozens* of different varieties of mushrooms jarred in a simple marinade. To serve, strain off the liquid, and mix with some fresh oil and vinegar. Add some sliced sweet onions for a nice contrast of textures. Try shiitakes as a good starter, or nameko (*opyata*) or butter mushrooms (*maslyata*) if you're more adventurous.

MILK CARAMEL вареная сгущенка

Milk caramel (page 363) is sweetened condensed milk that has been cooked down to a thick caramel, and used for everything from filling oreshki (page 320) to stirring in your coffee to folding into brownie batter. Called *sguschonka* in Russian, it's the same as dulce de leche in Hispanic markets.

MUSTARD POWDER горчичный порошок

In Eastern European markets, mustard powder is made from brown mustard seeds. Conventional grocery store mustard powder is made from yellow mustard seeds. This may seem like a minor distinction, but it makes all the difference. To make a truly spicy, nasal-passage-clearing mustard (page 355), brown mustard seed powder is a *must*. Can sometimes be found in Asian markets as well.

PRYANIKI пряники

These little round sweets are somewhere between a cookie and cake—just the thing for your morning tea. Sweetened with honey, and flavored with just a hint of gingerbread spices. *Pryaniki* should be pleasantly dry, dense, and contain real honey—avoid soft-feeling cookies and artificial ingredients.

POPPY SEEDS мак

Finding good poppy seeds is surprisingly hard to do. First off, they go rancid very quickly. Secondly, they absorb the flavors of what's around them very easily. And lastly, many specimens can be exceedingly bitter or musty. Only buy poppy seeds in well-sealed containers, and check the expiration date. At home, store them in the freezer, and give 'em a whiff and a taste before using.

RUSSIAN MUSTARD горчица
Russian mustard is spicy in the nasal-passage-clearing way. It is always most intense right after opening, and will lose potency over time. Grab the Zakuson brand—if you don't try making your own (page 355).

SEA BUCKTHORN BERRIES облепиха
Native to Siberia, these small bright orange berries are quickly becoming the superfood of the minute. And with good reason—they are brimming with vitamin C and all sorts of healthy fats (this is a berry that can actually yield an oil). Sea buckthorn is traditionally used for medicinal purposes (skin poultices and tonics), but more and more people are exploring how to best harness its punchy sourness in the kitchen (I love using these bright berries to make caramels and curds, or pairing them with meats, like the sea buckthorn relish, page 362). Usually found in the freezer aisle.

SMETANA сметана
How can a market have *an entire refrigerator* full of what seems to be, essentially, sour cream? Smetana in Russia is a foundational ingredient, and it's taken *seriously*. I could rant for quite a while about fat content and true culturing and flavor complexity. But suffice to say: it's worth it to get the real stuff (if you're not culturing it yourself—page 359). And just because you're buying something labeled *smetana* doesn't mean you're out of the woods—read your labels, avoid additives, and look for the highest fat content.

SUSHKI сушки
These little baked rounds are meant to be dipped into tea. They're traditionally (and adorably) sold tied on a string, and remind me of ever-so-slightly sweetened hard pretzels (the name translates to "little drieds"). Look for ones that are well-packaged— I've met more than a few stale *sushki* in my life.

SPRATS шпроты
Sprats (*shproti*) are beautiful little fish that hail from the Baltic Sea, hot-smoked in Latvia before being canned or jarred. Look for Riga Gold brand in glass jars.

SULGUNI сулгуни
A Georgian cheese similar to halloumi, available plain or smoked. California-based Karoun Dairy makes an excellent version, widely distributed in the United States.

SUNFLOWER OIL масло подсолнечное
A defining flavor of Ukraine—sunflower oil there is like olive oil in Italy. Look for refined oil (**рафинированное**) for cooking or where you want neutral flavors. Pick up a bottle of unrefined (**нерафинированное**) for a fantastic burst of sunflower flavor in dressings and such.

SUNFLOWER SEEDS семечки

Semechki are not just a snack, but practically a way of life. In Russia, you'll find streets littered with the shells. In our family, sunflower seeds often come out on the table after dessert. I'm a fan of the smaller, more flavorful jet-black Ukrainian variety—but they do require a bit more oral dexterity.

TVOROG творог

This fresh curd cheese often goes by the name "farmer's cheese"—but make sure it's the moist, fresh curds, like ricotta, and not the semi-firm slicing cheeses that are sometimes given the same name. Quark is an acceptable substitute. When cooking with tvorog, I prefer the Lifeway brand, which is consistent and not too runny. Tvorog is also an excellent breakfast option, with some cracked black pepper and cucumbers, or peach preserves.

UTSKHO SUNELI уцхо-сунели

A Georgian spice known as blue fenugreek in English—though that isn't too helpful since you virtually cannot find it in the States. Search it out online, if you'd like to make an authentic adjika (page 358), or various rubs and seasonings.

VOBLA вобла

Think beef jerky, but with fish—tiny whole fish. Sounds daunting, but it's the ultimate beer snack. Look for vacuum-packed dried fish, rather than stuff in the deli case (the moisture in the case ends up slightly rehydrating the fish, which is not ideal). *Vobla* is one species of fish, but the same method is used for many other fish: *taranka, bichki,* etc.

WAFERS вафли

Essential for turning plombir (page 315) into ice-cream sandwiches or making cakes (or DIY Kit Kats!). Basically flat sheets of the same stuff wafer ice cream cones are made of.

MENU IDEAS

LAZY SUMMER NIGHTS

Designed to minimize time spent over a stove during the height of summer. Simple, straightforward food that's light on its feet and highlights summer's bounty.

- Dill Flower Vodka (page 32) and Moscow Mules (page 30)
- Dacha Salad (page 99)
- Chicken Thigh Shashlik (page 246)
- Boiled new potatoes
- Lobio (page 96)
- Kompot (page 58) floats

AFTER THE BANYA

Hitting the sauna for a daylong Russian-style *shvitz*? These recipes can be made ahead, so all you need to do is heat up some oil when you get home. Also welcome after vigorous wintertime activities like skiing, or not-so-vigorous wintertime activities like watching the Super Bowl (in case you don't have a sauna in your backyard).

- Brindza Pashtet (page 106) with Lepyoshki (page 252) or pita bread
- Chebureki (page 187, or store-bought)
- Adjika (page 358)
- Vinegret salad (page 105)
- Zhigulevskoe beer (or other light lagers)
- Baba Sima's Tonics (page 46), mandarin oranges, and Chocolate Kolbasa (page 318)

IMPROMPTU GUESTS AT THE DOOR

If you have a well-stocked Russian pantry, you can build dinner seemingly out of thin air. In true Russian fashion, feel free to improvise.

- ✦ Sprat Buterbrodi (page 121)
- ✦ Pickles
- ✦ Pelmeni (homemade, pages 198–200, from the freezer—or store-bought if you haven't had the chance)
- ✦ Side salad of leafy greens with sliced radishes
- ✦ Russian candies (page 346)—or pull out that backup Poppy Seed Chocolate Roll (page 336) from the freezer to start proofing (or run to the store for one!)

QUICK WEEKNIGHT DINNER

Easy, healthy, delicious.

- ✦ Pork Kotleti and Grechka (page 279)
- ✦ Sauerkraut (page 84—or storebought)
- ✦ Moldovan Eggplant Salad (page 112—made ahead, or pick up a jar)

SUNDAY BRUNCH BUFFET

Smoked fishes and fresh dairy? Russian food was *made* for brunch.

- ✦ Beet and Horseradish–Cured Black Cod (page 128) and Smoked Trout Salad (page 141) with bagels, cream cheese, etc.
- ✦ Potato and Carrot Babka (page 274)
- ✦ Shkvarky with Buckwheat Blini and Lingonberry Mustard (page 180)
- ✦ Sirniki with Raspberry Kissel (page 325)
- ✦ Cranberry Mors (page 64)
- ✦ Bloody Mashas (page 22)

FOUR COURSE FORMAL DINNER PARTY TO IMPRESS YOUR BOSS

Or, you know, anytime you're feeling fancy.

- ✦ Buzhenina with Shaved Celery Salad and Toasted Caraway Vinaigrette (page 145)
- ✦ King Salmon Ukha (page 226)
- ✦ Roasted Veal Chops and Caviar Beurre Blanc (page 304)
- ✦ Bird's Milk Cake with Glazed Apricots (page 311)

ACKNOWLEDGMENTS

There would be no Kachka and therefore no book without my parents, Seymour and Luba. You two are the glue in our lives. I can only hope that I can be as unwavering and unconditionally supportive for my children as you are for me.

Thank you to my brother, Simon, my aunts Asya and Galina, my babushka Sima, and countless other family members whom I have pestered for ideas, recipes, techniques, and tchotchkes. To my dad's cousin Sasha, for always taking such good care of us when we visit Minsk.

To my beautiful boys, Isaac and Noah, thank you for your patience and understanding when I couldn't play or read to you when I was coming up against deadlines or testing recipes. I hope you're proud of your mama and will want to one day cook this food for your children.

To Israel, my husband, business partner, and best friend. Thank you for being my sounding board, inspiration, voice of reason, and all-around life raft throughout this process. And thank you for always getting up with the kids in the morning (that has nothing to do with writing this book, but deserves recognition nonetheless).

My Kachka family: Thank you for your unbelievable dedication and hard work. I am genuinely honored that you choose to work for us. I want to specifically mention Olga Mazurenko, my chef de cuisine. Olga, I am lucky to have you in my life. Thank you for being the good cop, the bad cop, and the ringmaster of this crazy circus. Thank you for getting me. Thank you for being you.

To my agent, Betsy Amster, who was nuts enough to believe that I could write this thing and held my hand through every bump and curve. You are an outstanding human, a true mensch.

To Will Schwalbe, Kara Rota, and the entire team at Flatiron Books: Thank you for taking me under your wings. I have tremendous respect for the way in which you have guided me through this process. Thank you for asking all the right questions and questioning all the right things.

To Leela Cyd: You are magic. I want to make another book simply so we can make more photos together. Thank you for drinking my Kool-Aid and making my vision yours.

Karen Koch, you have put together a design that is not only incredibly beautiful, but captures the soul of Kachka. Thank you for creating something worth cherishing.

Roman Muradov, you are a genius. Thank you for coming to our rescue in the eleventh hour and understanding our vision so absolutely. Your illustrations transport me to my childhood—stirring my pseudo-Soviet soul.

To our recipe testers, who gave their time and feedback, and shuttled countless small sample bites back to me for tasting: Jesse Friedman, Rebecca Gagnon, Adrian Hale, Joanna Stein, Amy Baird, Masha Levin, Danielle Centoni, Jessica Stumpf, Sarah Schneider, and Molly Thomas-Jensen.

And most of all, I really can't give enough gratitude to Deena Prichep, who has taken my commercial kitchen–sized recipes and clumsy little stories and sculpted them into something other people might actually want to read. You are not only a gifted writer, but a genuinely beautiful person. Thank you for embarking on this little journey with me.

FROM DEENA PRICHEP

Thanks to my family: To Bengt Halvorson for the love and support, and being (mostly) good-natured about all of the dairy. To the memory of Evelyn and Sidney Schwartz and Emanuel and Lillian Prichep for a fine legacy of deli meals, cabbage salad, and sour cream cake—and to Eileen Prichep, Barry Prichep, and Bonnie Leach for continuing the tradition. And to Odessa, who has a lifetime of good meals ahead of her.

To my fellow writers Marisa Robertson-Textor, Anne Ford, and Daniel Estrin for lending their keen editorial eyes, wit, and wisdom; and Jason DeRose for his guidance in learning how to find the heart of a story (and for his patience while I finished this one).

To Betsy Amster, Will Schwalbe, Kara Rota, the Flatiron Books team, Leela Cyd, Karen Koch, Roman Muradov, and our recipe testers: I echo Bonnie's gratitude and admiration.

And most of all to Bonnie Frumkin Morales. I've heard more amazing stories than we could possibly capture on these pages, and eaten more delicious food than I can possibly recall. You are an amazing chef, true partner, and storyteller in your own right. It's been a gift to pull up a chair at your family table.

INDEX

Page numbers in italics refer to photos